BEYOND THE RISK PARADIGM IN MENTAL HEALTH POLICY AND PRACTICE

BEYOND THE RISK PARADIGM
Series Editor: Nigel Parton

This important new series argues that a risk paradigm has come to dominate many human services in Western countries over the last 20 years, giving the impression that the social world is calculable and predictable. Each book critically engages with this paradigm, demonstrating the intended and unintended consequences of such an approach for those using and working in services, as well as for wider society, in order to open up new ways for taking policy and practice forward. Designed to challenge readers to think critically and creatively about risk, this fascinating series will develop the understanding and knowledge of students and practitioners alike.

Also available:

Beyond the Risk Paradigm in Criminal Justice, edited by Chris Trotter, Gill McIvor and Fergus McNeill
Beyond the Risk Paradigm in Child Protection, edited by Marie Connolly

Nigel Parton is Professor of Applied Childhood Studies at the University of Huddersfield, UK, and has been writing about and researching the issues of social and child welfare for over 20 years.

BEYOND THE RISK PARADIGM IN MENTAL HEALTH POLICY AND PRACTICE

EDITED BY

SONYA STANFORD, ELAINE SHARLAND,

NINA ROVINELLI HELLER AND

JOANNE WARNER

First published 2017 by
PALGRAVE

Palgrave in the UK is an imprint of Macmillan Publishers Limited,
registered in England, company number 785998, of 4 Crinan Street,
London, N1 9XW.

Palgrave® and Macmillan® are registered trademarks in the United States,
the United Kingdom, Europe and other countries.

ISBN 978–1–137–44135–5 paperback

This book is printed on paper suitable for recycling and made from fully
managed and sustained forest sources. Logging, pulping and manufacturing
processes are expected to conform to the environmental regulations of the
country of origin.

A catalogue record for this book is available from the British Library.

A catalog record for this book is available from the Library of Congress.

CONTENTS

CONTRIBUTORS

Gerry Bennison is a user educator and researcher who has endured complex lived experience relating to mental health. He has experience of educating on courses relating to positive risk management within academia. He is a peer reviewer for *Social Work Education* and the *Journal of Qualitative Social Work*. He also acts as a service user member of the editorial board for *Social Work Education*, and he has acted as co-editor for a special edition. Gerry has also been published in *Social Work Education* and *Critical Social Policy*.

Robert Bland is Professor of Social Work at Australian Catholic University. Social workers, as well as people and families with a mental illness, know him as a long-term advocate and supporter first in clinical practice for 17 years, then for 30 years in academia. He is regarded as a pioneer and foremost authority in Australian mental health. He was awarded a member of the Order of Australia (AM) in 2006. Robert's book, with Noel Renouf and Ann Tullgren, *Social Work Practice in Mental Health* (2nd edition), is a widely used text in Australian social work education.

Jim Campbell is Professor of Social Work at University College Dublin. He was co-editor (with Professor John Pinkerton) of the *British Journal of Social Work* from 2010–15. Jim has two broad teaching and research interests. He has published in the fields of mental health social work and policy, with a particular interest in related socio-legal studies. He also has a longstanding interest in exploring the relationships between social work and political violence. His co-authored book, Davidson, G., Campbell, J., Shannon, C. and Mulholland, C. *Models of Mental Health* (Basingstoke: Palgrave Macmillan), was published in 2015. For further details of his publications see www.ucd.ie/research/people/socialpolicysocialworksocialjustice/professorjimcampbell/.

Gavin Davidson is a senior lecturer in social work at Queen's University, Belfast. Before moving to Queen's in 2008 he worked for 12 years in adult mental health services. His main areas of research are in mental health including: the use of compulsory powers; the interface between mental health and child protection services; mental health and inequalities; and the associations between childhood adversity and mental health. He is the social work representative on the Reference Group for the Mental Capacity Act Northern Ireland 2016, which should provide a new legal framework based on decision-making ability rather than mental disorder and risk.

Catherine Hartley is qualified social worker and an approved mental health professional with more than 25 years' experience. She was a service manager in the NHS for 13 years. She has been a member of the Mental Health Tribunal since 2003 and of the Social Entitlement Tribunal since 2014. She is a course designer and trainer for the Judicial College where she currently trains tribunal members on risk. She has a Masters in Organisational Consultancy from the Tavistock and she has written about managing change in the NHS for *The Journal of Social Work Practice.*

Nina Rovinelli Heller is Dean and Zachs Professor at the University of Connecticut School of Social Work in Hartford, CT. Her research interests include mental health theory and practice, integrative psychological theories and suicide prevention, all informed by her years as a practising clinician. She has served on the National Action Alliance for Suicide Prevention Taskforce for Clinical Workforce Preparedness and on the Connecticut Suicide Advisory Board, where she authored the state suicide prevention plan. She is the co-editor of *Enhancing Psychodynamic Theory with Cognitive Behavioral Techniques*, and *Mental Health and Social Problems: A Social Work Perspective.*

Natalie Hendry is a lecturer in the School of Education at Deakin University and a PhD student in the School of Media and Communication at RMIT University. She is a secondary teacher, with experience in community, mainstream and hospital education settings. Her research explores the intersections of health, education and media, particularly focusing on visual social media practices, notions of youth identity and connection, and affective labour related to mental ill-health. Her current project focuses on developing pedagogy for school contexts that draws on digital media scholarship.

Chris Lee is an internationally performed and award-winning playwright with over 20 productions in seven different countries. He is a qualified social worker and approved mental health professional with more than 20 years' experience. He was a service manager in the NHS for 10 years. Chris is currently a Mental Health Act Reviewer for the Care Quality Commission in the UK. He has been a member of the Mental Health Tribunal since 2012 and of the Social Entitlement Tribunal since 2014. He has written for the *British Journal of Social Work, Journal of Social Work Practice* and *British Journal of Wellbeing.*

Shepard Masocha is a Lecturer in Social Work in the School of Psychology, Social Work and Social Policy at the University of South Australia. His research focuses on the critical study of social work with ethnic minorities, immigrants and asylum seekers, and the intersecting discourses of race, racism, culture and social citizenship. His most recent publications include 'Divergent Practices in Statutory and Voluntary Sector Settings?' (2016) with Dr Kim Robinson, and his book *Asylum Seekers, Social Work and Racism* (Palgrave, 2015).

Brady Robards is Lecturer in sociology at Monash University, Melbourne, Australia. His research explores how young people use and produce social media like Facebook, Instagram, Snapchat and Reddit. Brady's work appears in journals including *New Media & Society*, *Young*, *Continuum* and *Sociology*. Recent books include *Youth Cultures & Subcultures: Australian Perspectives* (Ashgate, 2015), *Mediated Youth Cultures* (Palgrave, 2014) and *Teaching Youth Studies Through Popular Culture* (ACYS Publishing, 2014). For more, visit Brady's website: bradyrobards.com.

Kim Robinson is a social work lecturer and has been a social work practitioner and manager in community health and refugee services for over 25 years in Australia and the UK. Her Masters in Public Health examined domestic violence and service settings, and her PhD focused on social work with refugees. Publications include 'Working with Refugees and Asylum Seekers in Australia and the UK' (2013) and 'Divergent Practices in Statutory and Voluntary Sector Settings?' (2016) with Dr Shepard Masocha. Recent work has focused on unaccompanied minors: 'Appeals Rights Exhausted: Care Leavers Facing Return to Afghanistan' (2015) in *Refuge* with Dr Lucy Williams.

Anne-Maree Sawyer is a sociology lecturer at La Trobe University, Melbourne, Australia. Prior to commencing an academic career, she was a mental health social worker in a psychiatric crisis team for 17 years. Through experience on the frontline, Anne-Maree developed a critical interest in the rise of risk management as a social intervention and its effects on the provision of community-based care. Anne-Maree's current research focuses on trust issues in suicide risk assessments, risk management and care ethics, and women's narratives of infertility and emotion management in an online support group.

Elaine Sharland is Professor of Social Work Research at the University of Sussex. For many years her main area of research interest was children, young people and risk, in particular child protection. More recently she has become interested in exploring how ideas about risk can frame and distort everyday family, professional and organizational practices. She brings to this her other areas of research interest, in disciplinarity and interdisciplinarity and in knowledge production and utilization. As Economic and Social Research Council Strategic Adviser for Social Work and Social Care Research (2008–10) Elaine led a UK-wide initiative to develop a strategy to improve research capacity and quality in the discipline and field. Elaine is one of the co-founders and will be Chair of the European Social Work Research Association, 2017–19.

Sonya Stanford is a lecturer in social work at the University of Tasmania, Australia. She has contributed to social work education for over 20 years. While working as a social worker in the fields of sexual assault, disability and ageing, Sonya developed a critical interest in the politics and ethics of 'risk work'. Her research 'speaks back' to risk by examining how risk thinking and risk practices impact the wellbeing and outcomes of people who use and deliver health and welfare services. Currently, Sonya's main research focuses on trust issues in suicide risk assessment, care ethics and mental health peer support practice.

Dawn Talbot is a user/carer educator and researcher who has experienced long-term stigma and discrimination based on mental health issues. She has experience of the complexities of social justice and its association with risk. She also educates at academic institutions and is engaged in user networks to develop guidelines and policy pertaining to user experience in mental health. Dawn has published ethnographic work relating to emotional labour and social supports in *Critical Social Policy*. Her work on user education in social work was published in *Social Work Education*.

Joanne Warner is a senior lecturer in social work at the University of Kent, UK. A registered social worker, Jo began her career in community development and generic practice before becoming an academic. Her research focuses on sociocultural approaches to risk and emotions, particularly the impact of cultures of inquiry, fear and blame and the way 'risk work' has increasingly shaped professional practice and the experience of service users. Her recent book, published by Policy Press, is entitled *The Emotional Politics of Social Work and Child Protection*.

Marianne Wyder is a social worker with a background in sociology. Over the past 20 years she has worked in various research and clinical positions in the government, non-government and university sectors. Her research experiences span the health sector and include expert knowledge on mental health, capacity building, inequality, involuntary treatment, family breakdown, translational research, gender, drug and/or alcohol abuse and suicidal behaviours. She is currently employed as a senior research fellow in Metro South Addiction and Mental Health Services where her role involves conducting and facilitating practice-based research and evaluations and to support clinicians and peer workers in conducting research.

ACKNOWLEDGEMENTS

This book has been some time in the making and there are many people we wish to thank for enabling us to bring it to fruition.

Firstly, we owe a debt of gratitude to Marie Connolly, Cathy Humphries, Chris Trotter and Rosemary Sheehan, who brought us together for the first 'Beyond the Risk Paradigm' colloquium in Italy, in 2012. That adventure, and its sequel in 2013, both hosted by the superb staff at the Monash Prato Centre, gave us the opportunity to forge new research relationships and to reinvigorate existing ones, centred around our common desire to re-envisage risk and mental health. The excitement of those early conversations has continued to energize us throughout the process of producing this book.

We would like to thank Palgrave for their confidence in us and our project, and their patience and guidance at key stages. Louise Summerling especially gave us sound advice and much-appreciated encouragement.

Nigel Parton gave us his generous supportive comments and gentle steer – thank you, Nigel, for your wise words. The care of special colleagues, friends and family also sustained us all along the way – many thanks to you all (you know who you are).

Finally, we are immensely grateful to all our contributors who have enabled us to achieve what we hoped for. Bringing together their diverse voices has allowed us to look afresh at risk and mental health, through the lens of social justice and human rights, and to point the ways forward – beyond the risk paradigm.

1

THE HISTORICAL CONTEXT OF THE RISK PARADIGM IN MENTAL HEALTH POLICY AND PRACTICE: HOW DID WE GET HERE?

Joanne Warner, Nina Rovinelli Heller, Elaine Sharland and Sonya Stanford

Introduction

The chapter begins by briefly setting the 'rise of risk' in mental health policy and practice in its wider context. It demonstrates that the idea of risk not only dominates mental health policy, practice and experience; it is also the major organizing paradigm in health and welfare services more widely. Of even greater significance is the fact that risk dominates public, political and cultural life in general. The language of risk is everywhere: in debates about health, childcare, pensions planning, banking, child protection, crime, what we eat, how we use our leisure time, what we buy. The idea of risk also characterizes organizational cultures and institutional life, where concern for the 'reputation risk' of those that occupy positions of power plays a particularly significant – and problematic – role (Power, 2004).

While the use of the term 'risk' has become increasingly widespread, it has been defined in a number of different ways. In the broadest sense, risk can be understood as either 'real' or 'constructed'. On the one hand, risk is treated as an objectively measurable and controllable entity, where, with the right expertise and tools, risks can be predicted, managed or even eradicated altogether. On the other hand, risk is 'constructed', in so far as the risks we identify as important – the way we perceive and respond to them – are all determined by social and cultural values. This distinction is an important one for this book. The starting point for our exploration of how we can 'move beyond the risk paradigm' is that we take it to be a paradigm: a mode of thinking and acting that is political, social and moral. We are not proposing that we move beyond (eradicate or stop caring about) objective dangers or harm, but that we find ways of thinking and acting with them in different ways when working for human rights and social justice in mental health. It is in this sense that we often use the term 'risk' as shorthand for the idea of risk.

The chapter considers the key theoretical accounts of risk, including Beck's 'Risk Society', that help us to understand the processes that have been at work and the growing significance of neoliberal agendas in welfare policy. The chapter then charts the rise of risk's 'peculiar' expression in mental health (Pilgrim & Rogers, 1999) through critical analysis of the trends in mental health policies towards 'deinstitutionalization'. These policies essentially signalled the replacement of asylum-based confinement with 'care in the community'. The discussion considers the problematic and contested nature of both community and care. It argues that community care policies, while progressive in important respects, were both symptomatic of, and also the cause of deep cultural anxieties about, 'madness' linked to the apparently increased visibility of people experiencing mental distress. The chapter highlights the disproportionate attention that was given by the media and policymakers to certain risks, in particular to the perceived increase in the risk of violence by people with mental health needs living in the community. This disproportionate focus on one particular kind of risk has simultaneously served to obscure from view the range of other risks to which mental health service users are exposed and that they live with each day.

The discussion then moves on to explore risk in mental health practice by tracing the relationship between risk and the much older concept of dangerousness in psychiatry. The targeting of services for individuals judged to be 'high risk' (especially to others) has meant that significant areas of professional practice revolve around processes of assessment based on calculating probabilities and risk factors. Being deemed 'high risk' can result in risk management practices, such as preventive detention, that have important implications for social justice and human rights. But the designation 'low risk' can mean exclusion from any form of support at all, with equally significant implications for human rights and justice.

In the concluding section of the chapter we emphasize that the dominant focus on risk has had major implications for social justice and for the human rights of people who experience mental distress. We briefly consider where challenges to the dominance of the risk paradigm have come from and where they may come from in the future. Specifically, we highlight the importance of refocusing attention on social suffering and the forms of power that influence responses to mental distress. When human rights and social justice are compromised by the policies and practices of the risk paradigm, the impact is felt directly by service users through experiences such as stigma, shame and the loss of dignity. Social suffering 'results from what political, economic, and institutional power does to people and, reciprocally, from how these forms of power themselves influence responses to social problems' (Kleinman *et al.*, 1997, p. ix). The chapter ends with a brief summary of the chapters that are to follow and the contribution they each make to 'moving beyond the paradigm of risk'.

Risk society, the 'other' and neoliberalism

We have been described as living in 'an age of anxiety' (Dunant & Porter, 1997) where, since the 1990s, 'safety has become the fundamental value' (Furedi, 1997). One of the most influential works on risk from a sociological perspective is Beck's (1992) *Risk Society*, where the issue of risk is elevated to the status of a new political theory. According to Beck, society is no longer structured as it was in the past, in terms of the distribution of 'goods'. It is instead organized according to a preoccupation with fears for the future and the distribution of 'bads' in the form of potential harm. The potential harms Beck has in mind are those that arise from industrialization and modernization; they are global in their impact – such as nuclear accidents and climate change – and they are incalculable in terms of their consequences. In Beck's account, the risk society is one that is concerned with safety and preventing 'the worst' and so it is motivated by a 'commonality of anxiety' about the future rather than a 'commonality of need' as in the past (1992, p. 49). In this preoccupation with the future, the focus falls on increasingly sophisticated attempts to calculate the probabilities of adverse events occurring. Through risk calculations, a lack of certainty about the future becomes quantifiable (Rose, 1998, p. 181) and this gives a measure of confidence about how to act in the here and now, even if that confidence is misplaced. Beck's (1992, p. 21) definition of risk is centred on the way modern risks are dealt with: 'Risk may be defined as a systematic way of dealing with hazards and insecurities induced and introduced by modernisation itself.'

Beck's argument is underpinned by the view that Western civilization is indeed faced with the threat of self-annihilation. For Beck and also for Giddens (1990, 1991, 1998), it is greater knowledge about risk that has fuelled anxieties about modernization – particularly technological developments – and made us morbidly aware of the risks we may face in the future. As Wilkinson (2001, p. 103) puts it:

> For both of these theorists the significance of public knowledge of risk lies in the extent to which it makes us more uncertain about the future. Where our minds are filled with thoughts of risk, then we are understood to acquire an amplified sense of doubt with regard to our personal ability to live in safety.

As Hollway and Jefferson (1997, p. 258) suggest, the importance of Beck's argument lies in the fact that 'risk is understood as pervasive in late modernity', and they emphasize the importance of addressing risk issues in terms of the political context for their recognition and management.

The risk society argument suggests that the focus on risk in mental health needs to be understood as part of a much wider development in which heightened levels of anxiety are endemic in modern society in general. However, as well as fuelling anxiety in the way that Beck and others suggest, knowledge about risk is understood by cultural theorists such as Mary Douglas as being part of the *antidote* to anxiety (Wilkinson, 2001). For cultural theorists, it is important to note historical changes in the meaning of risk in order to grasp the socially constructed nature of the concept and its modern-day use in relation to *blame*. Douglas (1992) traces the concept of risk back to the seventeenth century, where the probabilities and magnitude of both gains and losses in gambling were calculated mathematically. From this, the concept of risk subsequently evolved to become the basis for decision making in scientific environments. Douglas argues that this historical association with scientific calculation and the credibility that comes with it partly explains the modern use of the term 'risk'. Risk is now only associated with the possibility of negative outcomes and its political use is as a forensic resource in working out accountability for abuses of power:

> Risk is invoked for a modern-style riposte against abuse of power. The charge of causing risk is a stick to beat authority, to make lazy bureaucrats sit up, to exact restitution for victims … . (Douglas, 1992, p. 24)

In addition to risk's appeal as a concept that can be used to invoke blame, cultural theorists have also highlighted its power in relation to cultural processes such as 'othering'. The concept of the 'other' can be defined as 'that which is conceptualized as different from the self' (Lupton, 1999, p. 124). Otherness is rooted in observations of strangeness and danger in 'them', in binary opposition to the safety and familiarity associated with 'us'. The concept has been used to explain how and why different social groups become the focus of anxieties about particular kinds of risk so that they come to be seen as 'the marginalised and stigmatised risky other' (Lupton, 1999, p. 124). As we see in a later chapter, an equivalent process is defined in psychoanalytic terms, where othering involves splitting as a defence against anxiety and guilt. Regulation of the other has been identified as a central feature of the 'history of madness'. Otherness associated with mental disorder has been identified as a particularly potent force when combined with otherness associated with 'race'. To be black and to have been diagnosed with a mental illness is to experience two forms of otherness that are mutually reinforcing (Scott, 1998; Wilkinson, 1998). The significant over-representation of young black men in the most dehumanizing and coercive parts of the mental health system testifies to the social suffering that results from the social construction of the 'black other' (Frost & Hoggett, 2008). Through discourses of risk, the 'welfare other' is designated 'at risk' of dependency or 'a risk' to others, with the supposed moral deficits of 'Non-white Others in welfare policy' a sustained focus (Stanford & Taylor, 2013, p. 488).

Risk has also been linked closely with economic policies of neoliberalism. The meaning of the term 'neoliberalism' has shifted over time, but in its contemporary form it is mainly associated with the assumption that markets are inherently superior. Neoliberalism is underpinned by values of extreme individualism and self-interest with the expectation that citizens have agency actively to fulfil certain duties responsibly (Stanford & Taylor, 2013). Where citizens fail in their duty to look after themselves and, specifically, fail to plan for and guard against future risks, then they become blameworthy. Under neoliberalism, state welfare systems are viewed as burdensome, especially because they are seen to generate dependency among welfare recipients. Key to understanding the relationship between risk and neoliberalism is the idea that the neoliberal project has benefited from the 'fear of the future' generated by a climate of a particular kind of individualized risk (Culpitt, 1999). The role of the state is no longer to own risk, but to attribute it to, and to regulate and blame, others. In this way risk has come to dominate all forms of human services as well as welfare provision (Stanford & Taylor, 2013). As part of wider sociocultural and political shifts that have taken place in Western industrialized societies, risk has supplanted care in terms of becoming the main focus of professional activity (Turner & Colombo, 2008). Psychiatrists, social workers, mental health nurses and support workers are all engaged to some extent in procedures and policies relating to risk assessment and risk management.

One of the difficulties with defining risk is that it is closely associated with a number of different processes, including perception, assessment, management and communication. In mental health, risk has found a particular expression, which has been described as 'peculiar' (Pilgrim & Rogers, 1999, p. xiv). This is partly because the concept of risk in mental health policy and practice has increasingly been identified with one dimension more than any other: the risks *posed to others* by people with a mental health problem as opposed to the risks they overwhelmingly *face*. The preoccupation with the risk of harm to others is in contrast with other fields of social welfare, such as learning disability and older people, where the vulnerability of people 'at risk' is a more prominent feature. The question of how far this is new or simply a reworking of old fears about 'madness' and dangerousness has been the subject of some debate. When we ask how the particular and 'peculiar' expression of risk in mental health can be understood, part of the answer is linked to the major changes in ideas about care and in particular the shift away from asylum to 'community care'. From the 1960s large-scale institutions in the form of asylums, which had been a feature of the landscape across Europe and the US throughout the nineteenth century, began to lose their credibility in the minds of policymakers. The pace at which change took place was variable, but as Pilgrim and Rogers (1999) have argued, the overall trend towards deinstitutionalization was broadly the same.

Community care and the 'shift to risk'

One important reason for particular constructions of risk in mental health links to the policies of deinstitutionalization in mental health systems that have been implemented across Europe, North America and Australasia – that is, the shift from asylum to community in terms of the location of formal service provision. While this movement can be understood as progressive, it can also be understood as a further reflection of neoliberal ideology and the push towards marketization of welfare that has featured more widely across Western democratic states. 'Care in the community' may have its roots in an ethical stance about mental health service users as citizens, but there is also an argument that the driving force behind policies has been economic. One of the most plausible explanations is the 'fiscal crisis' thesis proposed by commentators in social policy, such as Lewis *et al.* (1995), where it is argued that limited resources demanded a focus on those deemed most 'in need/high risk'. As Pearson (1999, p. 164) has pointed out, however, the implications of this development for mental health compared with most other policy areas have been quite distinctive:

> Where the mental health field is concerned, however, this fiscal squeeze has come to be associated not with the 'invisible welfare state' of family obligations, but with the newly demonised vision of unchecked madness rampaging the streets.

At this point in our discussion we should note that community care, or, more specifically, the twin concepts of 'community' and 'care', are contested and themselves subject to intense debate. Both community and care have received detailed attention in social policy and social welfare literature (Bornat *et al.*, 1993; Bytheway *et al.*, 2002; Symonds & Kelly, 1998). Although there is insufficient space here to explore these areas in depth, one of the most helpful insights for present purposes is the distinction that can be drawn between community care as 'care' and community care as 'control' (Bartlett & Sandland, 2000). Community care for people with mental health needs in its most recent form represents a 'dual construction' of both care and control, making it paradoxical:

> mental health policy simultaneously constructs mentally disordered persons as being both 'of' the community, needing and deserving of its care; and as 'outsiders' from whom the community is in need of protection. (Bartlett & Sandland, 2000, pp. 296–7)

As Rose (1998) observes, it is through the idea of risk and the forms of practice associated with risk that this inextricable link between care and control in the community has been forged. Concerns about community care in relation to mental health have increasingly centred on the belief that the policies have failed and have resulted in increased risks for both service users and others in the community. It has been argued that the policy agenda in mental health has thus been dominated by the perceived failure of community care as 'control' rather than as 'care' (Bartlett & Sandland, 2000, p. 73), with an increasing emphasis on some kinds of risks rather than others. Since the implementation of community care policies in the early 1990s there has been an increasing focus on a perceived increase in the risk of violence to others by people with mental health problems. Following the closure of a number of long-stay psychiatric hospitals and the movement of people with serious and enduring mental illnesses into the community, other people living in such communities are *perceived* as being at greater risk of violent assault than before. This has led to the conclusion by many that there has been a 'conflation of violence with mental illness' (Pilgrim & Rogers, 1999. p. 185). It is risk assessment that has come to be seen as *the* procedure which should safeguard the safety of the public, at the same time as ensuring the wellbeing of persons who are ill and 'dangerous' (Grounds, 1995).

The emphasis on risk of violence to others is typified by the focus on homicides by people with mental health problems in the community, which arguably reached its zenith in the culture of mandatory inquiries in the UK during the 1990s. The focus on homicide represented a shift away from the attention given to 'scandals' involving poor quality *care* in large psychiatric institutions during the 1960s and 1970s (Laurance, 2003). It is also argued that the replacement of the 'dramatic architectural presence of the asylums' (Laurance, 2003, p. 381) with the newly dispersed nature of mental health care into 'the community' has led to a tendency to judge community care in absolute terms (as 'success' or 'failure') rather than relative terms (Leff, 2001). Evidence for its successes was certainly available.

A 14-year follow-up study of 670 people who had been inpatients at two of the UK's largest psychiatric hospitals concluded that community care had worked well for most of them, with minimal ill effects for society (Trieman *et al.*, 1999).

Those who sought to defend community care policies maintain that the perception of them as having failed is a misconception of the facts about post-asylum care: a misconception largely promoted through the media (Leff, 1997). Public perceptions of dangerousness exceed the evidence and a major source of the belief in increased risk associated with mental disorder is media reporting of rare, extreme events, particularly homicide (Jorm *et al.*, 2012). The belief that people with a mental illness are dangerous is particularly common in the US compared with other developed countries (Jorm & Reavley, 2014). The prevalence of this belief has been explicitly linked to the nature of media reporting and, specifically, the 24-hour rolling nature of modern news coverage of dramatic events such as mass killings. As Jorm and Reavley (2014, p. 215) have argued, 'In this way, the USA may be exporting stigma to the rest of the world.' Stigmatizing attitudes have also been promoted through policies, procedures and legislative change that have in part been formulated in response to media reporting and public anxieties. A notable example was developments in the UK in the 1990s as we have already discussed. The Glasgow Media Group study in the UK was a wide-ranging study (for a good account see Tummey & Turner, 2008, pp. 197–202). Among its main findings was the high prevalence of stories in the media that explicitly linked people referred to as 'mentally ill' with violence to other people. Stigmatizing attitudes are closely related to the processes of othering that we discussed earlier in this chapter.

The shift from asylum to community care has been important in policy and practice terms but also symbolically in the wider sociocultural sense. Risk as it intersects with mental health is 'spacialized' in the sense that the spaces and places associated with mental health care and/or surveillance – 'asylum' and 'community' – are, as we have seen, of central importance. This issue has been explored in detail in the literature on mental health in geography (Moon, 2000). In tracing the history of the spacial organization of mental health care throughout the eighteenth and nineteenth centuries into the twentieth and twenty-first centuries, it is observable how policies of deinstitutionalization generate new discourses of risk and danger, together with systems for their management (Philo, 2000). Regardless of the 'true' levels of risk associated with the supposed movement away from institutional care, powerful anxieties have been fused together during the *spacial* reorganization of mental health care, and the focus has been on particular kinds of risk and particular groups associated with those risks. As Warner and Gabe (2004) argue, mental health service users are identified with 'the street' as a specific site within urban spaces, symbolically as well as literally. Certain groups of service users, particularly young men with a diagnosis of schizophrenia, are more likely to be accommodated in poorer localities within urban spaces, where the base rates for violence, including street crime, are also higher (Rogers & Pilgrim, 2003, p. 160). However, the street is *symbolically* important, too, because of its general association with threat, danger and refuse, and because of the powerful fears associated with attacks by strangers on the street (Wilkinson, 1998, p. 210). Concerns to manage these risks means that deinstitutionalization has for many service users meant **'transinstitutionalization'** where service users have effectively been incarcerated within their own homes in the community (Kelly & McKenna, 2004). There has therefore arguably been a return to confinement (Philo, 2000), where deinstitutionalization has simply resulted in the transfer of the main functions of social control from the asylum to a new location (Kemshall, 2002, p. 98).

Far from becoming 'integrated' into communities, it is argued that mental health service users remain as alienated as they were under the asylum system, but in an alternative site (Coppock & Hopton, 2000; Taylor, 1994/5). The fixed distinction that could previously be made between those in the walls of the asylum and those outside it was replaced with a 'complex topography of community' (Rose, 1998, p. 179). This comprised day centres, supported accommodation, small-scale residential accommodation and so forth. Rather than mechanisms of control being limited to those diagnosed and enclosed in the hospital or prison, these practices now operated 'within wider networks of control, disseminated across the community' (Rose, 1998, p. 181). The direct link between these wider networks of control and the increasing domination of risk thinking in mental health practice is important. We next turn to a more detailed analysis of these developments.

Risk, dangerousness and prediction in mental health practice

Since the implementation of policies of deinstitutionalization, the intensification of anxieties about people with mental health needs and the state of mental health services has manifested itself in particular ways in mental health practice. One of the most significant factors has been the explicit shift in focus towards people defined as 'severely mentally ill' (Department of Health, 1994), and the targeting of resources on those regarded as 'most in need'. This shift in focus has been interpreted by many commentators as a way of rationing scarce resources so that *only* those with needs that can be defined as 'high risk' or high dependency receive a service (Lewis et al., 1995). It is argued that such targeting has led to an increasingly narrow definition of risk and the focus of organizations and individual practitioners on 'high-risk' individuals (Davis, 1996; Kemshall, 2002). The focus on the risks posed to others by mental health service users has also meant that the risks they routinely face have been systematically ignored or obscured (Kelly & McKenna, 2004). Yet little is known about what practitioners have in mind when they consider someone to be 'high risk' and what characterizes 'high-risk' individuals.

As we emphasized at the beginning of this chapter, risk can be treated both as 'real' and as 'constructed'. However, the predominant model in practice is realist, leading to calculative rationalities. Much of the research into risk assessment by professionals in the context of social welfare has similarly been undertaken within a realist paradigm. This means it has been based on the idea that 'risk' is objectively measurable and can therefore be assessed and managed. This approach to risk has been driven by a policy agenda that is concerned to improve professional decision making about risk and strengthen professional accountability (Kemshall, 2000). This policy agenda has been defined as the 'bureaucratic solution' (Alaszewski, 2002) because of the emphasis it places on organizational control of professional behaviour. It has been criticized because it assumes that improving risk assessment practice will result in fewer poor outcomes, such as homicide, by successfully identifying and managing the risks presented by 'high-risk' individuals. This latter view has persisted despite well-documented evidence of the tendency to over-predict rather than underestimate the risk of violence from people who are diagnosed as mentally ill, and the notorious difficulties inherent in the task of predicting and preventing events, particularly rare ones (Crichton, 1995). The rarity of extreme events such as homicide means that there will consequently be a high number of false positives, posing serious ethical dilemmas in a field such as mental health (Munro & Rumgay, 2000; Petch, 2001; Szmukler, 2000). The idea that clinicians make objective judgements about risk is fundamentally flawed. There are issues around the way professionals interpret probabilistic information, according to how it is framed or presented to them. For example, in a recent study of psychiatric decision making, Jefferies-Sewell et al. (2015) found that decisions by psychiatrists about admitting service users to hospital were affected by the mode of presentation of risk information rather than the content. If the *same* information was presented numerically and with a label of 'high' rather than 'low' risk, respondents were more likely to choose admission.

If we ask how new is 'risk' and risk thinking in relation to mental health, we need to understand that the most important shift has been from 'dangerousness' to risk (Rose, 1998). As Rose (1998) observes, 'madness', 'insanity', and the like have all always been associated with unpredictability and danger. Equally, from the mid-nineteenth century, the person who is deemed dangerous is assumed to suffer from some sort of madness (Foucault, 1978). But, as Rose maintains, the links between madness and danger have in more recent times undergone a major realignment in terms of the switch from the language of dangerousness to that of risk. This turn is not just a linguistic one: it represents a real and significant change in the way mental health problems are understood and consequently how we respond to them.

Whereas dangerousness was seen as a characteristic of particular pathological individuals, this meaning 'mutates' through the 1970s and 1980s so that 'dangerousness becomes a matter of factors, of situations, of statistical probabilities' (Rose, 1998, p. 178). In practice, this shift signalled an important change of focus from clinical to actuarial methods of prediction. Rather than assessing dangerousness based on clinical judgement of individuals, actuarial methods involve risk assessment based on statistical probabilities based on aggregates. Using this approach, it was argued, predictions of future violence could be made using probability calculations. Powerful proponents of this change were researchers in the US, Monohan and Steadman (1996). Importantly, this dominance of risk as an organizing idea was not confined to decision making about whether or not certain individuals required admission or imprisonment. It extended into the everyday lives of *all* service users and professionals:

> In practice, to put it crudely, all psychiatric patients can, and should be allocated to a level of risk, risk assessed, risk classified, risk managed: high risk, medium risk, low risk – but rarely no risk. (Rose, 1998, p. 179)

The overriding responsibility of professionals is now to classify individuals in making predictions of future conduct – how risky a person is deemed to be in the community and how these risks can be effectively managed. Service users can be divided into 'good' and 'bad' patients, where their capacity for self-management is the paramount concern (Rose, 1996, p. 14). The 'good' subjects of psychiatry are compliant with medication and attend appointments, the 'bad' 'do not "play the game" of community care' (Rose, 1996, p. 4). In this process of classification, 'high risk' has been more closely associated with service users who are deemed to represent a risk to others rather than to themselves (Warner, 2008). It is in this light that we can observe the moral dimensions of the operations of the risk paradigm and the implications it has for social justice. The injustice is in the moral ascription that conflates both 'mad', and risk, with 'bad'. Most important of all from our point of view, narrow definitions of risk and the focus on service users who are deemed 'high risk' has led to new forms of disadvantage and exclusion in community mental health practice. As Sawyer (2008) has argued, service users deemed to be 'low risk' are often excluded from services altogether. The need and social suffering that the dominant risk paradigm obscures is therefore as significant as the risks that it brings so sharply and disproportionately into view. The lived experience of stigma and discrimination by mental health service users, and the feelings that these forms of social suffering entail are, we argue, the starting point for an alternative paradigm.

The chapters: Challenges to the dominance of 'risk'

The particular focus of the next chapter, Chapter 2, is the use of mandated legal powers in mental health services and the contested risk paradigms that drive decision-making processes in this arena. The authors argue for a situated ethical stance in this area of practice, in which holistic methods of assessing risk and the basis for coercion are adopted.

Chapter 3 explores how the priorities of mental health social work organizations are dominated by risk thinking and practices, and how these are shaped by new managerialism and neoliberal economic policies. The authors bring direct experience of managing mental health services and also draw on psychodynamic insights in their analysis. Chapter 4 demonstrates how thinking about risk as a human rights and social justice issue creates new ways for thinking about mental health problems and responses to them. Drawing on sociocultural theories, the authors offer an alternative lens to the risk paradigm that is a continued theme in succeeding chapters. In Chapter 5, independent scholars with lived experience of mental health problems explore the challenges posed when narrow conceptualizations of risk dominate mental health services. They reflect on the value of a human rights and social justice perspective in challenging this dominant paradigm of risk and the suffering that results from it. In its focus on suicide prevention, Chapter 6 takes a critical approach to the conventional focus on individual risk assessment. It advocates a broader conception of risk that can also encompass macro-level issues and dilemmas. For example, some in the disability community argue that service provider attitudes towards people with severe chronic illnesses often preclude attention to their individual suicide risk.

Chapter 7 draws on research on the lived experience of service users to consider responses to people diagnosed with psychotic illness, suggesting new ways of responding to risks that advance more socially just outcomes and human rights. The specific focus of the chapter is recovery, and how the focus of the recovery paradigm that is now so prevalent might shift to include risks to recovery and a recovery focus in the assessment of risks. Drawing on research involving in-depth interviews with managers and practitioners, Chapter 8 explores the complex ways in which they negotiate the interface between managing risk and providing care. The author highlights how risk management strategies can both enhance social justice ideals and work against them. The focus of Chapter 9 is leadership and management in mental health services. The authors reflect on their own experience of resisting dominant cultures of risk to find critically reflective space in an organizational context. Chapter 10 also draws on empirical research to explore the experiences of young people with mental health needs through social media such as Facebook and Tumblr. The focus is on the risk and recovery identities of young people and how we might think beyond the social media panics that often frame responses to them.

In Chapter 11, attention is focused on the concept of asylum in global contexts, and specifically the risk discourses and processes of othering faced by refugees and asylum seekers. The discussion explores the complex relationship between poor mental health outcomes and migration, and provides insight into how professional practices can disrupt dominant risk paradigms in this arena. The main themes of the book are reviewed in Chapter 12, our concluding chapter. Here, we reflect on the potential of reconfiguring an understanding of risk within a paradigm founded on human rights and social justice principles.

Conclusion

In this introductory chapter we have highlighted the nature and character of the risk paradigm that currently dominates mental health systems across Europe, North America and Australasia. We have briefly analysed the development of the paradigm in historical terms, by charting the way the idea of risk has evolved and grown in its influence culturally, politically and socially. The concept of risk has been explored in terms of the major theoretical contributions to our understanding; the policy agenda and how the idea of risk has become so dominant a force; and, finally, we have observed how risk and its associated systems of classification have transformed practice. Good practice has essentially been redefined as risk-averse, or defensive practice. In the chapters that follow, each of these major themes are developed and elaborated on by the different contributory authors in a range of ways that will further elaborate our argument for a new paradigm that has human rights and social justice at its heart.

References

Alaszewski, A. (2002) 'Risk and Dangerousness', in B. Bytheway, V. Bacigalupo, J. Bornat, J. Johnson and S. Spurr (eds) *Understanding Care, Welfare and Community: A Reader* (London: Routledge), 183–91.

Bartlett, P. and Sandland, R. (2000) *Mental Health Law: Policy and Practice* (London: Blackstone Press).

Beck, U. (1992) *Risk Society: Towards a New Modernity* (London: Sage).

Bornat, J., Pereira, C., Pilgrim, D. and Williams, F. (1993) *Community Care: A Reader* (Hampshire: Macmillan).

Bytheway, B., Bacigalupo, V., Bornat, J., Johnson, J. and Spurr, S. (2002) *Understanding Care, Welfare and Community: A Reader* (London: Routledge).

Coppock, V. and Hopton, J. (2000) *Critical Perspectives on Mental Health* (New York: Routledge).

Crichton, J. (1995) *Psychiatric Patient Violence: Risk and Response* (London: Duckworth).

Culpitt, I. (1999) *Social Policy and Risk* (London: Sage).

Davis, A. (1996) 'Risk Work and Mental Health', in H. Kemshall and J. Pritchard (eds) *Good Practice in Risk Assessment and Risk Management* (London: Jessica Kingsley), 109–20.

Department of Health (1994) *Health of the Nation Key Area Handbook: Mental Illness* (London: HMSO).

Douglas, M. (1992) *Risk and Blame: Essays in Cultural Theory* (London: Routledge).

Dunant, S. and Porter, R. (1997) *The Age of Anxiety* (London: Virago).

Foucault, M. (1978) 'About the Concept of the "Dangerous Individual" in Nineteenth Century Legal Psychiatry', *International Journal of Law and Psychiatry*, 1, 1–18.

Frost, E. and Hoggett, P. (2008) 'Human Agency and Social Suffering', *Critical Social Policy*, 28, 438–60.

Furedi, F. (1997) *Culture of Fear: Risk Taking and the Morality of Low Expectation* (London: Cassell).

Giddens, A. (1990) *The Consequences of Modernity* (Cambridge: Polity).

Giddens, A. (1991) *Modernity and Self-identity* (Cambridge: Polity).

Giddens, A. (1998) 'Risk society: The Context of British politics', in J. Franklin (ed.) *The Politics of Risk Society* (Oxford: Polity).

Grounds, A. (1995) 'Risk Assessment and Management in Clinical Context', in J. Crichton (ed.) *Psychiatric Patient Violence: Risk and Response* (London: Duckworth), 43–59.

Hollway, W. and Jefferson, T. (1997) 'The Risk Society in an Age of Anxiety: Situating Fear of Crime', *British Journal of Sociology*, 48, 255–66.

Jefferies-Sewell, K., Sharma, S., Gale, T. M., Hawley, C. J., Georgiou, G. J. and Laws, K. R. (2015) 'To Admit or not to Admit? The Effect of Framing on Risk Assessment Decision Making in Psychiatrists', *Journal of Mental Health*, 24(1), 20–3.

Jorm, A. F. and Reavley, N. J. (2014) 'Public Belief that Mentally Ill People are Violent: is the USA Exporting Stigma to the Rest of the World?', *Australian and New Zealand Journal of Psychiatry*, 48(3), 213–15.

Jorm, A. F., Reavley, N. J. and Ross, A. M. (2012) 'Belief in the Dangerousness of People with Mental Disorders: A Review', *Australian and New Zealand Journal of Psychiatry*, 46(11), 1029–45.

Kelly, S. and McKenna, H. (2004) 'Risks to Mental Health Patients Discharged into the Community', *Health, Risk & Society*, 6(4), 377–85.

Kemshall, H. (2000) 'Conflicting Knowledges on Risk: the Case of Risk Knowledge in the Probation Service', *Health, Risk & Society*, 2, 143–58.

Kemshall, H. (2002) *Risk, Social Policy and Welfare* (Buckingham: Open University Press).

Kleinman, A., Das, D. and Lock, M. (eds) (1997) *Social Suffering* (Berkeley: University of California Press).

Laurance, J. (2003) *Pure Madness: How Fear Drives the Mental Health System* (London: Routledge).

Leff, J. (1997) *Care in the Community: Illusion or Reality?* (Chichester: Wiley).

Leff, J. (2001) 'Why is Care in the Community Perceived as a Failure?', *British Journal of Psychiatry*, 179, 381–3.

Lewis, J., Bernstock, P. and Bovell, V. (1995) 'The Community Care Changes: Unresolved Tensions in Policy and Issues in Implementation', *Journal of Social Policy*, 24, 73–94.

Lupton, D. (1999) *Risk* (London: Routledge).

Monohan, J. and Steadman, H. J. (eds) (1996) *Violence and Mental Disorder: Developments in Risk Assessment* (Chicago: University of Chicago Press).

Moon, G. (2000) 'Risk and Protection: the Discourse of Confinement in Contemporary Mental Health Policy', *Health and Place*, 6, 239–50.

Munro, E. and Rumgay, J. (2000) 'Role of Risk Assessment in Reducing Homicides by People with a Mental Illness, *British Journal of Psychiatry*, 176, 116–20.

Pearson, G. (1999) 'Madness and Moral Panics', in J. Peay and N. Eastman (eds) *Law Without Enforcement: Integrating Mental Health and Justice* (Oxford: Hart), 159–72.

Petch, E. (2001) 'Risk Management in UK Mental Health Services: An Overvalued Idea?', *Psychiatric Bulletin*, 25, 203–5.

Philo, G. (2000) 'Preface: Post-asylum Geographies: An Introduction', *Health & Place*, 6, 135–6.

Pilgrim, D. and Rogers, A. (1999) *A Sociology of Mental Health and Illness* (Buckingham: Open University Press).

Power, M. (2004) *The Risk Management of Everything: Rethinking the Politics of Uncertainty* (London: Demos).

Rogers, A. and Pilgrim, D. (2003) *Mental Health and Inequality* (Hampshire: Palgrave Macmillan).

Rose, N. (1996) 'Psychiatry as a Political Science: Advanced Liberalism and the Administration of Risk', *History of the Human Sciences*, 9(2), 1–23.

Rose, N. (1998) 'Governing Risky Individuals: The Role of Psychiatry in New Regimes of Control', *Psychiatry, Psychology and Law*, 5(2), 177–95.

Sawyer, A. (2008) 'Risk and New Exclusions in Community Mental Health Practice', *Australian Social Work*, 61(4), 327–41.

Scott, H. (1998) 'Risk and Community Care for People with a Mental Illness', in B. Heyman (ed.) *Risk, Health and Health Care: A Qualitative Approach* (London: Arnold), 303–13.

Stanford, S. and Taylor, S. (2013) 'Welfare Dependence or Enforced Deprivation? A Critical Examination of White Neoliberal Welfare and Risk', *Australian Social Work*, 66(4), 476–94.

Symonds, A. and Kelly, A. (1998) *The Social Construction of Community Care* (Hampshire: Macmillan).

Szmukler, G. (2000) 'Homicide Inquiries: What Sense do they Make?', *British Journal of Psychiatry*, 24, 6–10.

Taylor, R. (1994/5) 'Alienation and Integration in Mental Health Policy', *Critical Social Policy*, 42, 81–90.

Trieman, N., Leff, J. and Glover, G. (1999) 'Outcome of Long Stay Psychiatric Patients Resettled in the Community: Prospective Cohort Study', *British Medical Journal*, 319, 13–16.

Tummey, R. and Turner, T. (eds) (2008) *Critical Issues in Mental Health* (Basingstoke: Palgrave Macmillan).

Turner, T. and Colombo, A. (2008) 'Risk', in R. Tummey and T. Turner (eds) *Critical Issues in Mental Health* (Basingstoke: Palgrave Macmillan), 161–75.

Warner, J. and Gabe, J. (2004) 'Risk and Liminality in Mental Health Social Work', *Health, Risk and Society,* 6(4), 387–99.

Warner, J. (2008) 'Community Care, Risk and the Shifting Locus of Danger and Vulnerability in Mental Health', in A. Peterson and I. Wilkinson (eds) *Health, Risk and Vulnerability* (Oxford: Routledge), 30–47.

Wilkinson, I. (2001) *Anxiety in a Risk Society* (London: Routledge).

Wilkinson, J. (1998) 'Danger on the Streets: Mental Illness, Community Care and Ingratitude', in A. Symonds and A. Kelly (eds) *The Social Construction of Community Care* (Hampshire: Macmillan), 208–19.

2

UNDERSTANDING RISK AND COERCION IN THE USE OF COMMUNITY-BASED MENTAL HEALTH LAWS

Jim Campbell and Gavin Davidson

Introduction

We use this chapter to explore the contested risk paradigms that can be used to understand the organization and delivery of mental health services, with a particular focus on the use of mandated legal powers. These debates have influenced our ideas as former Approved Social Workers in Northern Ireland, and now academics who have worked in the UK, Ireland and Northern Ireland. Our experiences have coincided with fundamental changes to the way in which politicians, professionals and the wider public view risk and coercion in community settings. We believe now is an opportune moment to discuss these issues as it is a time when policymakers across the developed world, in tandem with populist discourses that focus on dangerousness (Corrigan *et al.*, 2014; Laurance, 2003) are driving decision-making processes in mental health services. These processes are primarily focused on the 'management of risk' and the increased use of coercive, community-based laws. As a result, the ways that practitioners use mental health laws imply complex decision-making processes involving judgements about risk and professional ethics. This chapter is particularly focused on substitute decision-making processes in two areas of mental health law: the use of Community Treatment Orders (CTOs) and the application of capacity laws. We begin with a review of the literature on substitute decision making in these fields, which reveals a range of personal, organizational and societal factors that influence judgements made by professionals. The chapter concludes with an argument for a situated ethical stance in these areas of practice, one that acknowledges the ambiguities embedded in these mandated roles, and the need for professionals to use holistic methods of assessing risk and legal coercion.

Risk and mental health and coercive laws

We begin this chapter, as have others in this book, by reflecting on some of the complex, shifting discourses on risk and mental health. In our case we seek to illustrate the fluid and value-laden nature of professional decision making in these areas by reference to two areas of law: mandated forms of care and treatment in the community, and the application of capacity laws that involve a range of substitute and supportive decision-making processes. These two areas of law have been chosen because they are relatively new to many practitioners and service users and are often subject to intense, sometimes controversial, debates about their purpose and efficacy. Importantly, in the context of this book, we argue that a more analytical, reflexive approach is needed to considerations of risk in these circumstances – risk to the service user as well as to practitioners and the wider public.

Perhaps more than other dimensions of mental health services, the origins and functions of mental health laws are worthy of historical interrogation. Scull's (2015) recent contribution to histories of 'madness' once again reminds us of the social, political and cultural narratives that sustained a century of incarceration, when large numbers of people, viewed to be at risk, were confined in institutions and others were subject to surveillance and management in the community (Bartlett & Wright, 1999). Regardless of wherever care, treatment and coercion took place, the overarching proposition that eventually informed the development of mental health services was that mental illnesses could be diagnosed and to some extent predicted, and that associated risks could and should be managed. The way in which the law was, and is, used tends to reinforce these sets of interlinked assumptions. This partly explains how and why mandated roles for mental health professionals developed and grew in the twentieth century. This sense of professional confidence and competence in assessing mental health and risk is reinforced by systems of professional education and practice. Actuarial approaches to risk assessment are founded upon the notion of evidence-based calculations and validated tools. This technology helps reveal patterns of identity, thoughts and behaviours that become part of the rationality of risk assessment (Langan, 2010). This, it is argued, can also be achieved through the more subtle development of practitioner knowledge and skills that enables the professional to assess and construct a picture, a representation of the 'patient', informed by biographical, familial and social contexts.

Optimism about the ability of professionals to fully understand mental ill-health and calculate risk, we believe, is misplaced (Campbell, 2010). Traditional notions of risk that have been the cornerstone of decision making are increasingly contested. For example, it is evident that too many false positives occur as a result of professional judgements made about those perceived to be of high risk, and too many false negatives of those identified as low risk (Large *et al.*, 2014). Consequent decisions to use compulsory powers therefore become more tenuous (Callaghan *et al.*, 2013). Fazel *et al.* (2012) conducted a systematic review and meta-analysis of the predictive validity of tools used to assess the risk of violence, sexual offences and other criminal behaviour. They concluded that although these types of tools are widely used, in both clinical and criminal justice settings, the current evidence does not support their use as the sole determinant of detention. Szmukler (2012, p. 173) has summarized the arguments succinctly: 'Rare events, such as suicide or serious violence – no matter how tragic they are or how much our society wishes us to prevent them – are impossible to predict with a degree of accuracy that is clinically meaningful.' Szmukler and Rose (2013) have also highlighted that the economic costs of focusing on risk assessment and management in mental health care are often neglected, but they include: cost of training on risk; the opportunity costs of spending time on risk; and the service costs of detaining many people who are false positives. Other costs, no less tangible, are: the associated neglect of those considered low risk; the impact on the relationships between workers and service users, especially in terms of trust; and the possible reinforcement of the stigma associated with mental health problems.

Our view, one that is pursued in this chapter, is that ideas and practices about risk and mental health can best be understood, not as fixed or easily defined entities, but as constantly shifting. They can be viewed as patterned and constructed in particular milieu, reinforced by political, social and populist discourses (Sawyer, 2009). When deconstructed in this way, predominant discourses about risk, which were heavily reinforced in the media in the 1990s (Laurance, 2003), become less persuasive (Stanford, 2008). As we have implied above, histories of the development of mental health services tend to focus on how professionals are required to deal with the risky or dangerous behaviours of service users. If anything, there is a greater preoccupation in contemporary societies about the dangers attributed to people with mental health problems than was the case in the past. We argue below that there is indeed a requirement for professionals to manage risk and dangerousness, particularly when laws are being used. What is missing in the analysis of these issues, however, is a broader concept of risk where the iatrogenic effects of interventions and their adverse impact on the lives of service users and carers is made more transparent, for example in terms of restrictions of liberties, inequalities that result from processes of labelling and social stigma (Ryan *et al.*, 2010; Warner, 2007). As others have argued elsewhere in this book, these are the types of risk to mental health service users that are often not recognized, nor well understood, when policymakers and professionals discuss these situations. Instead, there tends to be a focus on risk to the public or risk of self-harm for the service user, often with unforeseen consequences for particular populations (Warner & Gabe, 2008).

An example of the lack of transparency about impact is when practitioners, intentionally or otherwise, use informal types of coercion to change service user views and behaviours. It is a challenging and, perhaps for many practitioners, a surprising claim that various forms of coercion in the community take place in informal settings where mandated powers are not used but sometimes alluded to by professionals. Here coercion can be viewed as the subtle use of authority by the professional to override the rights of the client (O'Brien & Golding, 2003). Davidson and Campbell (2007) found that generic community mental health teams were more likely to engage in higher numbers of coercion strategies, which include compulsory admission, verbal direction, money management, bargaining and other forms of leverage, than specialist assertive outreach services. Across time and both types of team, all workers reported using at least one such coercive strategy in their practice. In order to deal with such perverse outcomes we believe that a broader vision of risk and risk management is needed, one that is more explicit about competing demands and ethical principles, and which includes a more encompassing discussion about the need to maintain public safety, protect the rights of patients, and, eventually, to offer reciprocal services to compensate for the loss of liberty (Roberts *et al.*, 2002).

We now examine two areas of practice where this intersection between legal coercion and the assessment of risk takes place: firstly where CTOs are used, and secondly when professionals use the law to assess service users' capacity to make judgements about their lives.

Mental health and legal coercion in the community

If we were writing this chapter two decades ago we would explore the legal processes that lead to compulsory admission to psychiatric hospital. This of course continues to be an area of practice that often has a profound impact on the lives of clients and their families and friends, as well as those professionals involved in these difficult decision-making processes. Instead we wish to develop our ideas about risk and mental health in the area of community-based forms of legal coercion that are more recent types of mental health law. CTOs (and Outpatient Commitments (OPC), as these forms of law are described in the US and parts of Europe) have been increasingly used by mental health professionals to manage situations of risk. They were introduced in Victoria, Australia in the 1980s, and since then have become commonplace across Australasia, some provinces in Canada and everywhere in the UK, apart from Northern Ireland where they have now been included in draft legislation (Department of Health, Social Services and Public Safety and Department of Justice, 2014). Despite policymakers' intentions to limit CTOs and target particularly problematic populations (for example, 'revolving door' patients who have frequent compulsory admissions to hospital), the history of their application throughout the world indicates a continuous, upward trend in usage. Following their introduction in England and Wales the Royal College of Psychiatrists noted, with some concern, that an initial estimate of 400–600 service users in receipt of CTOs per year had quickly grown to over 4,000 with incremental increases year by year (www.mentalhealthlaw.co.uk/ Statistics). Similar trends are evident in Australia and Canada (Brophy *et al.*, 2003; O'Brien & Farrell, 2005). Although there is variation in processes and accompanied professional duties (Campbell *et al.*, 2006) depending on the jurisdiction, CTOs generally require service users to comply with restrictions and conditions which, if these are not met, usually results in a return to hospital from the community setting. Typically, CTOs permit approved professionals to compel patients to accept medication, attend facilities and live in designated residences.

The arguments for and against CTOs have been summarized by Castells-Aulet *et al.* (2013). Critics argue that CTOs tend to have the effect of changing a previous set of status assumptions about the citizen's right to live freely and in consensual arrangements with professionals, for example by being able to refuse care and treatment. Service users sometimes experience negative, coercive threats if they do not comply with the conditions of the CTO. When combined, these factors tend to undermine the therapeutic relationship between the service user and the professional. Advocates tend to view the positives that CTOs can bring to service users' and carers' lives. Most notably they are considered less restrictive than laws that compel citizens to enter psychiatric hospitals and often attract better, concentrated services and resources. The hope is that by creating a more supported community context, but in the restrictions of the Order, there is less chance of relapse and recourse to hospital. Given the complex and controversial nature of these arguments it is perhaps not surprising that evidence of effectiveness and efficacy is contested (Burns *et al.*, 2013; Churchill *et al.*, 2007). A key rationale for the use of CTOs is that they offer a less restrictive alternative to institutional care and treatment and avoid the iatrogenic harm that is often associated with detentions in psychiatric hospital. However, a systematic review (Churchill *et al.*, 2007) and findings from the most recent randomized control trial (Burns *et al.*, 2013) tend to undermine this central claim for the efficacy of CTOs. These studies found no causal relationship between CTO use and reduction in hospital admissions.

It may be the case that some service users can benefit from the experience of having been placed on a CTO where social and personal needs are being met in community rather than hospital settings. The corollary is that, where such services and conditions are not in place, CTOs are less likely to achieve their aims and could potentially introduce additional risk factors. Worryingly, specific populations are more likely to be subject to CTOs, including younger men with dual diagnoses and people from black and minority ethnic groups. There are relatively few studies of the views of service users, but where these are carried out there is evidence of failures by professionals to listen to the voices of clients and that therapeutic relationships may be damaged when CTOs are introduced (Brophy *et al.*, 2003; Petrila & Christy, 2008).

We now wish to focus on one other, important area of community-based mandated powers. The legal criteria for CTOs tend to focus on mental disorder and risk but there are also legal frameworks, based on a person's decision-making ability, which enable compulsory intervention. These are usually framed as some form of mental capacity law, and their use to make substitute decisions and how this may offer an alternative to the current preoccupation with risk will be explored.

Mental health, capacity and risk

The introduction of capacity laws to Australia and the UK has challenged traditional criteria that generally exist when compulsory mental health laws are used. Thus most jurisdictions require professionals to assess for the evidence of a mental disorder alongside a degree of risk that is of a sufficient level that requires compulsory admissions either to hospital or, as we have explained above, placement on a CTO. Policymakers have challenged the rationale for these criteria in the last decade. For example it has been argued by Dawson and Szmukler (2006) that mental health laws which allow the compulsory treatment of people with mental health problems and the substitute decision making involved, even when the person has the ability to give and withhold consent, are discriminating against people with mental health problems. The debate has been intensified by the publication of the United Nations Convention on the Rights of Persons with Disabilities (2006) (CRPD), ratified by the UK in 2009. The CRPD prohibits all discrimination on the grounds of disability (Article 3) and it includes those with mental health problems in its scope:

> Persons with disabilities include those who have long-term physical, mental, intellectual or sensory impairments, which in interaction with various barriers may hinder their full and effective participation in society on an equal basis with others (Article 1).

It can be debated whether this would extend to all forms and duration of mental health problems (Kelly, 2014), but it would certainly seem to apply to those for whom compulsory treatment in hospital and/or the community is being considered. The CRPD goes on, in Article 12(2), to require that 'States Parties shall recognize that persons with disabilities enjoy legal capacity on an equal basis with others in all aspects of life'. Legal capacity tends to refer to a person's standing before the law and power to act, though sometimes it is also extended to mean ability to act. Again, the interpretation of 'legal capacity' and the related terms of 'substitute and supported decision making' is the subject of ongoing debate, but there seems to be a reasonable consensus that compulsory powers based solely on a person's disability status are not compatible with the CRPD. Dawson and Szmukler (2006) have asserted that in order to avoid the discrimination involved in compulsory intervention based on a mental disorder criterion, it is preferable to have a legal framework for everyone, regardless of disability, which only allows compulsory intervention, of any description, if the person is unable to make the relevant decision. In other words, a functional test of decision-making ability rather than a status test of mental disorder is needed.

In some jurisdictions attempts have been made to merge or read across capacity and mental health laws. For example, in Scotland, in addition to evidence of mental disorder, it must also be the case 'that because of the mental disorder the patient's ability to make decisions about the provision of such medical treatment is significantly impaired' (Section 57(3)(d), *Mental Health (Care and Treatment) (Scotland) Act 2003*). In Ontario, a separate law, the *Health Care Consent Act 1996*, does not allow for compulsory treatment if the person is able to consent and has refused. Unlike other jurisdictions in the UK, Northern Ireland is proposing to replace the current *Mental Health (Northern Ireland) Order 1986* with a capacity-based law that does not have a mental disorder criterion. Adding a decision-making ability criterion to mental disorder, or having it as the gateway criterion for any compulsory intervention for all, would seem to address the concern about only people with mental health problems being compelled to have treatment they have the ability to refuse. This approach attends to Article 12(3) of the CRPD that requires that 'States Parties shall take appropriate measures to provide access by persons with disabilities to the support they may require in exercising their legal capacity'. This suggests that, in addition to having the appropriate non-discriminatory criteria for compulsion, there is a requirement to positively support and enable people to make their own decisions. Even if decision-making ability is used as the gateway criterion and all possible decision-making supports are provided, there will still be some circumstances in which a person is unable to make the required decision. A process to determine what type of intervention is necessary, proportionate and the least restrictive is therefore still needed.

As in the case of CTOs, a professional judgement about risk is necessary where service users lack capacity. So in Victoria, Australia, the treatment criteria includes the following:

> because the person has mental illness, the person needs immediate treatment to prevent – (i) serious deterioration in the person's mental or physical health; or (ii) serious harm to the person or to another person (5(b), *Victoria Mental Health Act 2014*);

In Ontario, Canada, the risk criterion is that:

> if the person does not receive continuing treatment or care and continuing supervision while living in the community, he or she is likely, because of mental disorder, to cause serious bodily harm to himself or herself or to another person or to suffer substantial mental or physical deterioration of the person or serious physical impairment of the person. (Section 33.1(4)(c)(iii), *Ontario Mental Health Act 1990* (most recently amended 2015))

And in Scotland treatment is dependent on the following criterion being met: 'if the patient were not provided with such medical treatment there would be a significant risk – (i) to the health, safety or welfare of the patient; or (ii) to the safety of any other person' (Section 57(3)(c), *Mental Health (Care and Treatment) (Scotland) Act 2003*). This review demonstrates that, as with CTOs, professionals need to be mindful of the complex nature of the assessment process when using capacity laws. They need to balance the rights of service users alongside a duty of care to the service user and wider public. As we have already argued, it is questionable whether mental health professionals are sufficiently able to accurately assess the risk of future harm, to self or others, in order to justify the use of risk as a basis for compulsory intervention. This is a point that we now develop in greater depth.

Risk, mental health and professional decision making

We began this chapter by describing the shifts that have occurred in mental health law and policy in developed countries, particularly over the last few decades. This has resulted in increased numbers of people living with mental health problems in the community, often in situations of real or perceived risk. The response by the state has been, almost invariably, to reach towards community laws that are often coercive in nature, or to repair existing laws to make them compliant with international conventions. A consequence is that increased numbers of professionals and service users are engaged in often problematic relationships that are shaped by a variety of discourses on risk. We are interested in exploring the way in which such legal processes can either enhance citizenship rights in the use of coercion, or, more likely, exacerbate the painful experiences that clients often encounter at times when the law is being used by professionals (Campbell & Davidson, 2009). So far we have highlighted the way in which contemporary practices require professionals to make types of judgements about risk, but we have at the same time argued that predominant discourses on risk should be challenged. We believe that the received wisdom that has informed legally mandated professional interventions in the past is now unsustainable, given the increasing demands of international human rights laws that seek to redress the power of the state when coercive laws are being applied in practice.

We now wish to explore how alternative ideas on risk, mental health and capacity can enable rather than restrict the lives of service users and encourage alternative professional practices. One approach in working with CTOs is to encourage the deconstruction of professional decision-making processes and to consider how they may, or may not, appropriately manage situations of risk and thus enhance the lives of clients (O'Brien & Farrell, 2005; O'Reilly 2004). A good example of this is represented in the work of Brophy and McDermott (2013) whose study sought to identify principles of social work practice in this area. They argue that CTOs can be purposeful if professionals use direct practice skills, embrace human rights perspectives, focus on identifiable goals and outcomes, aspire to quality service delivery and engage with key stakeholders. Even where these laws work well, the increasing expectations of international conventions is that consent and capacity have significant implications for debates about how we understand risk and risk assessment. This is the case where mental disorder and risk are no longer the most appropriate criteria for compulsory intervention (as we discussed above, some CTO laws now require an additional capacity assessment process).

In many jurisdictions these criteria are being replaced by alternative approaches to substitute and supportive decision making. An assessment of the decision-making ability of service users then becomes crucial when considering issues of risk. The two main overlapping possibilities seem to be that professionals should abide by the service user's view, based on the person's will and preferences, or make a judgement about their best interests. Article 12(4) of the CRPD requires processes that:

> respect the rights, will and preferences of the person, are free of conflict of interest and undue influence, are proportional and tailored to the person's circumstances, apply for the shortest time possible and are subject to regular review by a competent, independent and impartial authority or judicial body.

New capacity laws, as a result, seek to lead policymakers and practitioners away from the supposed causal relationships between risk and mental health when issues of coercion are to be considered. Hence we return to the argument used at the start of this chapter about the need for a broader, contextual understanding of risk, mental health and professional decision making. This notion is implied in the CRPD with its requirement for a non-discriminatory legal framework, not based on any form of disability, that could address some of the ongoing concerns about how the operation of mental health laws tends to stigmatize service users. This allows us to open up traditionally narrow debates that often contextualize risk in terms of choices made by individual service users on the basis of abnormal thoughts and behaviours caused by mental health. It is imperative that professionals understand more fully a broader narrative that acknowledges notions about the social construction of risk, in particular iatrogenic risks associated with legal coercions, for example in terms of associated experiences of stigma and iatrogenic harm.

The argument for a capacity test also implies a shift from a position of *parens patriae* (where the state assumes the responsibility for the rights of vulnerable citizens) towards a more inclusive set of arrangements between the service user, professionals and other stakeholders. The CRPD requirement for supported decision making should reinforce what is already good practice in terms of creating a positive right to receive support that can facilitate independent decision making and so respect people's autonomy and legal capacity. Decisions about whether or not compulsion should be used and accepted become focused more on the decision-making ability and will and preferences of the service user, and less on the assessment of mental disorder and risk. This implies a redistribution of power, away from the decision making of professionals that tends to focus on the limitations or deficits of the service user and their circumstances, and towards a more evenly distributed exchange of views and opinions. In both the use of CTOs and capacity legislation, the importance of sustainable community-based resources and reciprocal commitments by the state (Eastman, 1994) then become crucial. At the same time, although the evidence for risk assessment does not provide a justification for compulsory intervention on its own, there does seem to a societal obligation to respond, in some way, to anyone who is sufficiently distressed to communicate, in whatever way, that they intend to harm themselves and/or others.

Conclusion

In this chapter we selected two legislative areas, CTOs and capacity laws, that have a direct and considerable impact on the lives of people with mental health problems, to explore issues of risk and professional decision making. We can be fairly certain that these laws will continue to be part of the landscape of mental health services now and into the future; it is important, therefore, that we continue to critically discuss the complexities of the relationship between the underpinning knowledge used by practitioners to make judgments while, at the same time, seeking to protect the rights of service users. We believe the received wisdom that informed professional interventions using mental health laws in the past is now unsustainable, given the increasing demands of international human rights laws that seek to redress the power of the state in these fields. Traditional notions of risk, once the cornerstone of decision making, are increasingly contested in these new contexts. As we argued earlier in this chapter, the presupposed veracity of actuarial and clinical models of risk assessment are less secure, so practitioners should be more cautious and considered in judging risk.

A more critical, broader approach in assessing risk must take into account the potential iatrogenic harm that is often associated with compulsory care and treatment; this may even be exacerbated in community-based settings when CTOs are used. In any case, the conventional legal requirement of a necessary coincidence of mental disorder and risk that has traditionally informed professional judgement making in this field is no longer sufficient, as our discussion of the impact of the CRPD has made apparent. The assessment of capacity may indeed be a complicated and debated process, but what seems clear is that professionals need to be more careful and clear about the reasons why capacity is not assumed or is overridden. As a consequence, practitioners have to do their utmost to support the decision making of service users, and only in the last case resort to substitute decision making. Where, then, does this leave the issue of risk assessment and management? We argue for a more situated approach to decision making (Campbell & Davidson, 2009). Practitioners should be more thoughtful in their interactions with service users with mental health problems, where there are issues of risk and when they potentially lack capacity. Policymakers, managers and opinion formers need to promote broader human rights perspectives (Davidson *et al.*, 2016) that imply a greater investment in mental health services and acknowledge the everyday risks that mental health service users experience. Only then can we be more secure that community-based mental health laws will benefit people with mental health problems.

References

Bartlett, P. and Wright, D. eds., 1999. Outside the walls of the asylum: The history of care in the community 1750–2000. A&C Black.

Brophy, L., Campbell, J. and Healy, B. (2003) 'Dilemmas in the Case Manager's Role: Implementing Involuntary Treatment in the Community', *Psychiatry, Psychology and the Law*, 10(1), 154–63.

Brophy, L. and McDermott, F. (2013) 'Using Social Work Theory and Values to Investigate the Implementation of Community Treatment Orders', *Australian Social Work*, 66(1), 72–85.

Burns, T., Rugkåsa, J., Molodynski, A, Dawson, J., Yeeles, K., Vazquez-Montes, M., Voysey, M., Sinclair, J. and Priebe, S. (2013) 'Community Treatment Orders for Patients with Psychosis (OCTET): A Randomised Controlled Trial', *Lancet*, 381, 1627–33.

Callaghan, S., Ryan, C. and Kerridge, I. (2013) 'Risk of Suicide is Insufficient Warrant for Coercive Treatment for Mental Illness', *International Journal of Law and Psychiatry*, 36(5), 374–85.

Campbell, J. (2010) 'Deciding to Detain: The Use of Compulsory Mental Health Law by Social Workers'. *British Journal of Social Work*, 40(1), 328–334.

Campbell, J., Brophy, L., Healy, B. and O'Brien, A. M. (2006) 'International Perspectives on the Use of Community Treatment Orders: Implications for Mental Health Social Workers', *British Journal of Social Work*, 36(7), 1101–18.

Campbell, J. and Davidson, G. (2009) 'Coercion in the Community: A Situated Approach to the Examination of Ethical Challenges for Mental Health Social Workers', *Ethics and Social Welfare*, 3(3), 249–63.

Castells-Aulet, L., Hernández-Viadel, M., Asensio-Pascual, P., Cañete-Nicolás, C., Bellido-Rodríguez, C., Lera-Calatayud, G. and Calabuig-Crespo, R. (2013) 'Involuntary Out-patient Commitment: 2-year Follow-up', *Psychiatric Bulletin*, 37, 60–4.

Churchill, R., Owen, G., Hotopf, M. and Singh, S. (2007) *International Experiences of Using Community Treatment Orders*, Department of Health and Institute of Psychiatry (King's College London: London).

Corrigan, P. W., Watson, A. C., Gracia, G., Slopen, N., Rasinski, K., and Hall, L. L. (2014) 'Newspaper Stories as Measures of Structural Stigma', *Psychiatric Services*, 56(5), 551–6.

Davidson, G. and Campbell, J. (2007) 'An Examination of the Use of Coercion by Assertive Outreach and Community Mental Health Teams in Northern Ireland', *British Journal of Social Work*, 37(3), 537–55.

Davidson, G., Brophy, L., & Campbell, J. (2016). Risk, Recovery and Capacity: Competing or Complementary Approaches to Mental Health Social Work. *Australian Social Work*, 69(2), 158–168.

Dawson, J. and Szmukler, G. (2006) 'Fusion of Mental Health and Incapacity Legislation', *British Journal of Psychiatry*, 188, 504–9.

Department of Health, Social Services and Public Safety and Department of Justice (2014) *Draft Mental Capacity Bill (NI): Consultation Document*, (Belfast: Department of Health, Social Services and Public Safety and Department of Justice).

Eastman, N. (1994) 'Mental Health Law: Civil Liberties and the Principle of Reciprocity', *BMJ: British Medical Journal*, 308(6920), 43.

Fazel, S., Singh, J. P., Doll, H. and Grann, M. (2012) 'Use of Risk Assessment Instruments to Predict Violence and Antisocial Behaviour in 73 Samples Involving 24 827 People: Systematic Review and Meta-analysis', *BMJ: British Medical Journal*, 345.

Kelly, B. D. (2014) 'Dignity, Human Rights and the Limits of Mental Health Legislation', *Irish Journal of Psychological Medicine*, 31(02), 75–81.

Langan, J., 2010. Challenging assumptions about risk factors and the role of screening for violence risk in the field of mental health. *Health, risk & society*, 12(2), pp. 85–100.

Laurance, J. (2003) *Pure Madness: How Fear Drives the Mental Health System.* (Routledge: London).

Large, M. M., Ryan, C. J., Callaghan, S., Paton, M. B. and Singh, S. P. (2014) 'Can Violence Risk Assessment Really Assist in Clinical Decision-making?', *Australian and New Zealand Journal of Psychiatry*, 48(3), 286–8.

O'Brien, A. J. and Golding, C. G. (2003). 'Coercion in Mental Healthcare: The Principle of Least Coercive Care', *Journal of Psychiatric and Mental Health Nursing*, 10(2), 167–73.

O'Brien, A-M. and Farrell, S. J. (2005) 'Community Treatment Orders: A Profile of a Canadian Experience', *Canadian Journal of Psychiatry*, 50, 27–30.

O'Reilly, R. L. (2004) 'Why are Community Treatment Orders Controversial?', *Canadian Journal of Psychiatry*, 49(9), 579–84.

Petrila, J. D. and Christy, A. (2008) 'Florida's Outpatient Law: A Lesson in Failed Reform?', *Psychiatric Services*, 59(1), 21–3.

Roberts, C., Peay, J. and Eastman, N. (2002) 'Mental Health Professionals' Attitudes towards Legal Compulsion: Report of a National Survey', *International Journal of Forensic Mental Health*, 1(1), 71–82.

Ryan, C., Nielssen, O., Paton, M. and Large, M. (2010) 'Clinical Decisions in Psychiatry should not be Based on Risk assessment', *Australasian Psychiatry*, 18(5), 398–403.

Sawyer, A-M. (2009) 'Mental Health Workers Negotiating Risk on the Frontline', *Australian Social Work*, 62(4), 441–59.

Scull, A. ed., 2015. Madhouses, mad-doctors, and madmen: The social history of psychiatry in the Victorian era. University of Pennsylvania Press.

Stanford, S., 2008. Taking a stand or playing it safe?: Resisting the moral conservatism of risk in social work practice. *European Journal of Social Work*, 11(3), pp. 209–220.

Szmukler, G. (2012) 'Risk Assessment for Suicide and Violence is of Extremely Limited Value in General Psychiatric Practice', *Australian and New Zealand Journal of Psychiatry*, 46(2), 173–4.

Szmukler, G. and Rose, N. (2013) 'Risk Assessment in Mental Health Care: Values and Costs', *Behavioral Sciences & The Law*, 31(1), 125–40.

Warner, J. (2007) 'Structural stigma, institutional trust and the risk agenda in mental health policy'. In: Clarke, K. and Maltby, Tony and Kennett, Patricia, eds. Social Policy Review 19: Analysis and Debate in Social Policy 2007. The Policy Press/Social Policy Association, pp. 201–220.

Warner, J. and Gabe, J. (2008) 'Risk Mental Disorder and Social Work Practice: A Gendered Landscape', *British Journal of Social Work*, 38(1), 117–34.

3

RISK THINKING AND THE PRIORITIES OF MENTAL HEALTH SOCIAL WORK ORGANIZATIONS

Chris Lee, Catherine Hartley and Elaine Sharland

Introduction

Beck (1998) and Giddens (1994), in their analyses of contemporary 'risk society', see risk as having a democratizing effect, given our shared vulnerability to, and anxiety about, risk in the late modern era. However, governmentality theorists argue that meanings about risk are constructed and practised as an art of neoliberal government (Barry *et al.*, 1996) and, as Dean (1999) points out, the heterogeneity of risk has allowed forms of neoliberal governance to colonize diverse and discrete spaces and practices.

Critical perspectives of the operations of risk in social work have considered how the dominance of risk thinking impacts negatively on social work and on the work of other caring professions (Ferguson, 2008; Harris, 2014; Webb, 2006). Within neoliberal governance, risk is cast predominantly in economic, not social, terms. Linked to this, need has been re-moralized as indicative of individual failure (Webb, 2006) and 'articulations of need are forced to "stumble over" the more urgent logic of costs and apportioning of limited economic resources' (Culpitt, 1999, p. 12). Neoliberal marketization of welfare has championed the idea of 'service users', including those with mental illness, as 'consumers' (Duffy, 2010). While some have considered this repositioning in a positive light (Healy, 2005), there is overwhelming critique of the social injustices now legitimated through the rationality of 'neoliberal risk welfare policy' (Stanford & Taylor, 2013). Meanwhile, concern with public protection has corresponded with the rise of risk management of people with severe mental health problems; they are identified as a public threat posing a physical risk and/or a financial risk due to their 'lack of economic participation' (Culpitt, 1999; Ferguson, 2008; Kemshall, 2002). Seen through a neoliberal lens (Mirowski, 2013), risk now contributes to the twin images of the service user either as a customer or a costly deviant.

As mental health team managers in England, two of us have witnessed at first hand how risk thinking has skewed the way practitioners think about and undertake their work. We have seen risk used as a rhetorical device to demonize people who experience mental ill-health, as well as their families and our colleagues working with them. In this chapter we draw on this experience to reflect on the dilemmas of working within the risk paradigm, situating this within our own political and professional context in England, while mindful that similar experiences and challenges occur in other Western countries.

We begin by considering how the rise and dominance of risk thinking and the privatization of risk have changed the priorities of frontline mental health services. We argue that risk considerations have become a subset of neoliberal welfare policy that is overtly economic in its focus. In this context, we have seen the diminution of the importance of relationship building (Coles *et al.*, 2013) in favour of quick fix, measurable interventions (Harris, 2014). This reflects neoliberalism's application of technocratic solutions (Layard, 2005) to even the most complex of human problems. As the mental health sector has become dominated by a business model of service delivery (Mearns, 2014), the financial and performance status of health care organizations is now valued over the therapeutic focus on service users. Accordingly, we argue that risk has distorted the priorities of mental health services and that in this context fear and paranoia are rampant. We go on to consider how a Kleinian (1975) perspective can inform our understanding of the intra- and interpersonal dynamics that permit obvious disregard for people's wellbeing. Our argument is illustrated by two case examples, exemplifying the impossible positions this creates for people who experience mental illness and those involved in their care.

Managerialism and the rise of risk

From the late 1980s in England, the Thatcher government instituted a new managerialism that constructed an apparatus of command and control (Seddon, 2008) across the whole of the public sector and, with this, an ensuing culture of risk management. Within this framework, the National Health Service (NHS) and local authorities (local government with responsibility for the provision of social care) were to be judged against rigorous performance measures that, it was claimed, would provide greater assurance that service quality standards were met (Department of Health, 1994).

The use of performance targets to drive improvement in public sector services expanded when the New Labour government came to power in 1997 (Harris, 2003). The attention of the new regime was drawn to the particular problem of mental illness because of a series of high media profile scandals involving mental health service users who killed members of the public or a mental health professional (Blom-Cooper *et al.*, 1995; Ritchie, 1994). What was seen as scandalous was that those with professional responsibility had failed to predict and prevent such risk from being realized. New Labour's approach was to invest significantly in mental health care and to increase the level of scrutiny and accountability over how care was delivered. The *National Service Framework for Mental Health* (Department of Health, 1999) laid out a plan to set up crisis teams, early intervention teams and assertive outreach teams in each locality.

During its 13-year reign, the New Labour government expanded regulatory frameworks which sought to exert an ever tighter, centralized grip on health and social care systems. NHS Trusts were urged to embrace a private sector ethos, extending and expanding competition within and between service providers. Similarly, local authorities developed service delivery initiatives for implementing the new policy framework of 'personalization' and 'safeguarding' in adult social care. Adult service users in all categories, including those using mental health services, were encouraged to manage their own personal budgets to buy their care (Leadbetter, 2004). Effectively, 'personalization' was a mechanism that resulted in local authorities transferring money, and with it associated financial and safety risks, to individual service users. At the same time, adult safeguarding teams in local authorities translated certain duties and processes across from children's services to fill the perceived void in policy with regard to the risk of abuse to vulnerable adults (Department of Health, 2000).

The New Labour government was reaching the end of its tenure when the global financial crisis of 2008 impacted on health and social care. Replaced by an even more determinedly neoliberal Conservative/Liberal Democrat coalition government in 2010, a powerful rhetoric about the need to cut state spending overrode any consideration of maintaining social welfare investments (Leys & Player, 2011). A proliferation of risk concerns and anxieties now pervades the health and welfare systems. In the mental health context these include: risks to service users from potential abusers such as carers, family or neighbourhood members (Fyson, 2015); risks of violence from service users to the public (Morgan & Felton, 2013); risk of diminished organizational reputation and funding cuts to services as a result of finance and performance failures (Garrett, 2014); risks to the identity of social work through redefining the focus of social work interventions; and risks to trust and confidence in care professions like social work (Jordan & Drakeford, 2012).

The privatization of risk

Set within this wider context, ever since deinstitutionalization (see Chapter 1 of this book) risk work has effectively been a core focus of mental health social work. Risk work involves the assessment and management of risks that those with mental health difficulties pose to others, and risks posed to themselves that arise through their vulnerability and illness (Kemshall, 2010). In both cases, clinical risk assessments may be undertaken. There is wide-ranging debate about how best to assess mental health risks, for example risk of suicide (see Cole-King *et al.*, 2013) and about how useful such assessments are in preventing 'risk events' such as deaths by suicide (Walter & Pridmore, 2012). Notwithstanding this debate, the assessment of risk is perceived as a core duty of mental health services (Department of Health, 2008). Professional bodies such as the Royal Society of Psychiatrists in the UK are committed to practice that is informed by such research and based on the assumption that the accuracy of predicting the likelihood of certain risks eventuating can be improved (Royal College of Psychiatrists, 2008). While there is merit in determining how risks can be mitigated to support people's wellbeing, the preoccupation with doing risk assessments along with an uncritical belief in their power unilaterally to reduce risks has three main distorting effects on the priorities of mental health services and social workers, to which we now turn.

Blaming practitioners

First among these distorting effects is that, in fear of blame for their actions, social workers' practice becomes 'overly proceduralized and defensive' (Parton & O'Byrne, 2000, p. 1). Douglas (1992) argues that risk is inherently political: perceptions of danger are constructed to apportion blame to 'unpopular' social groups; social workers and those they work with may be counted amongst these groups. Risk assessments are used in part to control risks, such that they can be avoided. Professional expertise is scrutinized and the actions of mental health professionals are condemned when they are found to have failed to prevent risks (Horlick-Jones, 2004). Foster (2013, p. 120), for example, analysing the problems facing contemporary mental health teams in England, contends that mental health professionals are held almost wholly individually responsible and accountable and are at risk of being professionally and publicly named, blamed and shamed when things go wrong. It is partly for fear of blame, Foster argues, that practitioners co-operate with target regimes, in turn reducing their time spent with service users for fear of falling behind with required electronic form filling. Reduced contact with service users in turn has the effect of excluding them from decision making. When there is heightened tension in mental health teams to 'get risk right', service user engagement can be diminished. Added to this, the controlling influence of negative risk thinking encourages conservative approaches to harm minimalization, rather than creative professional practices that support 'risk taking' (see Sawyer, this volume) to achieve positive outcomes.

Responsibilization through personalization

Neoliberal social policies have tended to stress the importance of personal responsibility. Exposure to impoverishment through cutbacks in state welfare spending has been reframed as returning to individuals, families and communities control over their own welfare (Stanford & Taylor, 2013). Through this logic, 'personal failings', such as requiring economic assistance, cannot be attributed to failings of the social system. Instead, such failings must be internalized (Harvey, 2006).

Thus the second distorting effect of the risk paradigm's dominance over the priorities of mental health services is that the privatization of risk usurps a focus on the social vulnerability of service users. Personalization explicitly endorses the idea of a transfer of risk from the local authority to the consumer (Department of Health, 1995). Ferguson (2008) stresses that by promoting the idea of the service user as customer, personalization policies mark a significant transfer of risk from the state to the individual. If the service user is a customer, then their choices are market choices and any failings are merely purchasing disappointments rather than reflections of systematic flaws.

Business versus therapeutic focus

The management of public mental health services has been reoriented towards business models, and with this the focus of mental health social work has been reoriented towards the business of service delivery. New Labour's Performance and Innovation Unit was set up to force public sector organizations to behave more like private sector businesses and a crucial aspect of achieving this goal was the effective management of a wide range of risks (Webb, 2006). In the competitive world of business, organizations attempt to secure their place and to achieve market advantage.

However the risks to welfare organizations operating as business entities include hostile activities of other public sector organizations in the form of mergers or takeovers, and exposure of poor staff performance, either clinically revealed by inspection or measured against nationally or locally set targets. Two of us have direct experience of trying to manage 37 different targets, set for the NHS and the local authority and used to judge the performance of our team. As managers we could be chastised if our team members failed to hit these targets. There has also been significant investment in data monitoring, so that individual practitioners can be scrutinized remotely by management via new 'dashboard' technology (Harris, 2014) and disciplined if not inputting sufficient data. This move towards privatizing the public sector, combined with an obsession with risks, has resulted in the third distorting effect of risk on mental health social work: managers are pressured to focus on the business needs of their organizations rather than the therapeutic needs of service users (Harris, 2003).

Fear and paranoia: The impact of risk-distorted priorities on mental health policy, services and practices

Our experience has been that the privatization of risk has evinced fear and paranoia in mental health services, such that managers and practitioners are overwhelmed by their own sense of being 'at risk' of blame and of the withdrawal of financial and other essential supports. Lending weight to our claim, Seddon (2008) argues that paranoia about the performance of the organization obscures concern for the delivery of high quality services and that it is the recipient of public services who suffers as service priorities are distorted. Risk management therefore becomes the management of risks to the business, as opposed to focusing on the vulnerability of service users to risks that include those associated with the symptoms of illness. In England, this turn has been exacerbated by austerity measures in the form of savage spending cuts to frontline services. As Garrett (2013) demonstrates, by refusing to relax the regulation and accountability of public organizations while nonetheless reducing their resources, government policies have amplified the internal anxieties of organizations and practitioners, further threatening to defeat any commitment to vulnerable people.

Government and media reactions in the UK to serious incidents such as the Baby P case (Warner, 2013) demonstrate how blame is split off from any consideration of the impact of wider social policy, and is firmly placed at the door of service users and social workers. Baby P was a toddler killed by his mother and her boyfriend. Following their conviction, social workers who had been involved with the family were vilified by the press and by members of parliament in what Warner describes as an outburst of 'moral panic'. Social workers in all specialisms now live in fear of serious incidents like Baby P happening again, for they have all too often seen their colleagues blamed. Likewise, senior managers live in fear of their organization being seen as 'failing' and/or being taken over by another organization through a process of competitive tendering (Department of Health, 2006).

These stresses and sources of paranoia are compounded by others, affecting day-to-day work. Over the last dozen years the NHS and local authorities have become subject to increased scrutiny by external bodies, such as the Care Quality Commission (CQC), which inspects and regulates health and social services in England and Wales. The reputation and status of organizations depend on being given a 'clean bill of health' following a CQC inspection. Consequently, senior management may invest considerable resources to facilitate a favourable review: IT may be upgraded, offices refurbished and even temporary extra staff employed prior to a CQC visit. In this quest it seems that the reality of service provision is all-too-readily obscured: increasingly fewer inpatient beds are available to manage acute illness episodes, and staffing levels are inadequate to respond to demand for services.

We have sought to develop a critical understanding of how neoliberal risk rationalities and risk thinking have secured such a hold in mental health organizations and distorted mental health policy, service and practice priorities. We have also asked this question of ourselves in a very personal way by exploring the tensions that have arisen for two of us in our mental health team management roles. Our critical awareness of the systemic issues that undermine the quality of care to vulnerable individuals and families only partly answers our question of what it is that supports the power of risk thinking in our work. We are convinced of the need also to understand the intra-personal issues that can contribute to and amplify the fear and paranoia evoked by neoliberal risk welfare mechanisms. Here we have found Klein's object relations theory most useful for explaining the internal tensions and anxieties that are experienced on the frontline.

Klein's object relations theory: Creating the 'other' and splitting from suffering

At its simplest, difference can be understood as an awareness of the 'other'. For Klein (1975) this sense of 'otherness' develops during early infancy, when a baby becomes aware that it is separate from its mother and that the mother has a relationship with an 'other' – the father – in which the baby has no part. Taking a psychodynamic approach, Klein explains that the infant copes with the feelings of pain, anxiety and fear of rejection that this causes by resorting to 'paranoid schizoid defences'. Intra-psychically, the infant splits its external world, its objects and itself, into two categories: *good* (gratifying, loved, loving) and *bad* (frustrating, hated, persecutory). This makes it possible to 'introject' and identify with the good, and to 'project' outwards onto others the bad, and so to gain relief from internal conflict. Developmentally, Klein argues, the infant moves from the paranoid schizoid position to the 'depressive position', when they come to perceive that the 'other' who frustrates is also the one who gratifies. This recognition becomes accompanied by feelings of anxiety and destructiveness, as well as guilt, grief and the desire for reparation. Eventually, when the ego has sufficiently developed, the bad can be integrated and ambivalence and conflict tolerated. However, both the paranoid schizoid and the depressive positions remain present in the psyche throughout life and can be reactivated at any time. As adults we all continue to struggle with anxieties that are either persecutory and paranoid, or depressive and guilt inducing.

Menzies (1959) applied Klein's theory to institutions, suggesting that in public sector organizations staff have to deal with anxieties regarding the care given to service users; the more vulnerable the client, the greater the anxiety. Members of staff either feel attacked by bosses and by external systems, or guilty that they have not prevented service users from relapsing or dying. In order to deal with these feelings, Menzies suggested that defence mechanisms are developed: one of these defence mechanisms results in the service user being dehumanized and another results in the deflection of blame. Following Menzies, we argue that just as the infant is terrified of rejection by its mother, organizations in our case are terrified of criticism from the government or CQC. Criticism is cascaded down the organization from the top to the frontline practitioner. Klein (1975) calls this process 'projective identification'. It enables managers to split off from their own feelings of guilt at the pressure to which frontline staff are subjected; it also enables policymakers to split off from feelings of responsibility for the provision of too limited resources in the face of too high demands, and the pain this might cause. Operating in the paranoid schizoid position and being overwhelmed by anxiety makes critical thinking and reflection difficult. In our view, this might explain some of the lack of opposition by the social work profession to the changes to social work practice over the past 20 years, outlined earlier in this chapter. When all hours are needed to complete computer-based risk assessments for fear of being seen not to perform or not to calculate risk, social workers have little time, energy or fight left in them to think creatively about risk or to take positive risks with their service users.

Risk-distorted priorities: The impact on real practice and real lives

The two case examples that follow illustrate what can happen if the service user and the frontline worker are seen as 'the other', as described by Klein (1975). As managers of mental health social work teams, two of us provide professional and task supervision to our staff. Within this, it is standard practice to discuss allocated cases and to look at individual performance against key performance indicators. In telling these two stories, we have combined elements of several situations that have been discussed with us by social workers in supervision. The cases are therefore composites and are illustrative of typical problems that are faced by staff in frontline practice.

Mr J

With the implementation of 'personalization', Mr J was awarded a personal budget several years ago. At the time, the local authority was keen to maximize the number of service users receiving direct payments, as it had set targets for this to be reached by all mental health teams. Consequently there was little scrutiny of such applications or of the amounts that were awarded. It was hard to persuade Mr J to accept a personal budget and it was difficult to find activities on which he might spend his allocated funds. Eventually it was agreed that he would purchase a gym membership and would attend a day centre. A few years later, the local authority decided to change its policy on the kind of financial support that mental health service users could receive. Mr J was re-assessed and it was determined that he needed to contribute substantially to the costs of his own personal budget items. By this time he had begun to reap some of the benefits of attending the gym and the day centre; the payment he had originally been reluctant to accept was now important to him. He was issued with a bill and told that he would not be allowed to continue the activities unless he began to pay. He became angry and soon stopped attending the gym and the day centre. The local authority sent warning letters and threatened him with court action. His mental health deteriorated and he required an admission to hospital. Fearing that this scenario would occur, his social worker had asked for Mr J to be made exempt from charging, but his application for a waiver, supported by his manager, was turned down.

To sum up, Mr J had a personal budget reluctantly thrust upon him. He became a customer but very quickly was transformed into a debtor. In this case 'personalization' resulted in detention in hospital, at significantly greater cost to the public purse than his gym and day centre memberships combined.

Many practitioners, and some managers, feel deeply conflicted by personalization. Its origins lie in the disability movement and it was promoted as a way of empowering service users to take control of their own recovery. While it was true that many day centres were not recovery focused when Mr J first attended, these centres did have an important part to play in countering social isolation. Many such centres have since closed because service users like Mr J are now expected to pay to attend them. Seen through the Kleinian lens, public spending cuts have led local authorities into the schizoid position of having targets both for the number of service users receiving personal budgets and for reducing personal budget allocations. This leads to frontline staff being reprimanded on the one hand for failing to offer personal budgets to sufficient numbers of service users, but chastised on the other hand if these budgets are too expensive, or have been reduced or stopped at review. Additionally, the experience of witnessing service users' distress when they receive letters from debt collectors makes frontline staff reluctant to discuss personal budgets with them. Meanwhile service users, their wishes and their needs, get lost in the system; they end up being treated, albeit unconsciously, as 'the other' or the rival. In Mr J's case, the local authority had first uncritically welcomed personalization and then applied a charging policy without reflecting on the consequences. In Kleinian terms (1991) it had demonstrated 'hallucinatory gratification', by first identifying or 'omnipotently conjuring' people like Mr J as ideal objects for personalization and then, when austerity measures set in, by proceeding to 'omnipotently annihilate' the transformed object.

Ms T

Ms T had murdered her mother, resulting in her detention in a secure psychiatric hospital. Her social worker felt traumatized by what had happened. Prior to the murder, he had been concerned enough about Ms T's mental health to attempt to secure her admission to hospital, but on the night in question there had been no beds available for her to be admitted. The NHS Trust involved conducted an internal inquiry into the events that culminated in the homicide, and identified as precipitating factors both communication difficulties and differing interpretations of policies among the staff involved. Focus on this shifted attention away from whether or not a bed had been available, and towards whether or not the social worker and others had made sufficient efforts to escalate this as a priority case with senior managers. The social worker's input was further scrutinized by an external homicide inquiry and it was recommended that his practice be investigated by a senior figure within the organization. The reason given for this was that he had not kept fully up-to-date records on the electronic case-record system in the months preceding the incident.

During supervision the social worker expressed his fear that the organization was attempting to refocus blame away from resourcing failures and onto his own individual practice, as a way of scapegoating him and to mitigate damage to the organization's reputation. He disclosed that he felt exhausted by the pressure of work: he found it virtually impossible to meet the combined expectations of hitting all targets, providing planning data and seeing all his allocated service users. He felt demoralized by the investigation into his own practice. He broke down in supervision and wept.

In England, austerity measures have led to a reduction in the number of psychiatric hospital beds (Health and Social Care Information Centre, 2013). However, because senior managers have been forced to be complicit with this reduction, they are reluctant to mention or blame it for serious incidents. Instead blame is passed downwards until a suitable scapegoat is located. Of course in this incident the real victims were Ms T and her mother. The reduction in psychiatric inpatient beds means that it is very difficult for service users to be admitted to hospital informally, at a time of their choosing. Indeed they are often compulsorily detained to hospital beds miles away from their homes and families (Mental Health Act Commission, 2009). They can also be discharged home when they are still acutely unwell, sometimes into the care of overburdened crisis teams or community rehabilitation teams (Weinstein, 2014).

Again, Klein's insights can be helpful here. She explains how an infant's unsuccessful attempts to move from the paranoid schizoid to the depressive position can result in major mental illness in later life (Klein, 1991). Holding up the same critical lens to the case of Ms T, we can see that this shocking incident made the organization take flight from heightened anxiety, by splitting. The Trust exonerated itself by producing an internal report, which split off the organization from the rest the 'bad' team – projecting onto them its own sense of persecution. The organization's failure to accept any responsibility, or to try to progress to a depressive position where feelings such as guilt can be acknowledged, led to a deflection of guilt onto the bad object, in this case the team, and even the individual practitioner.

Concluding reflections

In this chapter we have charted the rise of risk thinking and its effects on mental health practice, against a backdrop of economic and social policy making dominated by a neoliberal belief system that promotes market solutions for social problems and individualism as the focus of any change. We have demonstrated how risk has distorted the priorities of mental health services. These distortions derive from the pervasive influence of a risk management paradigm that leads to defensive practice on the frontline, privatizes risk through responsibilizing individual service users (as 'customers') and practitioners, and places the primary focus of mental health organizations on financial stability and adequate performance. We have argued that the avoidance of failure or blame now takes precedence over the amelioration of social and service user problems. Risk to the organization as a business entity places stress on frontline workers who must prioritize data inputting over direct work with service users. But practitioners must also carry the anxiety for risk of harm to or from service users neglected through time diverted to administrative tasks (Harris & Unwin, 2009), since blame will inevitably reside with practitioners when things go wrong. It is left to frontline managers to work through, and to support their teams in managing the tensions of these competing priorities.

Two of us, as mental health service managers, have experienced this dilemma first-hand. We have found it helpful to draw on insights from Klein (1975, 1991), if not fully to resolve these tensions, at least better to understand and work with them. We have seen all too well, for example, how the risk consequences of the policies we have outlined, situated in context of resource cuts, become split off and denied in defence against the anxiety and the guilt they engender. Frontline practitioners, for their part, believe that managers persecute them; they blame management and policymakers for system failures and this helps to relieve the guilt they feel at being unable to care well for service users. But managers, for our part, feel persecuted too. It is easy to become overwhelmed and disabled by the anxiety in our organizations. So we too become prone to the splitting that is characteristic of the paranoid schizoid position: if clinical anxieties can be split off and placed with the frontline workers, as managers we can focus on the business anxiety of performance and productivity.

Our concluding reflection is that if both clinical anxieties and the business anxieties are to be held and contained, then care must be taken to avoid being overwhelmed. This means adopting what Klein calls the 'depressive position'. It involves thinking through the consequences of our courses of action, so that all of us recognize our shared responsibility towards service users and for failures of care. In addition, adopting the depressive position allows us to recognize and accept the impossibility of providing all we might wish for all those for whom we may wish it.

References

Barry, A., Osborne, T. and Rose, N. (1996) *Foucault and Political Reason. Liberalism, Neo-Liberalism and Rationalities of Government* (Chicago: University of Chicago).

Beck, U. (1998) *Risk Society* (London: Sage).

Blom-Cooper, L., Hally, H. and Murphy, E. (1995) *The Falling Shadow: One Patient's Mental Health Care* (London: Duckworth).

Cole-King, A., Parker, V., Williams, H. and Platt, S. (2013) 'Suicide Prevention: Are we Doing Enough?', *Advances in Psychiatric Treatment*, 19(4), 284–91.

Coles, S., Keenan, S. and Diamond, B. (eds) (2013) *Madness Contested: Power and Practice* (Ross-on-Wye: PCCS Books).

Culpitt, I. (1999) *Social Policy and Risk* (London: Sage).

Dean, M. (1999) *Governmentality: Power and Rule in Modern Society* (London: Sage).

Department of Health (1994) *Developing Managers for Community Care: Interagency Management Development Techniques* (London: Her Majesty's Stationery Office).

Department of Health (1995) *An Introduction to Joint Commissioning* (London: Her Majesty's Stationery Office).

Department of Health (1999) *The National Service Framework for Mental Health* (London: Her Majesty's Stationery Office).

Department of Health (2000) *No Secrets: Guidance on Developing and Implementing Multi-Agency Policies and Procedures to Protect Vulnerable Adults from Abuse* (London: Her Majesty's Stationery Office).

Department of Health (2006) *Our Health, Our Care, Our Say: A New Direction for Community Services* (London: Her Majesty's Stationery Office).

Department of Health (2008) *Refocussing the Care Programme Approach: A Policy and Positive Practice Guidance* (London: Her Majesty's Stationery Office).

Douglas, M. (1992) *Risk and Blame: Essays in Cultural Theory* (London: Routledge).

Duffy, S. (2010) 'The Citizenship Theory of Social Justice: Exploring the Meaning of Personalisation for Social Workers', *Journal of Social Work Practice*, 24(3), 253–67.

Ferguson, I. (2008) *Reclaiming Social Work: Challenging Neo-liberalism and Promoting Social Justice* (London: Sage).

Foster, A. (2013) 'The Challenge of Leadership in Front Line Clinical Teams Struggling to Meet Current Policy Demands', *Journal of Social Work Practice*, 27(2), 119–31.

Fyson, R. (2015) 'Building an Evidence Base of Adult Safeguarding? Problems with the Reliability and Validity of Adult Safeguarding Databases', *British Journal of Social Work*, 45(3), 932–48.

Garrett, P. M. (2013) *Social Work and Social Theory* (Bristol: The Policy Press).

Garrett, P. M. (2014) 'Re-enchanting Social Work? The Emerging 'Spirit' of Social Work in an Age of Economic Crisis', *British Journal of Social Work*, 44(3), 503–21.

Giddens, A. (1994) *Beyond Left and Right* (Cambridge: Polity).

Harvey, D. (2006) *Limits to Capital* (London: Verso).

Harris, J. (2003) *The Social Work Business* (London: Sage).

Harris, J. (2014) '(Against) Neoliberal Social Work', *Critical and Radical Social Work*, 2(1), 7–22.

Harris, J., and Unwin, P. (2009) 'Performance Management in Modernised Social Work', in J. Harris and J. White (eds) *Modernising Social Work: Critical Considerations* (Bristol: Policy Press), 9–30.

Health and Social Care Information Centre (2013) *Mental Health Bulletin: Annual Report from MHMDS Returns, England 2011–12*, www.hscic.gov.uk/catalogue/PUB10347, date accessed 7 August 2016.

Healy, K. (2005) *Social Work Theories in Context: Creating Frameworks for Practice* (Houndmills: Palgrave Macmillan).

Horlick-Jones, T. (2004) 'Experts in Risk ... Do They Exist?', *Health, Risk and Society*, 6(2), 107–14.

Jordan, B. and Drakeford, M. (2012) *Social Work and Social Policy Under Austerity* (London: Palgrave).

Kemshall, H. (2002) *Risk, Social Policy and Welfare: Introducing Social Policy* (Buckingham: Open University).

Kemshall, H. (2010) 'Risk Rationalities in Contemporary Social Work Policy and Practice', *British Journal of Social Work*, 40(4), 1247–62.

Klein, M. (1975) *Envy and Gratitude* (London: Routledge).

Klein, M. (1991) 'Notes on Some Schizoid Mechanisms', in J. Mitchell (ed.) *The Selected Melanie Klein* (Harmondsworth: Penguin), 175–200.

Layard, R. (2005) *Happiness: Lessons from a New Science* (London: Penguin).

Leadbetter, D. (2004) *Personalisation Through Participation: A New Script for Public Services* (London: Demos).

Leys, C. and Player S. (2011) *The Plot Against the NHS* (Pontypool: Merlin Press).

Mearns, G. (2014) 'The Neoliberal Agenda and Social Work Values: Using Critical Discourse Analysis to Explore the Role of Language in Processes of Cultural Hegemony', *Critical and Radical Social Work*, 2(2), 208–16.

Mental Health Act Commission (2009) *Coercion and Consent: Thirteenth Biennial Report 2007–2009* (London: The Stationery Office).

Menzies, I. E. P. (1959) 'A Case Study in the Functioning of Social Systems as a Defence Against Anxiety: A Report on a Study of the Nursing Service of a General Hospital', *Human Relations*, 13, 1195–1219.

Mirowski, P. (2013) *Never Let a Serious Crisis Go to Waste: How Neoliberalism Survived the Financial Meltdown* (London: Verso).

Morgan, A. and Felton, A. (2013) 'From Constructive Engagement to Coerced Recovery', in S. Coles, S. Keenan and B. Diamond (eds) *Madness Contested: Power and Practice* (Ross-on-Wye: PCCS Books), 56–73.

Parton, N. and O'Byrne, P. (2000) *Constructive Social Work: Towards a New Practice* (Houndmills: Macmillan Press).

Ritchie, J. H. (1994) *Report of the Inquiry into the Care and Treatment of Christopher Clunis* (London: HMSO).

Royal College of Psychiatrists (2008) *Rethinking Risk to Others in Mental Health Services: Final Report of Scoping Group* (London: Royal College of Psychiatrists).

Seddon, J. (2008) *Systems Thinking in the Public Sector* (Axminster: Triarchy Press).

Stanford, S. N. and Taylor, S. (2013) 'Welfare Dependence or Enforced Deprivation? A Critical Examination of White Neoliberal Welfare and Risk', *Australian Social Work*, 66(4), 476–94.

Walter, G. and Pridmore, S. (2012), 'Suicide is Preventable, Sometimes', *Australasian Psychiatry*, 20(4), 271–3.

Warner, J. (2013) 'Social Work, Class, Politics and Risk in the Moral Panic Over Baby P', *Health, Risk and Society*, 15(3), 217–33.

Webb, S. A. (2006) *Social Work in a Risk Society: Social and Political Perspectives* (Basingstoke: Palgrave).

Weinstein, J. (2014) *Mental Health* (London: Policy Press).

4

MOVING BEYOND NEOLIBERAL RATIONALITIES OF RISK IN MENTAL HEALTH POLICY AND PRACTICE

Sonya Stanford, Nina Rovinelli Heller, Elaine Sharland
and Joanne Warner

Introduction

A reflection from Sonya.

While writing this chapter, I happened to see an ABC24 news story shown here in Australia (ABC News, 2015). The story focused on the humanitarian plight of people risking everything to make their way to Germany to seek refuge. The news story reported Hungary's drastic attempt to 'fence off' its borders by building a wall approximately 173 kilometres (108 miles) long, some of it towering bundles of piercing, ripping and staked razor wire. I felt a long way away from the drama of the story, living as I do on the island state of Tasmania in Australia and a whole hemisphere away. Nevertheless I felt a connection. I thought about my country's inhumane and unreasonable response to asylum seekers via mandatory offshore detention. I thought how it contributes to the wide-ranging problems associated with managing the mass exodus of people fleeing war zones and other places where hope of survival or a better future has diminished or been extinguished. The story became closer still as the journalist interviewed an adolescent boy who had just passed through the German border.

He was 14 years old: he looked so much older. He had left Serbia alone. He had been constantly on the move for over 20 arduous days attempting to get to Germany. I tried to imagine what he might have endured whilst travelling alone without parents, amongst strangers and in hostile places. The journalist asked him what made him leave. He replied in the kind of English that we used to call 'broken' and I wondered if indeed at that time he himself might have been so. 'War. Syria. I-S. Fighting' was his response. The journalist then asked, 'Do you think Germany wants you?' Inhaling my breath sharply from the pain that sat at the heart of the question, I heard his reply: simply, in a word, 'No.'

I imagined the terror of his life at home and the immense struggle of his life to come. I thought about the risks he had faced and the risks he still had to face across all dimensions of his life and to his 'being'. Given the focus of this book I wondered how profound were the risks to his mental health. I then wondered how such risks for him and so many other people would be addressed. And I was struck by how limited local and global responses could surely be if driven by a neoliberal ethos that promotes fear and suspicion of those people who are considered a risk of failing to enact their economic citizenship. This mentality requires people to be politically disposed towards profiting from their own entrepreneurship. Those who fail in such endeavours are seen to pose a risk to the economic security of others. Individuality and the common good have become fused in neoliberal rationality, reconfiguring the ethos of civil society as one preoccupied with 'consumer citizenship' (McDonald, 2006) as opposed to social solidarity. I therefore feared that the risk seen to be posed by this 14-year-old boy and the hundreds of thousands of others like him would overshadow any invocation of social justice to address such dire need and to mitigate the acute and chronic risks to his safety and wellbeing. His mental suffering would consequently be commodified, making it one unit amongst many others, to calculate in terms of its potential to undermine the array of privileges accorded to others. And indeed, as the refugee crisis in Europe has continued to unfold, such discourse has been prominent.

In this chapter we, the editors, explain why it is important and what it means to adopt a critically reflective approach to the mentality of risk (Culpitt, 1999; Rose, 1996) that informs current neoliberal welfare approaches to the organization, management and resourcing of services that respond to mental health problems. In keeping with a key theme of this book, we position mental illness as a human rights and social justice issue. That is, we locate the lived experience of mental illness, and its associated risks, as structured. In this way we connect the subjective experience of mental health problems with social inequality, which requires critical reflection of the 'social misery' (Frost & Hoggett, 2008, p. 438) that both gives rise to and that arises from living with mental illness. As Harrison and Melville (2010) note, globalization and neoliberal economic policies have introduced a new range of risk inequalities that impact people's mental health worldwide. Our beginning point in the chapter is to explicate how neoliberal risk rationalities reinforce prevailing inequalities that are associated with mental ill health, limiting and in some cases precluding social justice. Next, we clarify the mutability of rationalities of risk, even though they are institutionalized in law, policy and practice. By understanding that risk forms a part of the rhetorical apparatus that supports the politic of neoliberalism, we are challenged to envisage how we might 'speak back' to its logic at macro (structural), meso (policy and organizational) and micro (interpersonal) levels. Sonya's story above illustrates the importance of using a critically reflective approach to reconnect with and advance mental health policy that is human rights focused and aims to achieve social justice. We therefore present our model for critically reflecting on neoliberal rationalities of risk and how they operate in mental health settings, and we consider the implications such critical analysis has for moving beyond the risk paradigm in mental health policy and practice.

Neoliberal welfare risk rationalities and mental health

Culpitt (1999, p. 117) argues that 'neoliberalism creates the climate of risk in order to justify its overall politic'. Webb (2006, p. 38) claims 'neo-liberalism is *the* political programme of risk society' and as a form of 'political rule and power' it enables an extreme focus on 'regulation and compliance'. In either case, both writers claim that we now live under the conditions of neoliberal risk society, where society is organized according to the concept of risk (Beck, 2003, 2004), and our private and public imagination is dominated by concern for assessing and managing risks. Risk thinking is therefore institutionalized in neoliberal risk society – it has its own logic for defining the foundations of how welfare provision is understood and distributed (McDonald, 2006). Moving beyond the current risk paradigm in mental health policy, mental health services and mental health practices requires understanding the composition of the rationalities of risk (Kemshall, 2010) that comprise the logic of neoliberal welfare, which we now consider.

Stanford and Taylor (2013) outline a typology of three risk rationalities that comprise the institutional logic of neoliberal welfare: theoretical, substantive and formal risk rationalities. Theoretical rationalities are the core abstract ideas and concepts that institutions use to make sense of social reality (McDonald, 2006, p. 40). The theoretical rationality of risk exists in the conceptualization of risk as an idea or 'way of thinking' (Parton, 1996, p. 98) that influences how the things that come to be associated with it (such as people with mental illness) are recognized and responded to. As mentioned throughout this book, it is now impossible to speak of mental health issues without evoking ideas of risk in the neoliberal welfare context. Ideas about risk overshadow how people living with mental illness are understood: fears abound about the risks they pose to themselves and to others (Rose, 1996, 2000; Warner, 2008). The theoretical rationality of risk in neoliberal welfare therefore screens out other ideas about the risks associated with mental health problems, including the experience of social suffering that arises from being subject to multiple forms of social injustice (Frost & Hoggett, 2008).

Substantive rationalities are the core values that guide actions in institutions, such as the institution of welfare (McDonald, 2006, p. 40).

The substantive rationality of risk is a 'logic of security' (Webb, 2006). In neoliberal risk society this primarily equates to economic security that requires economically prudent and responsible citizenship to secure against risks in the immediate and distant future. In the mental health context this translates, for example, to an emphasis on achieving and maintaining 'recovery' so that an individual's capacity for independence (via work, stable housing and lower hospital admissions) is strengthened. Increasing degrees of welfare conditionality (enforced conditions and criteria for the receipt of welfare benefits and services), a feature of neoliberal austerity measures, aim to secure against and control risks. By extension this means neoliberal welfare aims to secure against and control those people who are associated with risky situations, such as those who become mentally unwell. When the social contract (staying well) is compromised, benefits and services can be legitimately withdrawn (Culpitt, 1999).

An institution's formal rationality comprises the rules, laws and regulations that govern and guide its actions (McDonald, 2006, p. 40). Neoliberal welfare is characterized by actions and practices that are underpinned by formalized risk frameworks. As all chapters in this book attest, risk frameworks are prominent in mental health institutions and services throughout neoliberal welfare regimes. Risk is constructed primarily as a calculable object and specifically as probability (Giddens, 2003a; Hacking, 1991; Kemshall, 2010). Objectifying risk as a calculable entity renders it governable and controllable (Culpitt, 1999; Rose, 2000; Webb, 2006). Accordingly, those who do 'risk work' (Horlick-Jones, 2005), such as mental health professionals, render those who become associated with risk (people with mental health problems and their families) as calculable, governable and controllable. Paradoxically, mental health professionals themselves are similarly rendered calculable, governable and controllable (Rose 1996, 2000; Webb 2006).

Neoliberal welfare risk rationalities dominate how mental health problems are understood, which in turn defines the value base informing responses to these problems. Risk thinking has become so pervasive in world risk society (Beck, 2003) that it appears to have colonized mental health policy and practice, such that a form of risk imperialism is evident. Such a circumstance raises the question: is it possible to move beyond the risk paradigm?

Is it possible to move beyond neoliberal risk rationalities in mental health?

Lupton (2006, p. 15) reminds us that 'risk concepts are fluid and dynamic over time and space'. Adam and Van Loon (2000, p. 4) state that definitions of risk reflect the power and influence of those who come to participate in risk debates. What or who is defined as 'a risk' or 'at risk' bears the markings of a complex interplay of competing knowledge claims, interests, politics, ideologies, technologies, emotions and moralities (Stanford, 2010). Various social theorists have noted that meanings of risk have changed over time (for example, Beck, 2003; Douglas, 2003; Giddens 2003a, b), as have the dominance of different risk discourses (Kemshall, 2002; Lupton 2004). Consequently, there is nothing static about the construct of risk: the shape of risk society itself is said to be 'multiple and mutable' (Mythen & Walklate, 2006). We argue that by understanding the contestability of how risk is defined (theoretical rationality), enacted (formal rationality) and valued (substantive rationality) other ways of thinking about and doing risk work in mental health service delivery *do* become possible, and in this way it *is* possible to move beyond the risk paradigm.

Moving beyond the risk paradigm in mental health policy and practice requires identifying the limits of how neoliberal risk society is conceptualized (Mythen & Walklate, 2006). It means questioning the politics of risk (Franklin, 2006) across all domains including at the local–global interface. We propose that critical reflection is essential to this task. Fook (2002, p. 92) has argued:

> Much of the power of discourses to remain dominant lies in the extent to which they go unquestioned. Therefore much of the potential to unsettle that power lies in our readiness to question them, and in the extent to which we are prepared to question them further once they are exposed to scrutiny.

Critical reflection can trouble hidden assumptions about power and privilege located in risk rationalities in the mental health field. Critical reflection therefore offers a way of reflecting on taken-for-granted assumptions about risk in mental health, enabling these ideas to be reviewed, contested and reconstructed if necessary.

The United Nations (Department of Economic and Social Affairs, 2006, p. 9) has argued that in view of intensified inequality it is 'important to reflect deeply on the nature and use of power within both the human and institutional contexts'. We argue such examination requires an explicit focus on human rights and social justice. Next, we provide a brief overview of these terms and consider their relevance as a focus for critical reflection on mental health risks as they are framed by the logic of neoliberal welfare.

Critically reflecting on mental health and risk rationalities by focusing on human rights and social justice

Human rights encompass ethical, legal, political, cultural and philosophical dimensions (Harrison & Melville, 2010, p. 139) reflecting a 'political will to develop a humanised society' (Mullaly, 1997, cited in Nipperess &

Briskman, 2009, p. 61). Human rights – such as the rights to liberty and freedom, dignity and respect, and to protection – are deemed by many to be universal, indivisible and inalienable (UN General Assembly, 1948). This framing of human rights is also contested, as it is seen to reflect Western thinking that is harmful or irrelevant to other cultures (Harrison & Melville, 2010, pp. 147–50). However, polarizing universalist rights against culturally relative rights is problematic. As Ife (2007, p. 94, cited in Nipperess & Briskman, 2009, pp. 54–5) notes:

> the challenge is to develop an approach to the universalism of human rights that, while emphasizing our common 'humanity' and seeking to articulate what that humanity means, at the same time acknowledges different cultural traditions as providing contexts within which that humanity is constructed.

Consequently, the '*relative* universality of human rights, rather than their relative *universality*' (emphasis in original) must be considered (Donnelly, 2007, p. 292, cited in Harrison & Melville, 2010, p. 149).

Typically, social justice is framed as 'social fairness' requiring 'a framework of political objectives, pursued through social, economic, environmental and political policies' (Craig, 2002, pp. 671–2, cited Taylor *et al.*, 2015, p. 2) to address the impact of disadvantage, vulnerability, oppression and having exceptional needs. In other words, social justice is a moral framework of principles and values that guide the actions of governments as they aspire to achieve the 'equitable distribution of fundamental resources and respect for human dignity and diversity, such that no minority group's life interests and struggles are undermined and that forms of political interaction enable all groups to voice their concerns for change' (Basok *et al.*, 2006, p. 267).

Human rights and social justice values underpin the ethical frameworks of mental health professions. For example, principles of human rights and social justice are embedded in the self-definitions of the professions of social work (International Federation of Social Workers, 2014) and nursing (International Council of Nurses, 2012), with promotion of economic, social and cultural rights definitive to each profession. Psychiatry and psychology also include values of human rights and social justice in their codes of ethics (International Union of Psychological Science, 2008; World Psychiatric Association, 2005). Yet 'helping' professions have been criticized for making sweeping statements about human rights and social justice that belittle the contestability of these terms (Nipperess & Briskman, 2009; Taylor *et al.*, 2015). As Campbell and Davidson, and Bland and Wyder discuss in Chapters 2 and 7 respectively, there are significant challenges that occur when dealing with, and attempting to balance, competing risk imperatives, such as the right to safety (for people experiencing mental illness symptoms and/or other people's right to safety) and the right to liberty.

Critical reflection can assist in developing a nuanced perspective of the complexity and contestability of human rights and social justice values that are pertinent to mental health work. Such a perspective means: scoping the full range of human rights and social justice issues that are particular to service users, their families and other stakeholders (such as mental health practitioners, service managers and the public); noting how these issues are framed by stakeholder groups and critically considering who is advantaged and disadvantaged by such framings; identifying the tensions between claims to rights and justice of different stakeholders; and identifying how to balance conflict and tension between various rights that can promote the dignity of people with lived experience of mental illness.

Critically examining how human rights and social justice are framed by neoliberal risk rationalities in the mental health field is vital. According to Basok *et al.* (2006, p. 269) citizenship principles of membership and obligation to communities have become 'intensely governmental'. A feature of the mentality of neoliberalism is its reconfiguration of social citizenship to align with contractual and conditional political arrangements between governments and its 'privatized citizenary' (Culpitt, 1999, p. 80). Culpitt explains that claims to social justice, especially in the domains of distributive justice and collective/solidarity rights, have therefore been radically undermined, 'denying legitimacy to welfare claimants'. He comments that 'risk is used to justify these exclusionary tactics, which morally stigmatize whole groups of people, who have fallen outside the contractual arena' (Culpitt, 1999, p. 80). Neoliberal rationalities of mental health risks therefore do harm to people's dignity by diminishing how people might be recognized (in the moral sense) according to their humanity, which has implications for both human rights and social justice.

As mentioned earlier in this chapter, neoliberalism's substantive rationality is one of security. Seen through a risk lens, this rationality supports viewing people with mental health problems as needing to be 'secured' for their own or others' protection. The logic of neoliberal welfare therefore justifies limitations, infringements and abuses of people's human rights given its constructions of their diminished humanity. Accordingly, these risk-based identities 'contribute to (identity-based) social hierarchies' (Simpson, 2013, p. 708) sustaining numerous forms of social exclusion (poverty, homelessness, unemployment, lack of access to education and health services, and lack of safety) that undermine the social justice aspirations of civil society. The challenge for mental health practitioners, mental health service managers and mental health policymakers is to find ways of resisting the reasoning that underpins such pervasive logic.

By critically reflecting on mental health and risk, it is possible to identify and examine silenced and muted accounts of how human rights are denied and where social injustices prevail. Importantly, critical reflection provides insight into where and how principles of rights and social justice can be upheld. This is crucial given the current climate of neoliberal austerity where 'many in the social service field question how human needs can be met with fairness and dignity' (Baines, 2006, p. 20). In contexts of macro- and meso-level constraints, identifying opportunities for upholding principles of human rights and social obligation is paramount if mental health work is to move beyond the risk paradigm.

Morley (2009, p. 146), quoting Fook (2000, p. 133), states:

> Critical reflection is integral to critical practice because it challenges dominant power relations and structures by 'pinpointing the ways in which we might unwittingly affirm discourses that work against us, and the people we are working with', and emphasizes practitioners' own person agency to respond.

This means that critical reflection enables on-the-ground examination of risk thinking and practices and considers their connection to broader social, cultural, political, economic and historical contexts. In this way, macro-, meso- and micro-level targets for change can be identified, and change practices can be envisaged and enacted. We now present our framework for such analysis in mental health policy and practice before concluding this chapter.

Using critical reflection on mental health risk rationalities

As we have noted above, a critical and reflective approach enables the deconstruction of the truths of neoliberal risk rationalities, and of the ways these configure values of human rights and social justice to align with the ruling risk mentality. By using human rights and social justice as evaluative criteria, it is possible to enable and affirm an alternative moral framework to guide the socio-political goals of mental health policy and practice. We suggest that this requires addressing the following critical questions across all contexts relating to working with problems associated with mental health and risk:

1. Where is risk understood to be located? Is risk understood to be in people, in a particular behaviour, in a condition or diagnosis, in the environment and/or in a particular place or space? Who gets to make this claim? Who doesn't?

2. What are the proposals for how these risks should be managed? Who gets to make these proposals? Who doesn't?

3. Who benefits and who suffers from this way of making sense of the issue/s in terms of risk?

4. What is obscured and what is occluded in this analysis?

5. What happens to these ways of seeing risk if we analyse them through a lens valuing human rights and social justice? Whose rights come into focus? Whose rights are distorted or obscured? Whose justice prevails? Whose justice is ignored or diminished?

These questions can be applied in a systemic way to elucidate obscured ways of thinking about and responding to risk issues in mental health. An example is the complex issue of gun violence in the US, particularly single incident shootings that involve a high number of fatalities and casualties. In debates about this social issue, risk is often framed in terms of unstable and mentally ill individuals, demonizing them and, in doing so, stigmatizing all mental health service users as potential 'demons' (*Washington Post*, 2012). Framing risk in these terms has resulted in proposing draconian and distorted measures of surveillance, not of all gun holders but all mental health service users. This further stigmatizes them compromising their individual right to dignity and their social rights as active agents and citizens, and constructing fixed and restrictive risk identities for them. Emphasizing that people with mental illness embody the risk of gun violence in these terms occludes the humanity and lived experience of mental illness, as well as the lack of support available to people suffering mental illness and its associated problems, such as lack of access to housing, employment and health care. Additionally, such a view obfuscates any critique of the social, political and cultural mores that condone private ownership and use of weaponry that threatens right to life. Those who stand to benefit from framing risk of gun violence in these terms are not mental health service users and families, nor those who are the victims of gun crime, but those who are invested in the gun lobby.

Beyond macro analysis, our critical questions can be used in direct mental health practice to unveil and highlight hidden assumptions about risk that can be problematic. For example, Lemon *et al.* (2016) found that interpretations of suicide risk are subject to a range of idiosyncratic personal and professional contexts. One of their findings was that front-line mental health practitioners in non-government services relied predominantly on informal methods of suicide risk assessment; intuition, hunches and feelings were the mainstay of their assessment practices. We argue that our foundational questions for critically reflective practice can support practitioners to re-evaluate how their own and others' ideas about risk shape their day-to-day assessments and interventions. Using these questions can lead to developing new approaches that improve the veracity of mental health assessments and interventions.

We suggest adopting Fook's (2002) model of using a critical incident technique to reflect on practice 'stories' as the basis for this work. The process involves writing a one-page description of a significant practice experience. It need not be traumatic, but it does need to be meaningful and in some way to feel unresolved for the practitioner. Fook's (2002) approach includes dividing the practice story into three parts: the context and background that is pertinent to the practice incident, a description of the actual practice incident, and a statement of why the incident was important. The next step in the process is to reflect on questions that enable deconstruction, resistance, challenge and reconstruction of the story. Below are 10 questions that we have developed to guide critical reflection on risk issues in mental health practice. These questions could be used as a basis for personal reflection, professional supervision and group discussion.

1. How are ideas about risk evident in the ways all people are characterized in the practice story?

2. What strategies are used to tell the practice story to create these ideas about each character? Consider whose perspectives are presented in the story and whose perspectives are missing or minimized in the story.

3. What (if any) risky relationships are constructed between the characters of the story?

4. What emotions dominate the ways the practitioner thinks about risk in relation to other people and themselves?

5. What ideas, information and circumstances support the practitioner to tell their practice story of risk in these terms? Consider micro, meso and macro influences.

6. What are the consequences of thinking about people in terms of the risk they represent (being a risk, being at risk)? Consider who benefits and who doesn't benefit from this risk thinking, and what options become possible, limited or impossible for service users, their families and the practitioner.

7. In what ways are issues of human rights and social justice framed (if at all) in the story? Consider whose rights or sense of justice are emphasized and whose rights or sense of justice is de-emphasized in the practice story.

8. How does the presentation of human rights and social justice (or lack of it) compare with the practitioner's stated commitments to working in ways that support people in terms of their human rights and their being treated equally and fairly?

9. What other identities could have been ascribed that might have been more enabling of people?

10. What, if any, changes in the practice context might support the practitioner to work in ways that value human rights and social justice in mental health?

Conclusion

In this chapter we have considered the logic of neoliberal welfare and how it deploys rationalities of risk to shape how mental health problems are understood (who is a risk), how such problems come to exist (individual failure to self-manage potential risk of illness) and how to respond to these problems (risk workers assess and then manage/control risks). We have introduced the idea that a critical reflective approach to mental health and risk that focuses on human rights and social justice can assist in moving beyond the neoliberal welfare risk paradigm in micro, meso and macro contexts. Webb (2006, p. 200) claims: 'In a society in which the narrow pursuit of material self-interest is the norm, adherence to an ethical stance is more radical than many people realise.' Consequently, Webb (2006, p. 233) argues for a practice of value as a form of '"unruly practices" that can actively sabotage, resist and challenge neo-liberalism ... thereby harnessing the logic of resistance to neo-liberal rule'. Adopting such an approach means that mental health policymakers, mental health managers and mental health practitioners could focus on risks *to* the moral and substantive dimensions of human rights and social justice. In this way, it is possible to develop counter-discourses to neoliberal risk rhetoric and to the individualized and pathologized view of mental health problems that it promotes and sustains.

Our analysis in this chapter elucidates how risks to human rights and to social justice for people with mental health problems in local and global contexts has been obscured by the dominant logic of neoliberalism. Reinvigorating a human rights framework has particular salience in neoliberal 'world risk society' where risks are globalized, for, as Harrison and Melville (2010, p. 1) explain, there is now greater recognition that 'the idea of what happens to "them" has implications for "us"'. Socially just aspirations become values for global justice in this context.

Focusing on human rights and social justice through critical reflection brings into view the historical, social, cultural, political and economic dimensions of mental health problems. Neoliberal risk rationalities favour the claim that everyone, irrespective of circumstances, has equal opportunity. A contextual understanding of mental health problems brings into focus how, in everyday settings for people around the world, political conflict, climate change, poverty, violence, isolation, racism and unemployment all contribute to and exacerbate the experience of mental ill-health. Accordingly, a contextual understanding of mental health problems brings into view the need to develop a full range of responses that promote and support people's sense of personal and cultural dignity, as well as enhancing their capacity to live meaningful lives without fear of social and personal harms. Critically reflecting on how issues of human rights and social justice feature in mental health risk rationalities is foundational for moving beyond the significant political-ethical and moral, and material and practical issues that create such immense difficulty for individuals, families and communities who struggle with and work towards recovery from mental illness.

References

ABC News 24 (2015) *ABC News (television story)*, Sydney, 24 August.

Adam, B. and Van Loon, J. (2000) 'Introduction: Repositioning Risk: The Challenge for Social Theory', in B. Adam, U. Beck and J. Van Loon (eds) *The Risk Society and Beyond: Critical Issues for Social Theory* (London: Sage), 1–31.

Baines, D. (2006) 'If You Could Change One Thing': Social Service Workers and Restructuring', *Australian Social Work*, 59(1), 20–34.

Basok, T., Ilcan, S. and Noonan, J. (2006) 'Citizenship, Human Rights, and Social Justice', *Citizenship Studies*, 10(3), 267–73.

Beck, U. (2003) *World Risk Society* (Cambridge: Polity Press).

Beck, U. (2004) *Risk Society: Toward a New Modernity* (London: Sage).

Culpitt, I. (1999) *Social Policy and Risk* (California and New Dehli: Sage).

Department of Economic and Social Affairs (2006) *The International Forum for Social Development: Social Justice in an Open World: The Role of the United Nations* (New York: United Nations).

Douglas, M. (2003) *Risk and Blame: Essays in Cultural Theory* (reprint) (London: Routledge).

Fook, J. (2002) *Social Work: Critical Theory and Practice* (London, California and New Delhi: Sage).

Franklin, J. (2006) 'Politics and Risk', in G. Mythen and S. Walklate (eds) *Beyond the Risk Society: Critical Reflections on Risk and Human Society* (Maidenhead, Berkshire: Open University Press), 149–68.

Frost, L. and Hoggett, P. (2008) 'Human Agency and Social Suffering', *Critical Social Policy*, 28(4), 438–60.

Giddens, A. (2003a) *Modernity and Self-identity: Self and Society in the Late Modern Age* (reprint) (Stanford, CA: Stanford University Press).

Giddens, A. (2003b) *The Consequences of Modernity* (Stanford, CA: Stanford University Press).

Hacking, I. (1991) *The Taming of Chance* (Cambridge: Press Syndicate of the University of Cambridge).

Harrison, G. and Melville, R. (2010) *Rethinking Social Work in a Global World* (Basingstoke and New York: Palgrave Macmillan).

Horlick-Jones, T. (2005) 'On "Risk Work": Professional Discourse, Accountability, and Everyday Action', *Health, Risk and Society*, 7, 293–307.

International Council of Nurses (2012) *International Council of Nurses Code of Ethics*, www.icn.ch/images/stories/documents/about/icncode_english.pdf, date accessed 25 August 2015.

International Federation of Social Workers (2014) *Global Definition of Social Work*, http://ifsw.org/policies/definition-of-social-work/, date accessed 25 August 2015.

International Union of Psychological Science (2008) *Universal Declaration of Ethical Principles for Psychologists*, www.iupsys.net/about/governance/universal-declaration-of-ethical-principles-for-psychologists.html, date accessed 25 August 2015.

Kemshall, H. (2002) *Risk, Social Policy and Welfare: Introducing Social Policy* (Buckingham: Open University Press).

Kemshall, H. (2010) 'Risk Rationalities in Contemporary Social Work Policy and Practice', *British Journal of Social Work*, 40(4), 1247–62.

Lemon, G., Stanford, S. and Sawyer, A-M. (2016) 'Trust and the Dilemmas of Risk Assessment in Non-government Mental Health Services', *Australian Social Work*, 69(2), 145–57.

Lupton, D. (2004) *Risk: Key Ideas* (London: Routledge).

Lupton, D. (2006) 'Sociology and Risk', in G. Mythen and S. Walklate (eds) *Beyond the Risk Society: Critical Reflections on Risk and Human Society* (Maidenhead, Berkshire: Open University Press), 11–24.

McDonald, C. (2006) 'Institutional Transformation: The Impact of Performance Measurement on Professional Practice in Social Work', *Social Work and Society*, 4, 25–37.

Morley, C. (2009) 'Using Critical Reflection to Improve Feminist Practice', in J. Allan, L. Briskman and B. Pease (eds) *Critical Social Work: Theories and Practices for a Socially Just World* (2nd edition) (Crows Nest, New South Wales: Allen & Unwin), 145–59.

Mythen, G. and Walklate, S. (2006) 'Introduction: Thinking Beyond the Risk Society', in G. Mythen and S. Walklate (eds) *Beyond the Risk Society: Critical Reflections on Risk and Human Society* (Maidenhead, Berkshire: Open University Press), 1–7.

Nipperess, S. and Briskman, L. (2009) 'Promoting a Human Rights Perspective on Critical Social Work', in J. Allan, L. Briskman, and B. Pease (eds) *Critical Social Work: Theories and Practices for a Socially Just World* (2nd edition) (Crows Nest, New South Wales: Allen & Unwin), 58–69.

Parton, N. (1996) 'Social Work, Risk and "the Blaming System"', in N. Parton (ed.) *Social Theory, Social Change and Social Work* (London: Routledge), 98–114.

Rose, N. (1996) 'The Death of the Social? Re-figuring the Territory of Government', *Economy and Society*, 25, 327–56.

Rose, N. (2000) 'Government and Control', *British Journal of Criminology*, 40, 321–39.

Simpson, R. M. (2013) 'Dignity, Harm and Hate Speech', *Law and Philosophy*, 32, 701–28.

Stanford, S. (2010) '"Speaking Back" to Fear: Responding to the Moral Dilemmas of Risk in Social Work Practice', *British Journal of Social Work*, 40(4), 1065–80.

Stanford, S. and Taylor, S. (2013) 'Welfare Dependence or Enforced Deprivation? A Critical Examination of White Neoliberal Welfare and Risk', *Australian Social Work*, 66, 476–94.

Taylor, S., Vreugdenhil, A. and Schneiders, M. (2015) 'Social Justice as Concept and Practice in Australian Social Work: An Analysis of Norma Parker Addresses, 1969–2008', *Australian Social Work*, DOI: 10.1080/0312407X.2014.973554.

UN General Assembly (1948) *Universal Declaration of Human Rights*, 10 December 1948, 217 A (III), www.refworld.org/docid/3ae6b3712c.html, date accessed 25 August 2015.

Warner, J. (2008) 'Community Care, Risk and the Shifting Locus of Danger and Vulnerability in Mental Health', in A. Petersen and I. Wilkinson (eds) *Health, Risk and Vulnerability* (Abingdon, Oxon: Routledge), 30–47.

Washington Post (2012) *Remarks from the NRA Press Conference on Sandy Hook School Shooting (Transcript)*, www.washingtonpost.com/politics/remarks-from-the-nra-press-conference-on-sandy-hook-school-shooting-delivered-on-dec-21-2012-transcript/2012/12/21/bd1841fe-4b88-11e2-a6a6-aabac85e8036_story.html, date accessed 2 September 2015.

Webb, S. (2006) *Social Work in a Risk Society: Social and Political Perspectives* (Houndmills, Basingstoke, Hampshire and New York: Palgrave Macmillan).

World Psychiatric Association (2005) *Appendix D: Madrid Declaration on Ethical Standards for Psychiatric Practice*, www.wpanet.org/uploads/About_WPA/Manual_of_Procedures/appen-d-madrid-4th.pdf, date accessed 2 September 2015.

5

DIRECTIONS FOR POLICY AND PRACTICE FROM THE LIVED EXPERIENCE OF MENTAL HEALTH PROBLEMS

Gerry Bennison and Dawn Talbot

Introduction

The chapter begins with Dawn's reflections on an incident that occurred on one occasion when she was being admitted to hospital. Through this small and seemingly insignificant event, Dawn illustrates some key features about how the medical model of mental distress and risk thinking combine so that they dominate everyday experience and dehumanize normal interaction. Following this, Gerry reflects on his experience of professional responses to the risks that arise for him from the interaction between his physical and mental health needs. He shows how the failure to see these two domains as interrelated in the 'whole person' leads to misunderstanding and inappropriate labelling of him as 'a risk' rather than 'at risk'. In analysing our experience, we use the concept of social suffering, defined as follows:

> Social suffering results from what political, economic, and institutional power does to people and, reciprocally, from how these forms of power themselves influence responses to social problems. (Kleinman *et al.*, 1997, p. ix)

In social suffering, our attention is drawn to processes of power that are operated through risk work and risk thinking. Central to the concept is the lived experience of discrimination and oppression, and the feelings – such as anger, shame and humiliation – that arise from these experiences. We conclude by setting out what a path to social justice and human rights might look like from our perspective as service users.

Dawn's story: The social construction of a sandwich

I am a 53-year-old mother of three, and live with my partner Gerry and my son. I have been using mental health services on and off since the age of 17. Since coming into contact with secondary mental health services in recent years, and receiving a diagnosis in 2003 of a mood disorder, my life and control over it has changed dramatically. My contact with my neighbours is shaped by my diagnosis as they have seen me distressed. I live on a large estate and have had issues around social exclusion. Although I have gained a degree in social science and consider myself confident most of the time, it has been certain other experiences that have shaped my life.

My experience of services has been mixed, with some extremely good practitioners who have worked with risk in a very positive way, looking at relapse and recovery and helping me understand my triggers. This approach led to a great move forward for me, as I actually felt like a partner in decisions around my care. My experiences have highlighted what makes the difference between positive engagement and other situations where I have felt completely powerless. Often, these experiences occur in the context of everyday encounters and the nature of the smallest interactions between professionals and service users.

One such situation was a couple of years ago, when I was acutely unwell and having to be assessed to come in for inpatient treatment. It was early in the morning and having not been sleeping, I was asked if I wanted anything. I said 'I am quite hungry' and the practitioner who was assessing me later came back with an egg salad sandwich. I took one bite and decided it was a bit dry and that I just didn't fancy eating it, as it didn't have any mayonnaise. Nothing was said and I was then admitted on to the inpatient ward.

Some six months later I saw the same person again, who asked me, 'How is your paranoia now? When we met before, you wouldn't eat that sandwich.' The professional concerned had assumed my refusal to eat the sandwich stemmed from a paranoid belief it might be poisoned. I stared in disbelief but I was too stunned to say anything for fear of appearing to be ungrateful for being bought the offending sandwich. I couldn't actually say I didn't like it without mayonnaise, so I accepted the label and felt like a naughty child for not eating my food some six months later. I felt ungrateful, powerless and frightened to tell the truth. I am ashamed to say I took another label because I was afraid to take the consequences if I appeared ungrateful. In the next section of the chapter I reflect on the way in which such encounters exemplify a type of interaction that is common for many mental health service users.

'I am not a constellation of symptoms'

In my overall experience of being admitted to hospital, as described above, it felt that I was perceived as being just a constellation of symptoms. Rather than a genuine rapport developing between a practitioner who could see me as a whole person and a human being with ordinary preferences and life experiences, I eventually felt infantilized; like a naughty child unable to say 'no'. Such 'micro' experiences accumulate and mean that I feel, ultimately, as though I cease to be seen as an autonomous adult and a competent social actor with choices and rights. I consider that recovery and expression of human rights starts to take place when an individual feels respected and there is equilibrium of power created between professionals and service users. This translates to wider notions of self-determination and choice where fixed essentialist identities of risk can then be challenged, as expressed through new modes of interaction in everyday encounters.

My experience of admission into hospital highlighted for me the lack of dialogue and reflective interplay that often exists between practitioner and service users. In general, it seemed easier for the practitioner to shape and see my expression of trauma as a simplistic 'persecutory complex' based on a very narrow model of risk. To me they seemed unable to juggle the uncertainties of emotional interaction and open up a communicative space, which could have enabled me to express my feelings and thoughts openly. It seems as though there was a fear of seeing me as a human being and, specifically, of being too close to the pain that I was experiencing at that time. This presented a barrier to an empathic interaction that could have been based on trust and exploration with me as a person. It was easier for the practitioner involved in my care to perceive my pain from a fixed position of power and a narrow idea of risk. They did not explore more widely than this narrow construct and most certainly not through the lens of what I may have been feeling as a fellow human being. This kind of professional response simply serves to heighten stress and also strengthen the barriers to support I need for my physical health conditions, including diabetes. This is reflected in the struggle I have had in managing the side effects of medication, which may have contributed to hindering my self-esteem (Coppock & Dunn, 2009).

In my experience, a simplistic construction of risk objectifies people and therefore dehumanizes them. In contrast, someone can only have human rights if they are seen as a person not an object. This objectification takes place when a person is seen as a set of symptoms, a malfunctioning biomedical object far removed from the influence of social experiences. Interactions with professionals indicate they do not always see service users as human beings suffering from pain, including the pain of being socially excluded from communities, as discussed by Boardman (2010). They also do not take into account someone's skills, strengths and expression of human rights (Morgan 2013). Evaluation of human experience through risk assessment and predictability makes the objectification of service users inevitable.

Risk assessment

The use of risk assessment should focus on the everyday reality of living with a diagnosis and the consequences this brings; the focus should not be on a preconceived, all-enveloping construct. It should be based on an open dialogue that takes place in a relationship and with the understanding that we are competent social actors. The consequences of living with a diagnosis are seen in the way service users face the pressures of living on the periphery, often within a subculture of socially produced distress. In this sense we experience the 'double suffering' that Frost and Hoggett (2008) associate with social isolation. If someone is unable to participate in society fully, due to lack of resources, restriction of human rights and social injustice, this will have a massive impact on their whole life course. This impact will be on their wellbeing, and it needs to be acknowledged and readily challenged. This approach would support and facilitate a richer and purposeful conversation, seeing the whole person sited in their social location. However, a fixed, narrow definition of risk obscures inequalities and oppression because it locates 'risk' in the individual. The task facing mental health service providers is to become more responsive to the experiences of people who access services and informal carers, not least by acknowledging the social construction of inequalities and the risks these produce.

My experiences have taught me that power and control impact directly on opportunities for collaborative, positive risk taking and inhibit co-production and shared power. As a mature woman, I am acutely aware that I can become childlike when feeling disempowered. In certain situations, I start to doubt my own reasoning. It is important that people understand me as a woman with multiple roles in my life, in the context of different relationships. Looking back at my life, when I have experienced mental health services, I have wanted and needed to be seen as someone who is a partner, a parent and also a carer. It is important that these identities are seen as a part of the person I am when discussing and understanding risk. I also want people to understand that I have hopes, skills and strengths, and to see these aspects of me as a person. For there to be a move to another paradigm of exploring risk, there needs to be co-production of autonomy and social justice. Such a move requires confident practition-ers who can hold uncertainty, challenge fixed expectations about their roles, and fight for resources. The unpredictability of a life course in which I experience inequalities needs to be recognized. It is only then that the current fixed ideas of risk will move to a liberating sense of who service users are as human beings and a paradigm which is based on rights and social justice. In the next section Gerry presents his experiences to further develop the themes of this chapter.

Gerry's story: 'What has it got to do with me?'

As someone labelled with 'borderline personality disorder', I am con-scious that the concept of risk around self-harm is prominent among mental health professionals, but it is often based on fear and illusion. Understanding the pragmatic need for good care often gets lost in the neg-ative connotations of risk in managing my wellbeing. Here is an example that shows this 'heightened risk panic' in practical terms.

I went to see a psychiatrist to talk about my concerns about a mood stabilizer I had been put on. I was worried about being on the drug because I have a major heart condition and kidney and urological impair-ments, and I felt it was appropriate to have these discussions with mental health services as they had prescribed the medication. I knew that they already considered me to be a risk in relation to self-harm. Although it was never communicated overtly in my care, I felt they saw my relation-ship with services as being an emotional crutch that, from their perspec-tive, was based on dependency. On this occasion, as soon as I opened the door, I could feel the tension in the environment. The psychiatrist's response to my query about the medication was that I should see a doc-tor who dealt with kidney functioning, stating, 'What has it got to do with me?' This was said in a very unpleasant manner and made me feel very scared and intimidated, and I felt the appointment had been futile. My feelings were so intense that I started to self-harm. This was a very frightening incident for me and one that I knew was inappropriate for all concerned. However, there was no attempt to discuss what had happened, or de-escalate or to understand the cause of the events. The outcome of this incident was that it was decided that two professionals should be pre-sent for all my future appointments. This felt intimidating and it meant a further label of being 'a risk' was applied to me, which reinforced my existing label. Sometimes the fear of risk is a risk in itself: a risk to engage-ment, a risk to choice and a risk to the sharing of power and a role in care. It was the fear to address risk, in my example, which led to further stigma, misunderstanding and pain.

The power of uncertainty

The ideas of social justice, particularly agency and autonomy of voice, are central to the themes of empowerment considered in the experiences outlined in my vignette. If we explore the concept of social justice further we must examine the construction of the therapeutic interaction, and often the essentialism it is built on, just as Dawn did earlier in the chapter. It is clear through my reflection on my experience that the narrow definition of risk is a barrier to the attainment of social justice. My concerns about my physical health were not met in terms of my biographical narrative – what was important to me – but what was important for the service and the psychiatrist. This produced an acute form of 'double suffering' (Frost & Hoggett, 2008) through my reaction in the form of self-harm.

The presentation of my distress through self-injurious behaviour in reaction to the way the psychiatrist treated me produced an even sharper narrowing in terms of the way risk was conceptualized. While I acknowledge that my behaviour could be seen as problematic, there was, beyond this, an over-willingness to shape my individual attributes into a simplistic, dominant discourse about risk. This was the discourse surrounding both my biomedical label – as 'personality disordered' – but also the essentialist discourse of risk surrounding my presentation. The focus of our interaction quickly turned away from the fears I had come to express and towards the threat I might somehow pose to others or myself. The preconceptions about me that underpinned the professional response were negative and went unchallenged. There was no appreciation of my humanity and the way I was presenting as a person 'in context'. This is key when considering how negative ideas and risk-averse practices are constructed, often without the co-production of understanding based on key elements of a person's life story. When reflecting on the intersectionality between risk and social justice in mental health, an unwillingness on the part of practitioners to live with uncertainty damages potentially helpful interactions. This was certainly the case in this encounter, where my physical health needs were never understood as being part of my identity in the way biomedical constructs of my mental health were. My experience highlights the importance for practitioners in 'making the uncomfortable comfortable' by engaging with uncertainty beyond the essentialist categories of risk and diagnosis. Only by moving beyond these can we shape a move to the promotion of human narratives and, in turn, human rights.

When I reflect on my experiences accessing mental health service provision, it is important to explore how discomfort with uncertainty shapes understanding. This can be seen in my vignette in how my presentation of what we will term 'self-harm' was taken to fit a fixed and linear notion of my biographical narrative and life course. There was, quite literally, no time taken to reflect on what I was trying to say or what my concerns may have been about. The humility that was needed on the part of the practitioners in order to create space for such reflection was absent. This lack of time to explore and understand wider issues locks such outpouring of emotional distress into a narrow – and purely negative – definition and indeed advances further oppression. It also filters the complexity of life experiences through a formal record of standardized risk assessment that polarizes and detaches the narrative from its situational context and meaning.

The unilateral use of professional power in this way means that risk is not seen as something to be shared and negotiated but a practical problem to be 'dealt with' and managed. It also disempowers and further oppresses individuals who access services and their informal networks of care alike. In my example, no consideration was given to a wider set of discourses about how I had presented, specifically about self-harm as a coping mechanism. Most certainly, it was also based on the assumption of a fixed linear life course, with no contradictions or ambiguity. Exploring the ideas of social justice and human rights, and their relationship with risk, means considering the individual in context and embracing the idea that interactions are not 'set in stone' on a linear path along which risk probabilities are sacrosanct.

Challenging fixed ideas of risk through social suffering

Our argument is that the promotion of social justice and human rights can only be facilitated through anti-oppressive and anti-discriminatory practices that move away from the fixed categories of risk that seek to produce certainty. In Gerry's situation and life, the (sometimes unspoken) need of people working in services for certainty through categories of risk has led to forms of exclusion which have only amplified his negative experiences. The experiences faced by both Gerry and Dawn in mental health services might be characterized as forms of 'being done to', which results from power relations that are too readily accepted as natural (Frost & Hoggett, 2008, p. 442):

> Because the exercise of 'power over' others appears natural and legitimate, the hurt that produces shame and humiliation and the losses that lead to grief become detached from the social relations which generate them. The suffering that then results becomes individualized and internalized – built into subjectivity. Secondary damage is experienced when the defences an individual deploys to cope with hurt and loss have destructive consequences for self and others ...

In considering social justice and risk, those working with people experiencing emotional distress must recognize and reflect on their need to understand structural power and the inequalities it produces. For both Gerry and Dawn, these experiences had the effect of making them feel ashamed. For Dawn this shaming took the form of infantilization; for Gerry, it was shame that arose from being designated 'a risk'. In both instances, we would agree with Frost and Hoggett (2008, p. 445) when they assert that shame produces 'serious identity damage with ramifications for various aspects of selfhood'.

In our view, the role played by binary distinctions, such as 'in crisis' or 'not in crisis', as articulated through the power relations between service users and practitioners, must also be considered. This can be seen in how actuarial and clinical forms of risk measurement are often viewed outside the narrative of the individual and their insights, skills and experience. In Gerry's situation, his anxiety about his medication and its impact on his physical health, together with the lack of compassion shown to him, was a consolidation of his expectations of self and the wider life course. In his experience, this obtuse response was not exceptional but the norm. The complexity of his identity was reduced to a measure of standardized risk and a diagnostic category. This, in turn, facilitated exclusion from accessing knowledge and expertise that might have promoted agency and reduced self-stigma. Practitioners seldom interrogate the connections between professional power, shame, stigma and suffering, and the responses that the resulting hurt elicits. We argue that understanding these connections is central to moving beyond the current paradigm of risk.

A path to social justice and human rights?

The road to developing a paradigm of risk assessment and management that encompasses a human rights and social justice approach must not be so simplistic as to deny the existence of risk altogether. The need to recognize risk while promoting a rights-based approach is reflected in the work of Rose (2002, cited in Langan, 2008, p. 471). It has to be acknowledged that such change of practice relating to risk is not simple; it is complex on a number of levels. It needs to take into account the fact that individuals may not consider the social consequence of their actions during certain moments of their life course, nor the choices that may be open to them. It is important to consider, when promoting social justice and human rights, that perceptions of risk and behaviour are often unspoken through therapeutic relationships due to their emotional resonance or sensitivity. In exploring what are termed 'risk behaviours' and moving to a social justice perspective, further openness and honesty is needed in interactions between practitioners and service users. Langan (2008, p. 477) explains:

> Professionals of all backgrounds suggested that honesty about risk could help the service user to understand the rationale for professional involvement and facilitate a collaborative relationship within which risk could be managed.

This requires sharing responsibility and having capacity for critical reflection, and to work with individuals to explore their constructions of their risk, in whatever contexts it operates.

The role of health literacy and narrative is key to bridging the conceptual link between risk as a tool of power and the shift to a new paradigm that is characterized by self-determination and understanding of experience. In part, this is articulated through the concepts of 'positive risk management' and the 'strengths approach' developed in the work of Morgan (2013). In shifting the existing paradigm of risk, it is important to understand its position alongside concepts such as recovery. In order to develop a methodology that encompasses the individual and the ebb and flow of life experiences, there must be a recalibration to consider recovery and its role in the exploration of risk in mental health and how choice is framed.

There is also a need to consider the wider influences of the life course, and practically to use wider concepts of risk in order to explore inequalities and social exclusion. Such an approach, based on principles of social justice and addressing power inequalities, is reflected on in the work of Tickle and colleagues (2014, p. 97) who propose, 'Professionals should be encouraged to broaden their conceptualisation of risk to include issues such as social exclusion and poverty.' The move from the existing risk paradigm to one that encompasses a human rights and social justice approach depends on an appreciation of the importance of such broader conceptualizations of risk. This can be facilitated through users' narratives and experiences in education and training around mental health, among other strategies. Professional power relationships can be explored and altered by hearing the experience of service users first-hand and sharing the uncertainties that are entailed in encountering risk for both practitioners and service users.

Gerry and Dawn, as people who have experienced long-term exclusion and crude categorization in services, have each experienced a significant and long-lasting impact on their self-esteem, albeit in different ways. Through the ideas in this chapter, we have identified the importance of operating through networks of relationships and shared stories to identify the impact of inequalities. These ideas also validate our experience of social suffering, particularly 'double suffering', within mental health systems. In order for risk assessment processes to address and move to another paradigm that fosters social justice and human rights, these processes must evidence and acknowledge people in their entirety. This requires sharing power, which deconstructs fixed perceptions and moves to a fluid way of working with risk, thereby highlighting the underpinning value of the human being and their experience. It also promotes the sharing of these experiences, in terms of our autonomous voices and agency and how rights based on autonomy can be positively shaped.

Concluding thoughts: Learning to live with uncertainty

'Risk', together with its assessment and management, is infused with issues around power and control and what it means to be labelled 'patient', 'citizen' and 'service user'. Our experiences have highlighted how interactions with practitioners based on narrow conceptualizations of risk can produce anger, panic and confusion. Paradoxically, such interactions also serve to increase rather than reduce the risk of harms occurring. Furthermore, society makes its own 'risk assessment' in terms of the interactions people have with mental health service users – based on negative perceptions of somebody who is seen as irrational even when they are not.

The role of risk assessment and management is integral to how perceptions around mental health are formulated. The dominant perceptions of people with mental health needs are evident in the media, where the focus is largely on representations of 'dangerousness', often through crudely observed media stereotypes. Perceptions are also shaped by the ongoing 'standardization' of the life course and narrative in experiencing the inequalities duly associated with emotional distress. If we are to move to a new paradigm based on social justice and which promotes self-determination, there must be critical reflection that deconstructs risk assessment and management in its current forms.

The shift to a different paradigm must move beyond linear, quantified measurement of risk based on expectations of the individual and their networks. It also has to move from a tentative exploration to a full embodiment of notions of 'positive risk management' and the 'strengths' approach (Morgan, 2013). This is not easily achieved, but it can be practically implemented in day-to-day therapeutic interactions within mental health settings to foster a human rights and social justice perspective. The focus then falls on the smallest everyday interactions that take place, moment by moment. Individuals need to be understood in the context of their relationships with others. All of us live 'linked lives' whereby '[h]uman life is social. Indeed, one's life narrative is hardly one's own. Its strongest storylines are punctuated by and enmeshed with other people' (Settersten, 2015, p. 217). Risk should be considered as part of a therapeutic dialogue, which may not have expected therapeutic value during the time of interaction and the sharing of resonant stories. It is not enough to quantify and to create a singular narrative anchored to simplistic constructs of 'wellness' or 'illness' and to validate such presenting experiences narrowly through the lens of 'risk' and what is the norm.

In evolving risk assessment and management in mental health settings we can develop a triangulated paradigm which redresses inequality and is attuned to the rich stories and narratives which then inform fulfilment of social justice goals. The work of Langan (2008) shows how these concepts of sharing and evidencing narrative, as well as fostering the exploration of skills and experiences, can contribute to processes of social justice. This also promotes human rights in challenging the restraint imposed by a fixed set of assumptions of the individual and their values within their own life course and networks. Such an approach focuses on micro-transactions and shared risk assessment as a therapeutic tool in its own right, to facilitate the articulation of agency and voice and the promotion of self-esteem. Tickle *et al.* (2014, p. 105) reflect on how shared exploration of this sort is impacted by fears, uncertainty and concerns for the weighting of consequences, reminding us of the negative potential to 'marginalize the consideration of possible successes or gains as outcomes of risk that might contribute to recovery'. Their observations and our own experience highlight that to attain a shift to a paradigm which is founded on stories of the life course and transparent communication also requires acceptance of moments of uncertainty. Holding such uncertainty is an important dimension in taking the tentative steps towards a focus on human rights, agency and self-determination in place of the current narrow view of risk and its management.

References

Boardman, J. (2010) 'Social Exclusion of People with Mental Health Problems and Learning Disabilities: Key Aspects', in J. Boardman, A. Currie, H. Killaspy and G. Mezey (eds) *Social Inclusion and Mental Health* (London: RCPsych Publications), 22–46.

Coppock, V. and Dunn, B. (2009) *Understanding Social Work Practice in Mental Health* (London: Sage).

Frost, L. and Hoggett, P. (2008) 'Human Agency and Social Suffering', *Critical Social Policy,* 28, 438–60.

Kleinman, A., Das, D. and Lock, M. (eds) (1997) *Social Suffering* (Berkeley: University of California Press).

Langan, J. (2008) 'Involving Mental Health Service Users Considered to Pose a Risk to other People in Risk Assessment', *Journal of Mental Health,* 17(5), 471–81.

Morgan, S. (2013) *Risk Decision-making: Working with Risk and Implementing Positive Risk-taking* (Pavilion Publishing and Media: Oxford).

Rose, D. (2002) *User and Carer Involvement in Change Management in a Mental Health Context: Review of the Literature*. Report to the National Co-ordinating Centre for NHS Services Delivery and Organization (R and D. London: Department of Health).

Settersten, R. A. (2015) 'Relationships in Time and the Life Course: The Significance of Linked Lives', *Research in Human Development*, 12(3–4), 217–22.

Tickle, A., Brown, D. and Hayward, M. (2014), 'Can We Risk Recovery? A Grounded Theory of Clinical Psychologists' Perceptions of Risk and Recovery Orientated Mental Health Services', *Psychology and Psychotherapy: Theory, Research and Practice,* 87(1), 96–110.

6

THE LIMITS AND POSSIBILITIES OF RISK ASSESSMENT: LESSONS FROM SUICIDE PREVENTION

Nina Rovinelli Heller

Introduction

The management of the individual risk of suicide is arguably one of the most challenging practice dilemmas for mental health professionals and it is not an uncommon experience. Jacobson *et al.* (2004) and Heller and Parks (unpublished data), in studies of social workers in the United States, found that one in three had experienced the death of a client by suicide, and the overwhelming majority had worked with clients who were actively suicidal. While suicidality is a relatively rare, albeit increasing, event population-wide, it is not particularly rare in clinical practice. One of the core mandates for social workers is the enhancement of individual wellbeing, and work with the suicidal person tests our ability to fulfil that mandate. This work requires advanced clinical assessment skills, knowledge of the emerging suicide knowledge base and certainty about who is at risk, at what particular point, and under what conditions. Paradoxically, the worker must also be able to tolerate the ambiguities and uncertainties of suicide risk assessment and prediction, all while maintaining a crucial connection with the humanity and complexity of the individual at risk. At the same time, in the context of a dominant risk paradigm, the public, funding agencies and government regulators, managers and supervisors, and indeed we ourselves, demand certainty in our assessment and prevention efforts. Work with suicidal clients is not for the faint of heart.

Suicide risk assessment, fear and uncertainty

Composing this chapter about any negative, though unintended, consequences of utilizing the prevailing risk paradigm in regard to suicide has been the most challenging writing project I've attempted. Frankly, it scared me. On reflection, I recognize that my numerous starts and stops were related to my concerns that any critique of the risk paradigm as it pertains to suicide would be seen as a minimization of the very tangible devastation and impact of a death by suicide, inadvertent collusion with the hopelessness of the suicidal client, or an outright violation of the core social work principle of enhancing human wellbeing: in this case, saving lives. At moments, this fear, although not altogether rational, has been paralysing. My own writing about suicide, as is the case with the vast literature on suicide prevention and suicide risk assessment, has focused on the prevention of deaths by suicide. That is the bottom line – and success is measured by lives saved. Indeed, in the US the Zero Suicide movement recommended by the National Action Alliance for Suicide Prevention (NAASP, 2015) for health care systems is increasingly being adopted in order to provide institution-wide structural changes to suicide prevention and intervention activities. I do not argue here that this should not be the goal. However, the tension that I feel in writing this chapter is not unlike that experienced by the clinician who sits across from the suicidal client and is simultaneously dealing with their own concerns about risk and safety in a context that demands certainty.

I am writing both as an academic and as a mental health practitioner. Similar to an author, in my experience the practitioner has an audience in their head that threatens to condemn their potential failure, in this case to keep a client safe. That audience may include direct supervisors, a client's family member, government agencies, attorneys, and sometimes the client him- or herself. In these moments, those fears threaten to impede the practitioner's ability to listen closely and empathically to the client. At these times, there are risks inherent for both the practitioner and the client. Here, I argue the importance of understanding the forces that create this tension, such that the practitioner can 'meet the client' at their most vulnerable point, with a clear mind that is not cluttered with the clinician's own fears about risk, censure, reputation and litigation. In order to understand clearly the potential suicide risk that a client poses to him- or herself, as a practitioner one needs to be able to join, unencumbered, with the client's despair while simultaneously 'holding' another more hopeful view that the client is unable, at least at the moment, to imagine. At the same time, it is critical that the practitioner is able to use the best available knowledge of risk assessment, while being keenly aware of its current limitations.

A clear example of the danger of unexamined fear, in relation to the issue of risk on the part of the clinician, is the use of the *no-suicide contract*. Introduced several decades ago, this contract was given to suicidal patients by their clinicians and included a statement of the client's agreement not to harm (or kill) him- or herself, sometimes for a specific amount of time. Each party would sign it. As a member of a treatment team on a psychiatric unit, I remember feeling a sense of relief when we obtained such an agreement. However, there are, of course, many things wrong with this activity. For example, many clients may feel coerced into signing such a document, particularly when not doing so might mean the denial of discharge, privileges or a visit pass. More importantly, these contracts could actually cause more harm to patients (Kroll, 2000) and they may do more to protect practitioners than clients. For example, if a clinician falsely believes that the client is *less* suicidal on the basis of having signed a contract, that clinician, feeling somewhat relieved, might be less likely to monitor very closely the client's suicidal status, potentially placing the client at increased risk of harm (Simon & Hales, 2006).

It may also be simplistic to assume that it is the signing of such a contract that keeps someone safe. Indeed, nearly 20 years after I'd worked with a young woman who suffered a severe suicide attempt while under our care, she called me for an appointment for outpatient services. In our first session we talked about her life in the intervening years and the fact that she had been suicidal at times, but had not made another suicide attempt. The issue of the safety contract we had both signed came up. She credited the contract with her having 'stayed safe'. However, as we discussed this further, she insisted that:

> it really wasn't the contract at all – yes, I kept it, but it was the relationship with you that actually made the difference. Or maybe the idea of the relationship with you. Not the paper – that would have meant nothing … if I'd wanted to kill myself, I would have. (Heller, 2014, p. 1795)

In this case, the client had the ability to maintain a symbolic awareness of the *relational* meaning of the contract, sustain object constancy and maintain that as a way of managing her impulse control. However, many of our clients do not have the capacity to do this, particularly when compromised by cognitive distortions and affective lability that may be present in a suicidal state. Furthermore, given the changing practice arena for mental health services, clients are now apt to be offered very brief interventions with a succession of different providers. Both these factors work against the continuity of care and the opportunity for relational work that are particularly important for clients who struggle with suicidal thoughts and impulses.

Fortunately, *safety* contracts are now more likely to be offered than the no-suicide or no-harm contract, usually at the time of discharge or of heightened suicidal risk. These documents, typically developed by client and practitioner together, identify potential triggers such as interpersonal disruptions and symptoms like changes in mood or thinking that might result in increased suicidality. The contract lists action steps, like reaching out to designated support people or resources and engaging in identified self-care activities, such as taking a walk and having a nap. What distinguishes this safety contract from the no-suicide contract is the very active involvement and *expectation* of involvement of the client. This restores a sense of agency to an individual who is likely feeling powerless, hopeless and alone. At once, it increases the likelihood of the client's assumption of responsibility for his or her life, while providing the jointly constructed plans; the client is not *done to* but *worked with*, a major tenet of a human rights approach.

Before exploring further how a human rights and social justice approach may be helpful, there are a few principles of risk assessment with suicidal clients that are worth noting. First, the prediction of rare events, generally, is not particularly reliable and in the case of suicidality the stakes are very high. Payne (2011, p. 86) is clear about this: 'risk is a matter of probability; a risk is the likelihood, not the certainty, of something happening'. Second, while people share some common risk factors, some risk factors are idiosyncratic and others pertain to certain subgroups based on, for example, age, race and gender. Third, risk assessment must include attention to risk of suicidal thoughts, feelings and attitudes as well as behaviour, as the first three have complicated associations with eventual death by suicide. At the same time, a prior suicide attempt is consistently found to be the best available predictor of eventual suicide. Finally, throughout at least the last 70 years, our approaches to risk assessment have been primarily from a mental health perspective.

It is ironic that with significant attention being paid to risk and risk assessment of suicide, our attempts to predict suicide accurately are woefully inadequate. Luoma *et al.* (2002) reported that in their review of more than three dozen studies, a health care provider had seen an average of 45 per cent of people who died by suicide within the month prior to their death, while a mental health provider had seen 20 per cent. Likewise, Draper *et al.* (2008) found in an Australian study that 79 per cent of suicide decedents had seen a health care professional in the three months prior to their deaths. This suggests either that we are not effectively screening individuals who may be at risk or are not facilitating appropriate follow through referrals, or that there were no identifiable risk factors for those who died. The latter interpretation is unlikely, particularly given the elevated risk due to factors such as psychiatric diagnosis and previous

attempts, both relatively easily identified. It is perhaps at the point of consideration of the degree to which a service system adequately meets the
needs of suicidal individuals that a broader view is indicated.

More recently, a public health model for suicide prevention has come
to the fore alongside the mental health focus. This provides a way of
understanding risk at the population level, not only at the individual. The
public health approach also increases the likelihood that the role of social,
economic and other macro factors will be better understood, leading to
both more population-based prevention and risk assessment interventions
as well as attention to structural forces which place some groups at some
particular points of time at higher risk. Public health approaches broaden
the lens and focus for intervention and an examination of society and
social structures further extends our understanding for assessment, intervention *and* social change.

Suicide and structural factors

While the evidence for the association between psychiatric conditions and
death by suicide is convincing, it is less so for the sociological influences.
Heller (2014, p. 451) notes: 'While psychological and micro-etiological factors dominate the contemporary suicide discourse, the influence of economic, social and related micro issues are worth another look.' An early
pioneer in suicide studies, the sociologist Durkheim put forth the idea
that when there are changing rates of suicide, these should be the focus of
attention. According to Spencer (1997, p. 86), Durkheim believed that 'the
degree of integration between man and society is essentially protective
against self-destruction ... the shared unquestioned values of religion and
families are protective of ... "the collective sentiment"'. The lack of social
integration is theorized to raise the rate of suicidality. This view suggests
the influence of social structures and inequities on suicide rates; in fact, it
could be argued from this perspective that the rise of rates in psychiatric
conditions follows the same pathway as the rise in suicide rates, namely
both are associated with rapid changes in the social order.

In a period of global recession, increasing financial insecurities and
inequities, technological advances and attendant social role changes,
Durkheim's attention to the social structures or 'anomie' (a sudden and
unexpected change in a social position which poses new challenges) may
be particularly relevant. Judd *et al.* (2012) suggest that contemporary
examples of anomie might include financial ruin, or some shameful forensic event such as child pornography. They point out that the important
factor here is that we understand the complex and ever-changing relationship between structural societal changes and individual-level factors

and, related to this, the key question of whether the profile of suicide is changing or changeable. This suggests the importance of real-time examination of suicide data trends, as well as broader social and economic developments.

Social conditions vary by country and region and several authors have questioned the degree to which Western studies about the correlations between psychiatric disorders and suicide can be generalized to other regions (Mann *et al.*, 2005; Tondo *et al.*, 2003). Elevated suicide rates have been linked with trends in national economies (Yang & Lester, 2001) and employment (Andersen *et al.*, 2010). Reeves *et al.* (2012) note a rise in suicide rates of up to 60 per cent in Greece associated with the financial difficulties there. However, the literature is equivocal and Mishara (2008) suggests, among other things, that social solidarity in relation to stressful times may actually be considered a protective factor. Along with exposure to greater social vulnerability, may both unemployment and suicide result from other mental health-related factors? He also suggests that 'people in desperate situations' such as unemployment may turn to each other in what we might call mutual support.

In another examination of macro influences, Milner *et al.* (2011) found that high levels scored on a globalization index were associated with higher male and female suicide rates. Though the significance of the association lessened when they considered other social and economic factors, they urge further examination of the relationships between globalization, traditional societal structures and suicide rates. Blasco-Fontecilla *et al.* (2012) examined the trends and correlations between gross domestic product (GDP) adjusted for purchasing power parity per capita on global suicide rates by World Health Organization (WHO) regions. They conclude that economic growth is not invariably followed by a fall in suicide rates, and that public health interventions may be more appropriate for developing countries, while preventive measures directed towards the amelioration of psychiatric problems may be best suited for high-income countries. Similarly, Li *et al.* (2011, p. 608) in a review of attributable risks of psychiatric and socio-economic factors found that 'prevention strategies which focus on lower socio-economic strata (more distal risk factors) have the potential to have similar population-level effects as strategies which target more proximal psychiatric risk factors' in the prevention of suicide.

Clearly, the emerging research literature on the relationship between suicide rates and social structures and changes does not provide us with certainty either. Furthermore, incorporating global, economic, employment and social structural variables into both mental health and public health suicide risk assessments may be crucial, but it is not enough. Macro strategies that address and change these inequities are a critical component of a human rights and social justice approach. We must be forward thinking here. For example, prospective studies that follow emerging suicide data in the context of Syrian refugee immigration, which is impacting the 'social order' for both the immigrants and the population of the EU, some of whose countries fear their own social disruption, might benefit from a Durkheimian theoretical approach. If indeed 'the degree of integration between man and society is essentially protective against self-destruction' (Spencer, 1997, p. 86) what dangers in a breakdown in social integration might exist? The answers are not clear, but need to be answered.

Lethal means restriction: Examples from the United States and Asia

There are at least two contemporary examples of prevailing attitudes and behaviour towards lethal means restriction – in the US and Asia – that demonstrate the social construction of policies. Here, I discuss lethal means restriction from a human rights and social justice perspective.

Lethal means restriction, on the clinical level, refers to the activities that clinicians take to restrict access to means to take their own life from clients who are already identified as being at risk for suicide. This approach has only recently gained more traction as a core component of comprehensive public health approaches to suicide prevention, particularly in the US, although the approach has previously been used effectively in other regions of the world. Any discussion of means restriction also highlights the stark differences in suicide risk factors, phenomenology and methods across the globe, and hence foci for prevention, intervention and public health efforts. This underscores the importance of developing prevention priorities and strategies that emerge from the data and the understanding of complex social, cultural, political and/or economic influences in the countries where one practices.

The patterns of suicide deaths in some regions and countries will favour a macro or population approach to means restriction, while other areas will benefit from a more targeted, clinical-level approach. Therefore the issue of *means restriction* is considered central to suicide prevention efforts from both clinical and public health perspectives. Yip *et al.* (2012) discuss theories of means restriction, noting the central challenge of accurately identifying those individuals in a population who are at elevated risk. They write that: 'Applied to the population as a whole, [means restriction] typically affects people whose suicide risk is otherwise undetected and who do not seek therapeutic assistance to prevent their crisis or for life-saving interventions when necessary.' (Yip *et al.*, 2012, p. 2394) They further report that the limitation of access to lethal means used for suicide is an important population strategy and cite numerous studies that show this is effective. They argue that efforts at restriction will be most success-ful when the means is particularly lethal and common and the broader community supports the restriction. They acknowledge that some individ-uals may utilize other available means but that those means left available will be less lethal, and are associated with fewer fatalities.

Means restriction is not without controversy, some of which stems from cultural norms, such as in the US, which stress the value of inde-pendence, self-regulation and individual rights. These are individualistic notions of rights – in keeping with both very conservative and neoliberal ideologies. In the political language of the US, these are views that are cen-tral to both ultraconservatism and libertarianism. The progressives and the Democrats, on the other hand, argue that the right to be protected (from self and others) is of greater importance than the right to bear arms. In the case of suicide this becomes particularly thorny. Does the right to bear arms trump the right to be protected? And does a suicidal individual have the right to the access to firearms? Self-determination or protection of the state? In addition, some argue about the inevitability of suicide, suggest-ing that if someone is determined to kill him- or herself, they cannot be stopped by the lack of access to the preferred means. By this argument, they would simply choose another method. Against this is the argument that, if someone thwarted by lack of available means 'substitutes' another method, it is typically one far less likely to result in death, reducing both individual and population-level risk.

The approaches and foci of means restriction policies developed by different countries and regions are determined based upon the data about demographics, major methods of suicide and lethality, and avail-ability of means of suicide for each area. Some countries have achieved some success through restricting lethal means. In a review of the litera-ture, Lewiecki and Miller (2013) reported that means restriction resulted in declines in suicide rates by pesticides in Asia (Mann et al., 2005) and by sedatives in Australia (Oliver & Hetzel, 1972). They also reported that sui-cide rates have also been brought down by reduced availability of coal gas in the United Kingdom (Kreitman, 1976) and installation of safety fences at notorious jump sites in Taiwan (Lin & Lu, 2006).

In contrast the challenges for lethal means restriction are sig-nificant and distinctive in the US, where gun ownership is legal and firearm access is a leading risk factor for suicide. The country is an out-lier in its high rate of suicide by firearm, the method of choice for more than half of people who die there by suicide annually. In 2013, more than half of the more than 41,000 suicides in the US were fire-arm deaths (Centers for Disease Control and Prevention, 2016). Miller et al. (2007) examined the Centers for Disease Control and Prevention surveillance data and found that both men and women of all age groups were at elevated risk for suicide if they lived in states with high rates of gun ownership. After controlling for other variables such as rates of mental illness and substance abuse, they found that overall suicides were almost twice as high in the states with the highest levels of gun ownership as in the lowest prevalence states, although the non-fatal attempts were roughly equivalent. In contrast, in 2010, hangings, suffocation and poisonings in England and Wales accounted for the vast majority of suicides, with very few by firearm. In addition, according to Miller *et al.* (2007), there are data not only from the United Kingdom but also from Brazil, Canada, Australia, Austria and New Zealand confirming that legislation restricting firearm ownership is associated with a reduction in firearm suicide.

Lethality of method is also an important consideration. From a phenomenological perspective, this is important: death by firearm is both rapid and irreversible. It is tempting to think of a firearm attempt as associated with higher intent, given the elevated likelihood of fatality. The role of intent is less clear, however, with some studies finding no relationship between intent and method (Harvard School of Public Health, 2012; Plutchik *et al.*, 1988), while others did find a correlation. However, impulsivity is a critical factor in this discussion. In a study by Hawton (2007) as cited by the Harvard School of Public Health, 24 per cent of a US sample of attempters reported having taken less than five minutes to decide to make the attempt. A full 71 per cent took less than one hour to make the decision. Williams *et al.* (1980) found, in a large sample of survivors, that 40 per cent contemplated their attempt for less than five minutes before taking action. Clearly, this speaks to the notion of impulsivity among a large proportion of suicide attempters. When there is ready access to a firearm, the amount of planning required is minimal and individuals who are experiencing intense and disturbing affective states can readily take what will be irrevocable action.

The ready availability of firearms is a hotly debated political issue in the US, particularly following numerous mass shootings in the country in 2012. And yet, notwithstanding these killings and the record of suicides by firearm so contrasting with the reduction of lethal means successes of other nations, a fierce lobby still fights for the right of gun ownership in the US. There are inherent contradictions in these arguments – on the one hand, the neoliberal or conservative position justifies putting limits on the rights of people with mental illness to own firearms, while demanding that they themselves (allegedly without mental health issues) have unfettered rights. If we were to frame this as a human rights and social justice issue, where is the balance between individual responsibility and social responsibility? These questions underlie the attitudes and behaviours that practitioners and systems bring to bear on individual and population-level prevention efforts.

There are several lessons in these data for service providers, regardless of nationality. First, suicide prevention must be understood in the context of social, political and cultural environments. Lethal means restriction must have a prominent role in any suicide prevention plan, for both populations and individuals, and efforts should focus on all means, with a particular priority for the most lethal methods in a population. In the US, this means that the restriction of firearms is important in reducing fatalities. According to the Harvard School for Public Health (2012), 'means reduction does not change the underlying suicidal impulse, or necessarily reduce attempts, but it saves lives by reducing the lethality of attempts'. Yip *et al.* (2012) underscore this, while acknowledging the challenges to implementing means restriction at the population level. Service providers in high gun suicide locales must make screening for firearm access a standard part of assessment, particularly with high-risk clients. For those individuals at risk for suicide, the means should be restricted. However, service providers do not routinely practise lethal means counselling. This means education and protocols for practitioners to include access to lethal means, in this case firearms, as part of mental health screenings, intakes and assessments. Slovak *et al.* (2008) surveyed social work practitioners in Ohio, in the US, about their practices, knowledge and attitudes about client firearm assessment and safety counselling. They found that that the majority did not report assessing for firearms or counselling safety on any regular basis. The barriers to doing so included lack of risk awareness, discomfort with the topic, belief that this was not a social work role, and low priority given to the task. The authors argue that this is so, even in the face of preliminary evidence that firearm risk management is effective in prevention of suicide in high-risk psychiatric patients. In the case of the US, practitioners need to address the issue of gun control, nationally and at the state levels, as part of an overall suicide prevention strategy.

Giving further credence to the importance of understanding the relationship of means availability and suicide deaths, Asia struggles with the issue of suicides by pesticide ingestion. This is particularly problematic in rural populations of China, Sri Lanka and India, where it is the most common method of suicide deaths, as well as in rural areas of Korea and Taiwan, and, more recently, in South Korea (Chen *et al.*, 2012). Chang *et al.* (2012) report that pesticide poisoning accounts for one-third of deaths by suicide worldwide, but until recently the method has been under-investigated. They found some moderate evidence for the reversing of trends, in the aftermath of Taiwanese legislation banning a number of toxic pesticides. Vijayakumar and Satheesh-Babu (2009) studied four villages in the state of Andhra Pradesh in India that had stopped using pesticides in farming and compared them to four similar villages that continued the use of chemical pesticides. This region was known for its cotton production, which accounted for half of the pesticide consumption in India. Due to a variety of environmental, resource and economic factors, these villages adopted a no-pesticide approach to farming. The change had the desired effects: lower production costs, and increased revenue. The researchers then examined the rates of suicide before and after the no-pesticide initiative and identified a downward trend. Importantly, there was not a similar downward trend in terms of factors such as family disputes, alcoholism and mental health issues and domestic violence. In Sri Lanka, restriction of pesticides has resulted in a reduction of suicide in both men and women (Gunnell *et al.*, 2007).

The literature and evidence for the positive role of a range of means restriction activities is growing, leading to the World Health Organization (2012) recommendations which include: 'education on the dangers of pesticide ingestions; provision of lockable storage boxes for pesticides; reductions in the use of the most highly toxic pesticides; and use of alternative (natural) managements of land cultivation'. In any event, it is clear that lethal means restriction on a broad scale requires significant political will which may challenge, in the case of Asia, longstanding agricultural practices, or in the case of the US strongly held beliefs.

The right to suicide prevention: Voices from the Disability Community

As assisted suicide and right to die legislation is being debated in various places across the globe, there is one group that has raised critical issues that are commonly overlooked. Many disability activists have great concern about this legislation and its negative impact on persons with disabilities. Not Dead Yet, an advocacy group with chapters in the UK and US, devotes energy and resources to combat prevailing attitudes about the value of their lives, as they are portrayed in this debate:

> Disabled people have become aware of the dangers associated with the call for assisted suicide to be legalised. The idea that disabled people, including those who do not have long to live, are 'better off dead' is not new. We believe individual disabled people's suicidal cries for help come from a lack of proper practical, emotional and medical support needed to live dignified lives, rather than from the 'suffering' they experience as a result of a medical condition. Such loss of hope – which forces some to see death as their only option – is easily misinterpreted in a society that continues to see and treat disabled people as second class citizens. Individuals risk being easily exploited by the right-to-die movement or, worse, by family, friends and health care professionals. Their attitude

is not compassionate – it is prejudiced and disablist. We oppose policies that single out individuals for legalised killing based on their medical condition. (Not Dead Yet, 2016)

My own understanding of the human rights and social justice dimensions of assisted suicide legislation was significantly altered when I heard disability rights expert Catherine Ludlum testify about her opposition to a pending bill in the General Assembly in Connecticut. I had always argued that I wanted the right to die on my own terms and I favoured legislation that allowed this. Ludlum (2013) noted in her testimony that many people equate loss of physical independence with a loss of dignity. As a woman with an incurable and irreversible disorder, she says that her doctors have not infrequently stated that death was imminent. However, with necessary and costly technological and medical interventions she lives well. In her words:

> for those of us with physical disabilities, our lives could be characterized as a dance with death. Whether people come into our community through accident or illness, there was likely a vulnerable moment where it could have gone either way. Once someone has a disability, there will likely be times where problems arise and survival is not assured. Add to that the very strong cultural assumption that death is preferable to life with a disability, and you have a recipe for disaster. (Ludlum, 2013)

Ludlum's is a powerful voice for human rights and the minimization of social suffering. Indeed, her perspective challenges the notion of the 'social suffering' of people with disabilities as projected by 'able' people. She demands that those with disabilities be seen as human, whose dignity is measured not by a 'merciful' death, but by the right to live – and to receive adequate services when needed.

There is an erroneous assumption that suicidality in persons with physical disabilities is a common if not inevitable response to their physical limitations. People with disabilities can become suicidal for many of the same reasons that others do. However, added stresses can relate to role changes and functions, lack of access to needed services, social stigma and fears about being a burden to family members. Furthermore, attitudes of providers may complicate things. For example, a practitioner's projection of fears related to chronic illness, disability and potential associated losses may obscure their assessment of a patient's quality of life. An ability for reflexive practice and the willingness to explore their own fears of illness becomes critical in this work. For example, whether as a practitioner or just as a person, how often does one look at someone with profound disability and think, 'If I had to live like that I'd kill myself'? That reflex, unexamined, is likely to diminish the humanity of the disabled person; it also forecloses any possibility that the practitioner will take seriously the suicidality of a person with disabilities. Suicidality in this population is not, in fact, normative. Nor are those with disabilities immune from suicidal thoughts, behaviours and acts. That said, people with disabilities have a *right* to quality suicide prevention resources and interventions. Disability activists want at once to be seen as fully potentialized human beings with aspirations and dreams who are simultaneously dealing with challenging medical and physical conditions.

Conclusion

In this chapter, I write with two voices: as a practitioner and as an academic. This was not entirely by design. However, I think this underscores the importance in the work of preventing suicide in vulnerable people and populations of the acknowledgement of the imperfection of our ability to predict accurately who will die by suicide at a given time. A false reliance on imperfect predictors can lull us into complacency. As societies, we need to examine critically the political will to restrict lethal means, even when strong cultural ideals, such as the right to bear arms, persist. We also need to make the best possible use of empirical knowledge that examines factors that reflect every dimension of people's humanness. This includes psychiatric, demographic, environmental and societal/structural risk factors – and their interplay with each other. As professionals, we have dual commitments both to the alleviation of individual human suffering and to the identification and alleviation of structural and environmental conditions. This is especially important in our work with suicidal people. At the same time, we need to acknowledge our uncertainty while engaging in the very human experience of *being with* the suicidal person. Being suicidal is a lonely experience; engagement with an empathic other may be critical in tipping the balance between despair and hope.

References

Andersen, K., Hawgood, J., Klieve, H., Kõlves, K. and De Leo, D. (2010) 'Suicide in Selected Occupations in Queensland: Evidence from the State Suicide Register', *Australian and New Zealand Journal of Psychiatry*, 44(3), 243–9.

Blasco-Fontecilla, H., Perez-Rodriguez, M., Garcia-Nieto, R., Fernandez-Navarro, P., Galfalvy, H., De Leon, J. and Baca-Garcia, E. (2012) 'Worldwide Impact of Economic Cycles on Suicide Trends over 3 Decades: Differences According to Level of Development. A Mixed Effect Model Study. *BMJ Open*, 2, e 000785. DOI: 10:1136/bmjopen-2011-000785, date accessed 9 March 2015.

Centers for Disease Control and Prevention, (2016) www.cdc.gov/.

Chang, S-S., Lu, T-H., Eddlestone, M., Konradsen, F, Sterne, J. A. C., Lin, J-J. and Gunnell, D. (2012) 'Factors Associated With the Decline in Suicide by Pesticide Poisoning in Taiwan: A Time Trend Analysis, 1987–2010', *Clinical Toxicology,* 50(6), 471–80.

Chen, Y., Chien-Chang Wu, Il, Y. and Yip, P. (2012) 'Suicide in Asia: Opportunities and Challenges', *Epidemiologic Reviews,* 34, 129–44.

Draper, B., Snowdon, J. and Wyder, M. (2008) 'A Pilot Study of the Suicide Victim's Last Contact with a Health Professional', *Crisis,* 29(2), 101.

Gunnell, D., Fernando, R., Hewagama, M., Priyangika, W. D. D., Konradsen, F. and Eddelston, M. (2007) 'The Impact of Pesticide Regulations on Suicide in Sri Lanka', *International Journal of Epidemiology,* 36(6), 1225–42.

Harvard School of Public Health (2012) *Means Matter,* www.hsph.harvard.edu/means-matter/, date accessed 9 March 2015.

Hawton, K. (2007) 'Restricting Access to Methods of Suicide', *Crisis,* 28(S1) 4–9.

Heller, N. R. (2014) 'Risk, Hope and Recovery: Converging Paradigms for Mental Health Approaches with Suicidal Clients', *British Journal of Social Work,* 45(6), 1788–1803.

Jacobson, J., Ting, L., Sanders, S. and Harrington, D. (2004) 'Prevalence and Reactions to Fatal and Nonfatal Client Suicidal Behavior: A National Study of Mental Health Social Workers', *Omega,* 49(3), 237–48.

Judd, F., Jackson, H., Komiti, A., Bell, R. and Fraser, C. (2012) 'The Profile of Suicide: Changing or Changeable?' *Social Psychiatry and Psychiatric Epidemiology,* 47(1), 1–9.

Kreitman, N. (1976) 'The Coal Gas Story. United Kingdom Suicide Rates, 1960–71', *British Journal of Preventive Social Medicine,* 30, 86–93.

Kroll, J. K. (2000) 'Use of No Suicide Contracts by Psychiatrists in Minnesota', *American Journal of Psychiatry,* 157(10), 1684–6.

Lewiecki, E. and Miller, S. (2013) 'Suicide, Guns and Public Policy', *American Journal of Public Health,* 103(1), 27–31.

Li, Z., Page, A., Martin, G. and Taylor, R. (2011) 'Attributable Risk of Psychiatric and Socio-economic Factors for Suicide from Individual Level, Population Based Studies: A Systematic Review', *Social Science and Medicine,* 72, 608–16.

Lin, J. and Lu, T. (2006) 'Association between the Accessibility to Lethal Methods and Method-specific Suicide Rates: An Ecological Study in Taiwan', *Journal of Clinical Psychiatry,* 67(7), 1074–9.

Ludlum, C. D. (2013) 'Second Thoughts', www.cga.ct.gov/2013/PHdata/Tmy/2013HB-06645-R000320-Ludlum,%20Catherine;%20Second%20Thoughts%20CT-TMY.PDF, date accessed 9 March 2015.

Luoma, J. B., Martin, C. E. and Pearson, J. L. (2002) 'Contact with Mental Health and Primary Care Providers before Suicide: A Review of the Evidence', *American Journal of Psychiatry,* 159(6), 909–16.

Mann, J., Apter, A., Bertolote, J., Beautrais, A., Currier, D., Haas, A. and Varnik, A. (2005) 'Suicide Prevention Strategies: A Systematic Review', *JAMA: Journal of The American Medical Association,* 294(16), 2064–74.

Miller, M., Lippman, S., Azrael, D. and Hemenway, D. (2007) 'Household Firearm Ownership and Rates of Suicide across the United States', *Journal of Trauma*, 62(4), 1029–34.

Milner, A., McClure, R., Sun, J. and De Leo, D. (2011) 'Globalisation and Suicide: An Empirical Investigation in 35 Countries Over the Period 1980–2006', *Health and Place*, 17, 996–1003.

Mishara, B. (2008) 'Suicide and the Economic Depression: Reflections on the Great Depression', *International Association for Suicide Prevention Newsletter*, https://www.iasp.info/pdf/papers/mishara_suicide_and_the_economic_depression.pdf, date accessed 21 December 2016.

NAASP (National Action Alliance for Suicide Prevention) (2015) 'Zero Suicide Project', http://actionallianceforsuicideprevention.org/ZeroSuicideAdvisoryGroup, date accessed 9 March 2015.

Not Dead Yet (2016) http://notdeadyetuk.org/, date accessed 23 August 2016.

Oliver, R. G. and Hetzel, B. S. (1972) 'Rise and Fall of Suicide Rates in Australia: Relation to Sedative Availability', *Medical Journal of Australia*, 2(17), 919–23.

Payne, M. (2011) 'Risk, Security and Resilience Work in Social Work Practice', *Revista de Asistenja Sociala*, 10(1), 7–14.

Plutchik, R., van Praag, H. M., Picard, S., Conte, H. R. and Korn, M. (1988) 'Is There a Relation between the Seriousness of Suicidal Intent and the Lethality of the Suicide Attempt?', *Psychiatry Research*, 27, 71–9.

Reeves, A., Stuckler, D., McKee, M., Gunnell, D., Chang, S-S. and Basu, S. (2012) 'Increase in State Suicide Rates in the USA during Economic Recession', *The Lancet*, 380 (9856), 1813–14.

Simon, R. I. and Hales, R. E. (eds) (2006) *The American Psychiatric Publishing Textbook of Suicide Assessment and Management* (American Psychiatric Publishing).

Slovak, K., Brewer, R. and Carlson, K. (2008) 'Client Firearm Assessment and Safety Counseling: The Role of Social Workers', *Social Work*, 53(4), 358–71.

Spencer, D. J. (1997) 'Suicide and Anomie', *Journal of the Royal Society of Medicine*, 90, 86–7.

Tondo, L., Isacsson, G. and Baldessarini, R. J. (2003) 'Suicidal Behaviour in Bipolar Disorder: Risk and Prevention', *CN Drugs*, 17(7), 491–511.

Vijayakumar, L. and Satheesh-Babu, R. (2009) 'Does "No Pesticide" Reduce Suicides?' *International Journal of Social Psychiatry*, 55(5) 401–06.

Williams, C., Davidson, J. and Montgomery, I. (1980) 'Impulsive Suicide Behavior', *Journal of Clinical Psychology*, 36, 90–4.

World Health Organization (2012) 'Public Health Action for the Prevention of Suicide: A Framework', www.who.int/mental_health/publications/prevention_suicide_2012/en/index.html, date accessed 9 March 2015.

Yang, L. and Lester, B. (2001) 'Learnings from Durkheim and Beyond: The Economy and Suicide', *Suicide & Life-Threatening Behavior*, 31(1), 15.

Yip, P., Caine, E., Yousuf, S., Chang, S., Chien-Chiang Wu, K. and Chen, Y. (2012) 'Means Restriction for Suicide Prevention', *The Lancet*, 379, 2393–9.

7

WORKING WITH PEOPLE WHO HAVE PSYCHOTIC ILLNESS: BALANCING RISK AND RECOVERY

Robert Bland and Marianne Wyder

Introduction

For people impacted by the experience of psychotic illness, risks do appear to be everywhere. People who have low-prevalence psychotic illnesses, such as schizophrenia, bipolar disorder and depressive psychosis, are profoundly affected by the power of risk-focused approaches in mental health services. A risk-focused approach in mental health emphasizes the individual's risk of self-harm or of harming others. Accordingly, clinical practice is often oriented towards managing these risks. As people with psychotic illnesses are more likely to be seen as a threat to themselves or others than people who experience more high-prevalence disorders, such as depression, anxiety and substance abuse disorders, they are likely to be subject to the provisions of involuntary treatment (Kallert & Schutzwohl, 2008). There are consequently social and legal risks to people's human rights in this context; there are risks to people's liberty and their autonomy.

Social, cultural, political and economic risks of psychotic illnesses also exist and these are associated with stigma and discrimination. There is a strong connection between psychosis and social exclusion and many people, as a consequence of their illness, live in poverty for most of their lives. This has profound negative impact across all life domains (Morgan *et al.*, 2011). Families experience flow on effects of these risks. Many families also contend with the associated risks of stigma, discrimination and exclusion, and financial hardship is common for people providing care for a family member experiencing mental illness (O'Grady & Skinner, 2012).

Risk is understood differentially from the perspective of service providers, service users and families, and views on how risks should be avoided, assessed and 'managed' also differs. Clinicians, for example, generally focus on the risk of poor clinical outcomes for people experiencing psychotic illnesses. Conversely, service users and families are more likely to focus on the risks of social and interpersonal adversities (Centre for Values, Ethics and the Law, 2013). We contend that both perspectives need to be included in developing a comprehensive understanding of the risks associated with mental illness. We contend that both are critical and need to be included in our understanding. It is important to move beyond focusing on risk in isolation and to include the values and principles of recovery approaches. In this chapter we outline how a recovery approach can shed a new light on how to comprehend the risks of psychotic illness for individuals and their families. We will suggest new ways for responding to these risks so that they advance people's human rights and can potentially lead to more socially just outcomes for individuals and their families. We use our own research into the lived experience of receiving involuntary treatment in hospital settings, and consideration of the experience of families to indicate how a recovery focus that is cognizant of *risks to recovery* and that is *recovery focused in the assessment of risks* can illuminate more empowering processes and hopeful outcomes for people whose lives are impacted by psychotic illness. We begin the chapter with an overview of the recovery paradigm that is now so prevalent in mental health policy around the world.

The recovery paradigm in mental health policy and practice

In this chapter we propose that a recovery framework and principles can be used to improve mental health services' and mental health practitioners' understanding of risk. We claim that the recovery paradigm can help reframe how to understand and respond to risks associated with illness and that this alternative perspective is more enabling and ethical than the more problem-saturated risk perspectives that tend to dominate traditional methods of assessment and response to risks in mental health services.

People with psychosis are profoundly affected by the power of the problematized risk focus in mental health services. They are subject to a range of intervention processes such as ongoing risk assessment and examination of their psychotic symptoms such as delusions and hallucinations. There is a strong focus on risk and surveillance with an emphasis on compliance with treatment. Since the 1980s, Community Treatment Orders (CTOs) have been introduced worldwide (Churchill *et al.*, 2007). CTOs require psychiatric patients to comply with a set of conditions (such as compliance with their medication and outpatient attendance), which in turn allow them to live in the community. If they do not comply, however, these treatments can be administered involuntarily or the patients can be involuntarily hospitalized. While CTOs are intended to be a less restrictive alternative to involuntary hospital care, and despite having been in use for more than two decades, their use and acceptability remain controversial (Churchill *et al.*, 2007; Kisely & Campbell, 2006; Light, *et al.*, 2012). Involuntary mental health treatments are among the most powerful emotional experiences for service users and families alike (Hatfield & Lefley, 1987; Kallert & Schutzwohl, 2008; McSherry, 2008).

While there is disagreement in the service user, research and clinical literatures about the need for and appropriateness of involuntary treatment, mental health legislation in nearly all jurisdictions make provision for involuntary treatment and specify the circumstances under which such treatment should be provided (McSherry, 2008). Such legislation typically requires that involuntary treatment can only be provided where an individual has a mental illness and represents a risk to the safety and welfare of themselves or others, or that the person lacks the capacity to refuse treatment but that the treatment is in the best interest of the person (Centre for the Law, Values and Ethics, 2013). When considering risk it is important to incorporate the risk of harm to self or others and also the risk of social adversity, excess distress and compromised treatment. For example, a focus on risk to safety as the major criterion for involuntary care may leave many people who are in need of care without treatment. Conversely, focusing on managing risks associated with psychotic symptoms can also have the unintended consequences of institutionalization and socialization into a patient role. When focusing on managing symptoms this can objectify the individual concerned, presenting them as a passive victim of an active pathology rather than as an active participant in their own lives (May, 2004).

The recovery paradigm offers an alternative perspective to traditional, clinically based conceptions of, and responses to, mental illness. Recovery, simply defined as the ability to live well in the presence or absence of one's mental health symptoms, is now a central concept in mental health policy and has become the guiding principle in shaping contemporary mental health services (Jacobson & Greenley, 2001; Meadows *et al.*, 2012). Recovery occurs when internal conditions of recovery, such as empowerment, self-determination, hope, healing and connection, and external conditions, such as human rights, a positive culture of healing, and recovery-oriented services, are present (Jacobson & Greenley, 2001). Both the clinical and consumer literature emphasize that recovery from a mental illness occurs despite the enduring presence of symptoms (Leamy *et al.*, 2011). Recovery does not mean cure and beginning the journey of recovery does not depend on getting effective treatment first. A recovery philosophy emphasizes the importance of hope and optimism about the future, empowerment, choice, connectedness, identity, meaning in life, responsibility and exercising citizenship (Davidson *et al.*, 2005; Leamy *et al.*, 2011). Based on this philosophy, five cornerstones of recovery-oriented care have been formulated in Australian mental health policy and these are replicated in other places around the world.

Recovery-oriented care is underpinned by:

1. a focus on the uniqueness of the individual

2. real choices

3. attitudes and rights

4. dignity and respect

5. partnership and communication. (Commonwealth of Australia, 2013)

The starting point for a recovery focus is a concern with the lived experience of mental illness. The concept of *lived experience* is based on two important principles. The first is that mental illness is much more than a set of symptoms and syndromes that clinicians, from the outside looking in, seek to diagnose and treat. The lived experience is the view of mental illness from the inside looking out, as it affects all areas of life. A deep appreciation of the lived experience of psychosis underpins clinical competencies and acknowledges that diagnosis and treatment alone are insufficient to enable service users to move beyond illness and problem-dominated lives. The second principle of a lived experience perspective acknowledges service users as the experts in their own experience. This calls for relationships between professionals, service users and families that are inclusive, respectful and empowering as all work together towards recovery (Bland & Tullgren, 2015).

The exacerbation of psychotic illness and the subsequent personal crisis requiring medical intervention is perhaps the most extreme test of recovery principles as service users, families and mental health workers struggle to confront the distress of both intrusive symptoms and invasive and unwanted treatments. To unpack some of these ideas, we will describe how risk and recovery are experienced throughout an involuntary mental health admission.

Risk and recovery in involuntary settings

For people with the lived experience of mental illness, self-determination is a vital part of successful recovery (Commonwealth of Australia, 2013). Retaining a sense of agency, control and hope, however, can be difficult, particularly when people are experiencing a crisis and are acutely unwell. During these times it may be up to those around them to hold on to hope that recovery is possible (Glover, 2012). For many people, an involuntary mental health admission represents the culmination of acutely distressing symptoms of illness and the unwelcome experience of being confined to hospital and the imposition of treatments and restrictions. However, for others the involuntary treatment can also be a point from which recovery can gain direction and momentum (Bland et al., 2015).

There are many competing risks that are at play in these situations. The principles of right to treatment and protection compete with those of self-determination and individual civil liberties within a context of uncertain capacity. From a human rights perspective, involuntary treatment is a violation of a person's liberty, civil freedoms and physical integrity (Bland et al., 2015; McSherry, 2008). Alternatively, people who are experiencing a serious psychotic illness may also need involuntary treatment or admission to protect themselves or the community from the risk of harm to themselves or harm to others (Campbell, 2008; Fawcett, 2007).

There is currently considerable debate whether a mental health crisis requiring involuntary treatment is a threat to an individual's recovery or if it is a turning point on a recovery journey. When working with those who receive involuntary treatments it is important to consider tensions between these competing principles and to balance risk aversion with dignity of risk and self-determination with the need to protect from harm. Within this context it is important to find ways to maximize people's self-determination and ability to exercise control. It is important to find ways to reduce coercion, seclusion and restraint. Involuntary assessment and treatment will continue to be necessary when there are no less restrictive alternatives available to protect a person's health and safety (Meadows et al., 2012). The challenge for mental health workers is to find ways in which mental health service users, who may be temporarily unable to be self-directing in their treatment, can retain a maximum level of autonomy and control within the limits of involuntary care (Wyder et al., 2013). Another way to express this dilemma is to ask: how do mental health workers promote personal recovery within the crisis of involuntary treatment?

Drawing on our own research into the experiences of service users and families of involuntary hospital treatment we now argue that even in this most contested and difficult area recovery principles can challenge the power of the risk-averse mentality that has dominated mental health services. In this way there is a balance between duty of care and the support of individuals to take positive risks, and to make the most of new opportunities is possible.

The lived experience of involuntary treatment in hospital settings

We conducted research into the lived experience of receiving involuntary treatment under mental health legislation in Australia. For this study we interviewed 25 mental health services users who had been admitted under an endorsed Involuntary Treatment Order (ITO) and were close to discharge. We invited service users to reflect on their experience of involuntary treatment in the hospital, the aspects of care that were difficult or helpful for them, and their relationship with treatment staff. We were also interested in their experience of the legal processes that had been designed to protect their rights, such as periodic review of the involuntary treatment process. The study was part of a broader project that also considered the perspectives of families and mental health workers.

The service user data was analysed using an inductive approach that consisted of narrative restructuring and thematic analysis. In our study, the participants were almost equally divided between those who had accepted the need for the ITO (10 people) and those who resisted the ITO completely (12 people). A third cohort comprising three people reported a more mixed response. The more positive group viewed the ITO as an opportunity to get the treatment they needed, whereas the more negative group experienced the ITO as unwanted, coercive and intrusive and a violation of their autonomy. This group, despite feeling that their illness symptoms had improved, still described their involuntary hospital admission and treatments as an intrusion upon their liberty which compromised their physical and mental integrity. For some this experience had a profound negative impact on the way they felt about themselves. While their illness may have influenced some of these perceptions, other factors, such as the attitudes and actions of staff, lack of knowledge of legal rights, and rigidly applied ward routines, also appeared to significantly influence this experience.

All participants across all three groups expressed a clear desire to regain a sense of personal responsibility and control over their lives. They also described that when they were able to progressively re-assume control over their lives this increased their sense of agency and autonomy. We now highlight some of the major themes that appeared to facilitate this process.

The importance of mutually respectful and trusting relationships

Connectedness was important to all participants. Many people spoke about how the general busyness of the ward, the levels of staffing and staff's focus on biomedical tasks, monitoring practices and administrative and other duties impacted on their ability to interact with their patients. Furthermore, staff attitudes and behaviours had the potential to make a difference to their experiences of the ITO and being admitted to hospital.

Having a safe space to reflect on the experience

All participants spoke about the need to feel safe from their symptoms and from other patients on the ward. They also needed a space to make sense of events leading up to their admission and the experience of being admitted involuntarily to a psychiatric unit.

Co-ordinated or consistent inpatient programmes

While some participants spoke about programmes that facilitated recovery, the majority of participants described a sense of boredom while they were in hospital. They described the need to receive support and most importantly to have something to do. This was a particular issue when they were not allowed out of the hospital or when they started to feel better and needed something to do to keep them occupied.

Experiencing a sense of procedural justice

While for some people the ITO process had been fair and necessary, for others the ITO was experienced as an arbitrary process without any safeguards. Mental health legislation in different state or national jurisdictions in Australia provide explicit criteria for the assessment, detention and compulsory treatment of people with severe mental illness. While it is a clinical decision, involuntary treatment is essentially a legal decision. Various mental health legislation aims to provide statutory safeguards to allow for the lawful detention and treatment of patients while ensuring that the patient's rights are respected. These include: the promotion of autonomy; the establishment of a clear set of objective criteria for involuntary mental health admissions; and the provision of structural protections for involuntary committed persons such as the right to review and appeal compulsory treatment or hospital admission.

Despite these mechanisms, participants in the negative and mixed groups felt coerced into treatment and they did not believe that they were given any procedural justice. Many were also unaware of these mechanisms. It has consistently been reported that the perception of procedural justice and coercion are inversely related (Galon & Wineman, 2010).

Knowledge about ITO, ward expectations and treatment

Related to individuals' lack of understanding of the ITO processes was the lack of understanding of their ITO conditions, the ward expectations or their treatment. Many participants described feeling disempowered because they were given treatment against their will and also because they did not understand what was expected of them to have their ITO revoked and how to behave on the ward.

Working in partnership with the health care professionals

All participants described the importance of working in partnership with their health professionals. At the very least they expected information about their treatment. The majority of participants described the importance of being given some opportunities to make decisions for themselves. In this process it was critical that health carers not only listened to their concerns but that they included the concerns and suggestions of service users in providing care and treatment. These findings highlight that in an environment where people have little control, clear structures and having the ability to exercise some control and choices are essential.

From a rights and empowerment perspective, the service user should always know when and how an ending will occur as not knowing can lead to vulnerability and disempowerment especially when poor helping relationships have characterized people's histories. This clearly suggests that people need to have access to information about their rights and ITO conditions, and also around their treatment and ward expectations. Furthermore, the provision of this information needs to be seen as a process, as many of the participants described how they either did not receive it or they did not retain the information that was provided to them. This implies that clinicians need to be proactive in providing this information on an ongoing basis.

Traditionally, risk management approaches are concerned with protecting individuals from themselves and others; they are led by professionals and focus on monitoring, observing, taking control and imposing restrictions (Boardman & Roberts, 2014). Many mental health practices remain solely based on containing risks and behaviours without facilitating opportunities for autonomy and citizenship or for people to re-engage with their lives, or facilitating their transition back into the community. Our study suggests that such approaches have the potential to create power imbalances which potentially impact people's overall sense of well-being, which in turn may impact their recovery. In the next section we will focus on the experiences of the family.

The lived experience of families of people with psychotic illness

An important and often forgotten party is the family of those living with a mental illness. Partners, friends or others who have an active role in caring for a person with the lived experience of mental illness have often supported their loved ones for many years through periods of illness and recovery that might have included crisis and hospitalization. We use the term *family* rather than *carer* to describe this group as this focuses the attention to the relationships rather than the caregiving role.

Families often experience medicalized mental health risk discourses differently from those living with a mental illness (Lefley, 1993). Paradoxically, while service users often experience such discourses as too restrictive, families experience the opposite. In many instances families have tried to find support for their family member and expressed their views without being heard by the health care professionals (Machin & Repper, 2014). During times of crisis they may also have tried unsuccessfully to find support for their loved ones. One of the consistent arguments put forward by families is that the provisions of mental health law to arrange involuntary treatment for mentally ill family members are such that treatment services are too slow to intervene (Lefley, 1993). International mental health laws generally require that involuntary treatment can be provided when the person appears to be mentally ill and there is some risk of harm to self or others. The legal framework for involuntary treatment appears to be geared towards crisis management as opposed to early intervention. Families are understandably anxious to arrange treatment quickly when it is clear that a family member is becoming ill, particularly when a family member has had a number of episodes of psychosis and recovery, and it is clear that when they intervene quickly this can prevent a relapse. Their appetite for intervention may be keener than the workers in the treatment system.

Clearly, families have a right to express their own needs and suggestions to treatment staff, but at what point do their needs for safety and security override the service user's right to refuse treatment? Family advocate Harriet Lefley makes a strong case for the rights of families:

> Families ... suffer greatly when a relative's concept of self-determination means rejection of treatment, noncompliance with medications, substance abuse, or even homelessness ... The argument of self-determination, that leads mentally ill persons to reject involuntary treatment as an abuse of their rights, can also be used to support the self-destructive behaviours that make such interventions necessary. (Lefley, 1993, p. 8)

While unable to offer a solution to the dilemma of competing rights, Lefley suggests the need for ongoing dialogue among consumer groups, families, service providers and lawyers so that the needs of all groups continue to be addressed.

Bland *et al.* (2015) argue that another right that needs to be acknowledged is the individual's right to timely and effective treatment, whether voluntary or involuntary. Certainly the uneven quality of services that are known to exist across and within Australian jurisdictions challenges this right for many citizens (Mental Health Council of Australia, 2005) and this may also be the case in other countries. There is a strong connection between the aims of mental health law and the availability and quality of services. Without access to good services, less restrictive legal options, such as CTOs, cannot be effective (Brophy, 2012; Mechanic *et al.*, 2014).

Families' needs can be in direct opposition to those of their loved ones and it can be difficult to reconcile these (Lefley, 1993). Understandably many families are risk averse and, particularly during times of crisis, they may take on daily tasks such as controlling money, taking care of cleaning or ensuring their loved ones take their medications. Most families struggle with the dilemma of when protection is necessary and how much independence is realistic. Another issue is that they need to step down from the role of helper to a more equal relationship with their loved ones (Topor *et al.*, 2006). Families have the difficult task of balancing the concepts of holding control and minimizing risk with handing back this control and allowing consumers to take risks and potentially fail (Baxter & Diehl, 1988). This can be particularly difficult when their own needs are in direct opposition to those experiencing the illness (Hatfield & Lefley, 1987).

Clinicians typically recognize the support role provided by families to those living with a mental illness. While families are crucial to their loved one's recovery it is important to recognize their own needs. While there is a strong emphasis on their role as partners in the care and they are endowed with caring obligations they are also subject to conservative clinical interpretation of privacy legislation. At times this means that family carers do not have access to relevant information about their loved one's treatment, discharge planning or issues that are going on in their loved one's life. This lack of information often means that they are not always equipped with the information to make decisions and to support their children, siblings, partners and parents as best they can, and this can make their decisions more risk averse (Wyder & Bland 2014). It is important to acknowledge the impact that caring for someone with psychosis can have on their lives. Families not only provide recovery-oriented support but they also have their own recovery journey (Wyder & Bland, 2014). In the next section we will focus on to recovery-focused practices can assist in responding to the risk of a psychotic illness.

Towards recovery-focused practices when responding to the risks of psychotic illness

While recovery-oriented practice has become mental health policy in reality, most services still focus on containing risks. As a consequence, many clinical practices are driven by risk management rather than an objective assessment of the least restrictive alternative (Stickley & Felton, 2006). Similarly, families remain risk averse as they struggle to deal with the consequences of clinical risk taking and mental health services that are seen to be stretched and inadequate (Wyder & Bland 2014).

Our research indicates the importance of incorporating recovery-oriented care principles and finding ways to manage the risks that are supportive both of individuals and their families. There is a need to shift policies and procedures around risk assessment away from containment and risk management and towards what Boardman and Roberts (2014) call *recovery-oriented risk assessments* where individuals and clinicians jointly construct personal safety plans.

A focus on human rights and recovery provides an alternative framework to a preoccupation with the prevailing risk-averse agenda that has dominated mental health policy and practices for so long. A recovery focus suggests a number of important practice principles that can assist clinicians to practise more creatively and effectively.

Starting with a focus on lived experience

Recovery practice theory encourages workers to start, not with a list of symptoms and risk factors, but with a concern for what is happening in the life of the person with psychosis. As we have argued earlier in this chapter, this means working with the person's individual concerns in such areas as relationships, housing and employment. Risk discourses in mental health need to include risks such as loneliness, poverty and obesity. A focus on the lived experience starts with the question: what is happening to the person right now that is problematic and which the person wants changed? It also means incorporating the person's hopes and dreams. One of the ways clinicians can challenge the mentality of risk is to help the person imagine a better future, which might be a start for planning positive and desired outcomes.

Working at multiple points of intervention to promote recovery

Deeply held concerns for connection and relationship, secure housing and employment allow a focus on the consumer's strengths rather than their deficits. Shifting the focus from managing illness symptoms to other areas has the potential to actually mitigate the risk factors that would normally concern clinicians. For example, focusing interventions on strengthening and building friendships and connections to community would reduce the risks of personal isolation and self-harm. It would potentially reduce the risk of the stress of social exclusion while building relationships that would enhance resilience and problem-solving skills and resources.

A focus on sustaining relationships

Supportive relationships and connections are central to recovery (Leamy *et al.* 2011). The capacity to provide positive support for service users, even within the limits of coercive treatment in hospital settings, appears to be central to limiting the potential distress of involuntary treatment (Wyder *et al.*, 2015). Supportive and caring relationships become particularly important when people are acutely unwell. Establishing such supportive relationships between staff and service users has to be a central goal not only of involuntary treatment but also of all treatments. Such relationships need to be based on compassion, respect and hope-giving. Supportive relationships with workers are also critical to the experiences of families (Wyder & Bland, 2014).

A focus on rights, information and procedural justice

Self-determination and self-management are core components of the recovery paradigm and recovery practice aims to promote decision making that is person-led in accordance with their values, needs, resources and circumstances (Commonwealth of Australia, 2013). Our study, described in this chapter, has highlighted the importance of information giving in this process. For example, when using coercive powers it is important to acknowledge these, to explain the limits of these powers and discuss the consequences with the service user. Trotter (2006) has argued that the provision of clear information about the purpose of involuntary intervention and the social worker's dual role as helper and social controller are core components of social work's role. Similarly, the recovery paradigm promotes collaborative partnerships between the mental health professional and those with the lived experience of mental illness. As part of this process, the role of health care professionals is to provide service users with enough information, skills and support for people to manage their own condition and get access to the resources they need. Providing this information is also part of the process of establishing a relationship based on reciprocity and power sharing. When working in this way risk management can become a collaborative process that is founded on relationships between service users and the health care professionals that are based on mutual trust. This would encourage a focus on jointly finding solutions to problems.

A focus on agency and empowerment

The concepts of self-determination, personal responsibility and self-management are pivotal, regardless of a person's legal status or situation. Our research on the lived experience of involuntary treatment shows that even within the overwhelming experience of incarceration and coercion there were many times when people could exercise choice over aspects of their lives. For some people this was as little as having their concerns about their treatment being heard and considered by staff in providing care. These concepts of agency and empowerment are potentially as relevant for families struggling with the stress of illness as they are for service users. The challenge for staff working in coercive relationships, either in hospital or the community, is to seek out those spaces where choice and agency are possible. For families, choice and agency can be as simple as having the choice of being included in the treatment plan. For those with lived experience having small choices such as what activities to participate in or knowing the structure of their day appeared to make a big difference to how they experienced the involuntary mental health admission. Another way to support agency and empowerment would be through engaging service users in the development of their own recovery plans and advance directives.

Creating a sense of safety

Risk agendas encourage a sense of fearful anticipation and a more positive challenge to this is to emphasize the rather old-fashioned concept of therapeutic relationships generally, and hospitalization specifically, as places of safety. In our study many of the participants focused on the importance of a sense of safety as a feature of their experience. This included feeling safe from their symptoms and other patients on the wards but also having a place of safety to make sense of their experiences. Again, the emphasis is on the positive right to quality treatment rather than the negative right to freedom from coercion.

Sustaining hope and confronting despair

The recovery literature emphasizes the centrality of hope in the recovery journey for individuals (Davidson *et al.*, 2005; Leamy *et al.*, 2011) and also for family members (Bland & Wyder, 2014). Such is the centrality of hope to the recovery journey that a focus on being hopeful, and supporting the hopefulness of others, is a central challenge to the mental health worker. That commitment to hopeful engagement has to underpin any response to risk management so that workers become skilled in assessing and supporting positive risk taking in an individual's recovery.

The tension between relational and agency dimensions of recovery

Our research explored the way that involuntary treatment challenges the two dimensions of recovery – a sense of agency and empowerment on the one hand, and the relational dimensions of identity and hope on the other. The imposition of involuntary treatment removes a sense of personal agency. When this happens there is a clear risk that an individual's recovery journey is disrupted. The relational dimensions, however, remain a site for recovery. The individual can experience genuinely compassionate relationships with family, friends and health workers that reinforce an identity as a person of worth. These relationships can emphasize the capacity of others to understand and share the distress of psychosis and so be hope-supporting. The crisis of psychosis and involuntary treatment becomes a shared crisis, perhaps even an opportunity for recovery.

Conclusion

Risk remains a powerful concept in the provision of care and treatment for people with serious mental illness. A risk-focused approach in mental health emphasizes the individual's risk of self-harm or of harming others. Accordingly, clinical practice is often oriented towards managing these risks. Yet there are other aspects of risk here, such as the risk of social exclusion and the loss of control over one's life. In this chapter, we have explored the possibility of applying a recovery focus in that most contested and difficult of contexts – that of involuntary treatment. It is in this space that the dominant medicalized risk discourse is most powerful. Using our research into the lived experience of involuntary treatment, we have tried to describe the complexity and diversity of that experience. We have considered the experience of families, as well as service users, in understanding involuntary treatment. Our argument is that recovery provides a useful alternative to this discourse in key areas such as valuing the lived experience, agency and empowerment, and hope and relationships. Mental health workers can make a real difference in supporting service users through the crisis of psychosis and treatment. The relationships that workers can make with service users and their families are central to achieving good outcomes. A preoccupation with risk should not prevent an approach to care that encourages service users to maintain whatever personal agency is possible, to support their hopefulness and maintain significant relationships with family and friends.

References

Baxter, E. and Diehl, S. (1988) 'Emotional Stages: Consumers and Family Members Recovering from the Trauma of Mental Illness', *Psychiatric Rehabilitation Journal*, 21, 349–55.

Bland, R. and Tullgren, A. (2015) 'Lived Experience of Mental Illness', in J. Fitzgerald and G. J. Byrne (eds), *Psychosocial Dimensions in Medicine* (IP Communications), 43–56.

Bland, R., Renouf, N. and Tullgren, A. (2015) *Social Work Practice in Mental Health* (2nd edition) (Sydney: Allen & Unwin).

Boardman, J. and Roberts, G. (2014) *Risk, Safety and Recovery, ImROC Briefing*, https://www.centreformentalhealth.org.uk/risk-and-recovery, date accessed 11 September 2015.

Brophy, L. (2012) 'Involuntary Treatment in the Community', in G. Meadows, J. Farhall, E. Fossey, M. Grigg, F. McDermott and B. Singh (eds) *Mental Health in Australia: Collaborative Community Practice* (Melbourne: Oxford University Press).

Campbell, J. (2008) 'Stakeholders' Views of Legal and Advice Services for People Admitted to Psychiatric Hospital', *Journal of Social Welfare and Family Law*, 30(3), 219–32.

Centre for Values, Ethics and the Law (2013) *Risk, Capacity and Decision Making. A Report from the 'CTO Study'* (Sydney: University of Sydney).

Churchill, R., Owen, G., Singh, S. and Hotopf, M. (2007) *International Experiences of Using Community Treatment Orders* (London: Department of Health, Institute of Psychiatry).

Commonwealth of Australia (2013) *A National Framework for Recovery-oriented Mental Health Services: Policy and Theory* (Canberra: Australian Health Ministers Advisory Council).

Davidson, I., O'Connell, M., Tondora, J. and Lawless, M. (2005) 'Recovery in Serious Mental illness: A New Wine or Just a New Bottle?', *Professional Psychology: Research and Practice*, 36, 450–87.

Fawcett, B. (2007) 'Consistencies and Inconsistencies: Mental Health, Compulsory Treatment and Community Capacity Building in England, Wales and Australia', *British Journal of Social Work*, 37, 1027–42.

Galon, P. and Wineman, N. (2010) 'Coercion and Procedural Justice in Psychiatric Care: State of the Science and Implications for Nursing', *Archives of Psychiatric Nursing*, 24, 307–16.

Glover, H. (2012) 'Recovery, Life Long Learning, Social Inclusion and Empowerment: Is a New Paradigm Emerging?', in P. Ryan, S. Ramon and T. Greacen (eds), *Empowerment, Lifelong Learning and Recovery in Mental Health: Towards a New Paradigm* (London: Palgrave).

Hatfield, A. and Lefley, H. (eds) (1987) *Families of the Mentally Ill: Coping and Adaptation* (New York: Guilford Press).

Jacobson, N. and Greenley, D. (2001) 'What is Recovery? A Conceptual Model and Explanation', *Psychiatric Services*, 52, 482–85.

Kallert, T. M. G. and Schutzwohl, M. (2008) 'Involuntary vs. Voluntary Hospital Admission. A Systematic Literature Review on Outcome Diversity', *European Archives of Psychiatry and Clinical Neuroscience*, 258, 195–209.

Kisely, S. and Campbell, L. (2006) 'Community Treatment Orders for Psychiatric Patients: The Emperor with no Clothes', *The Canadian Journal of Psychiatry*, 51(11), 683–85.

Leamy, M., Bird, V., Le Boutillier, C., Williams, J. and Slade, M. (2011) 'Conceptual Framework for Personal Recovery in Mental Health: Systematic Review and Narrative Synthesis', *The British Journal of Psychiatry* 199, 445–52.

Lefley, H. (1993) 'Involuntary Treatment: Concerns of Consumers, Families and Society', *Innovations and Research*, 2(1), 7–9.

Light, E., Kerridge, I., Ryan, C. and Robertson, M. (2012) 'Community Treatment Orders in Australia: Rates and Patterns of Use', *Australasian Psychiatry*, 20, 478–82.

Machin, K. and Repper, J. (2014) *Recovery: a Carer's Perspective. ImROC Briefing*, https://imroc.org/resources/4-recovery-carers-perspective/, date accessed 11 September 2015.

May, R. (2004) 'Making Sense of Psychotic Experiences and Working Towards Recovery', in J. Gleeson and P. McGorry (eds) *Psychological Interventions in Early Psychosis: A Treatment Handbook* (West Sussex: John Wileys & Sons), 245–60.

McSherry, B. (2008) *Protecting the Integrity of the Person: Developing Limitations on Involuntary Treatment* (Annandale, Australia: The Federation Press).

Meadows, G., Farhall, J., Fossey, E., Grigg, M., McDermott, F. and Singh, B. (eds) (2012) *Mental Health in Australia: Collaborative Community Practice* (Melbourne: Oxford University Press).

Mechanic, D., McAlpine, D. and Rochefort, D. (2014) *Mental Health and Social Policy: Beyond Managed Care* (6th edition) (Boston: Pearson).

Mental Health Council of Australia (2005) *Not for Service: Experiences of Injustice and Despair in Mental Health Care in Australia* (Canberra: Mental Health Council of Australia).

Morgan, V. A., Waterreus, A., Jablensky, A., Mackinnon, A., McGrath, J. J., Carr, V., Bush, R., Castle, D., Cohen, M., Harvey, C., Galletly, C., Stain, H. J., Neil, A., McGorry, P., Hocking, B., Shah, S. and Saw, S. (2011) *People Living with Psychotic Illness 2010: Report on the Second Australian National Survey* (Canberra: Department of Health and Ageing).

O'Grady, C. and Skinner, W. (2012) 'Journey as Destination: A Recovery Model for Families Affected by Concurrent Disorders', *Qualitative Health Research*, 22(8), 1047–62.

Stickley, T. and Felton, A. (2006) 'Promoting Recovery through Therapeutic Risk Taking', *Mental Health Practice*, 9(8), 26–30.

Topor, A., Borg, M., Mezzina, R. and Sells, D. (2006) 'Others: The Role of Family, Friends, and Professionals in the Recovery Process', *American Journal of Psychiatric Rehabilitation*, 9(1), 17–37.

Trotter, C. (2006) *Working with Involuntary Clients: A Guide to Practice*, (California: Sage).

Wyder, M., Bland, R. and Crompton, D. (2013) 'Personal Recovery and Involuntary Mental Health Admissions: The Importance of Control, Relationships and Hope', *Health*, 5(3A), 574–81.

Wyder, M., Bland, R., Blythe, A., Matarasso, B. and Crompton, D. (2015) 'Therapeutic Relationships and Involuntary Treatment Orders: Service Users' Interactions with Health Care Professionals on the Ward', *International Journal of Mental Health Nursing*, 24(2), 181–9.

Wyder, M. and Bland, R. (2014) 'The Recovery Framework as a Way of Understanding Families' Responses to Mental Illness: Balancing Different Needs and Recovery Journeys', *Australian Social Work*, 67(2), 179–96.

8

NEGOTIATING THE INTERFACE BETWEEN RISK MANAGEMENT AND HUMAN RIGHTS-BASED CARE

Anne-Maree Sawyer

Introduction

Since the advent of deinstitutionalization and the shift to community-based models of care, Australia, and many other Western countries, have seen distinct and marked changes in public policy, legislation, and service delivery approaches in mental health. Each major shift in public policy and service delivery has been accompanied by different understandings and interpretations of risk and these, in turn, have reshaped practice, service priorities and procedures – and even the experience of being a professional. This chapter concerns two such recent changes in public policy and service delivery: the political shift to neoliberalism, often referred to as 'New Public Management', which transformed the public sector of Western democracies from the 1980s with the introduction of market-based principles into the provision of services and new demands for accountability and transparency (Hood, 1995; Osborne & Gaebler, 1992); and the emphasis on individualized service delivery, conceptualized as 'recovery-oriented' practice in contemporary mental health policy (Stanhope & Solomon, 2008; Yeatman, 2009).

Following close on the heels of the early community-based mental health services, New Public Management brought radical changes to the way public services were organized and made accountable. These changes produced a new regulatory regime, directed not only towards the goals of improving the efficiency, quality and performance of human services, but also towards the management of risks (Braithwaite, 1999; Hood, 1995; Webb, 2006). These governance systems were strongly influenced by private sector models and, as a consequence, focused on the 'forensic functions' (Douglas, 1992, p. 27) of risk: that is, on the protocols used to guide practice, establish accountability and apportion blame when things go wrong. In the case of an adverse event, a service could defend itself by demonstrating that the proper procedures had been followed, regardless of the outcome (Munro, 2004, p. 1090; Rose, 1998). These corporate-oriented functions of risk management tend to foster predominantly negative conceptions of 'risk', focused on anticipating, reducing, transferring or eliminating identified risks. In human services, however, this approach privileges the protection of service users and upholds organizational reputation, sometimes at the expense of service users' human rights: their opportunities for autonomy, freedom and social participation. Focused on the possibility of harm or danger, this negative approach to risk may obscure the value of risk-taking activities in the fulfilment of the service user's aspirations and needs as a self, and in the meeting of service goals – and it sets the stage for defensive and narrow practice (Titterton, 2011, p. 31).

A scenario from a support worker, interviewed in the study discussed below, will serve to illustrate the 'negative' and 'positive' dimensions of risk management which are analysed throughout this chapter. The service user, an elderly man with early dementia, expressed a wish to pay his own bills but his adult children were adamant that it was too risky because he might forget the account details and make mistakes, which could land him (and them) in financial chaos. Their stance represents a negative approach to risk management; protection at all costs. This frustrated the elderly man, who wanted to exercise some independence. Taking a positive view of risk and risk taking, in line with his agency's philosophy, the support worker eventually argued successfully that the man's needs as a self ought to be honoured:

> He felt like a lump of meat sitting in the corner, useless for everything, and he was getting really down. And I spoke to his daughter and I said, 'Look I'll be there, why can't he try and pay his own bills?' ... I finally convinced her ... she told him the pin number and that it was a credit and not a savings card ... We went out and he made one mistake; he thought it was a savings card ... He didn't forget the pin number, he didn't forget the bills, he did them all with the assistance of the shopkeepers and I only made one comment and that was, 'It is a credit card' the first time ... That's all I did. I sat back and he was empowered. He just said: 'I can do it. I can do it.'

In this scenario, the worker takes care of any risks that might arise by accompanying the service user on his bill-paying expeditions. In positive dimensions of risk management, strategies to manage identified risks are integrated within the broader aims of socially inclusive practice. The focus here is primarily on the service user's needs, on 'building capacity'

(Titterton, 2011, p. 33), whereas the 'safety-first' approach of negative dimensions of risk management may obscure and restrict a service user's needs and opportunities for autonomy and social inclusion.

Much of the early research in the field of risk and community care highlighted the negative impacts of the new regulatory regimes on service provision and professional practice, especially for those employed in statutory agencies. Kemshall (2002) has argued that risk management may lead to a narrowing of service responses, along with reduced flexibility and decline in service quality. A focus on risk may also create new exclusions and inequalities in service delivery because 'high-risk' service users are prioritized at the expense of 'low-risk' service users (Kemshall, 2002, p. 93; Sawyer, 2008). In a related vein, 'risk thinking' (Rose, 1998) produces an emphasis on assessment and crisis intervention, and marginalizes preventative work, early intervention and ongoing therapeutic work (Carey, 2007; Ferguson, 2007). As McDonald *et al.* (2008, pp. 1378–9) report, workers in statutory services have become heavily reliant on actuarial tools and administrative procedures, 'rather than working proactively and creatively'. In summary, researchers in both Australia and the UK argued that the reforms brought about by New Public Management significantly diminished professional discretion and autonomy, greatly increased administrative monitoring and supervision, and reshaped professional identities around managerial rather than therapeutic skills, leading to high levels of stress and frustration, and the deskilling of professionals (for example, Carey, 2007; Ferguson, 2007; McDonald & Chenoweth, 2009; McDonald *et al.*, 2008; Munro, 2004, 2010; Webb, 2006).

The second change in public policy and service provision concerns the growing endorsement of 'individualized services', based on what Yeatman (2009, p. 27) identified as the need for the new services 'to shape what they have to offer in relation to what is of subjective significance to the client'. Individualized service provision requires the reshaping of care at the level of interpersonal relationships. As Fine (2005, p. 257) so aptly defines it, care is 'the outcome of a relationship between the different parties in which mutual respect, and the fostering of the capabilities and autonomy of the recipient are foremost'. The service user is therefore 'entitled to have his or her sense of self or subjective experience taken seriously by those with whom s/he interacts' and this means that 'both the "what" and the "how" of the service need to be oriented to the individual considered as a unique centre of subjective experience' (Yeatman, 2009, p. 16). It follows, then, that the process of balancing the service user's freedom to choose how to live and the worker's 'duty of care' to protect him/her from risk is to be built on rational negotiation between two parties in the context of an open, trusting and mutually respectful relationship. This practice orientation demands a positive view of risk and risk taking, balanced with safety, while also meeting the worker's legal, professional and organizational responsibilities. The public policy emphasis on individualized care effectively ushers in a new paradigm that transforms the (traditional) asymmetries of power, knowledge and expertise between professionals and service users. Through individualized strategies, knowledge and learning are co-produced within therapeutic relationships and inter-agency partnerships (Titterton, 2011, p. 33).

Positive risk taking

In response to the policy emphasis on individualized service provision, and constraints on professional practice generated by negative approaches to risk management, researchers over recent years have begun to explore the challenges and dilemmas involved in 'positive risk taking' from the perspectives of practitioners, service users and organizations (for example, Barry, 2007; Baxter & Glendinning, 2013; Green, 2007; Heller, 2014; Munro, 2010; Robertson & Collinson, 2011; Stanford, 2010; Taylor, 2006; Titterton, 2005, 2011). Four key observations from this early, though limited, research are significant to the present discussion.

First, the relationship between the worker and the service user is critical to the practice of positive risk taking (Robertson & Collinson, 2011, p. 149). Hence 'relationship building' must be revalued at the organizational level *and* within the practitioner–supervisor relationship, in preference to an overriding emphasis on procedural compliance.

Second, positive risk taking involves a higher degree of risk and uncertainty than standard responses based on negative interpretations of risk taking that rest on a 'safety-first' approach (Titterton, 2005). Positive risk taking places greater demands on workers' emotions and their intellectual/ problem-solving capacities – and also means accepting that occasionally things will go wrong (Munro, 2010, p. 1145; Robertson & Collinson, 2011, p. 154). However, it provides greater intrinsic rewards and a framework to facilitate analytical and reflective practices consistent with the values of such disciplines as social work.

Third, coherent organizational approaches to positive risk taking, together with high levels of interpersonal trust across different levels of the organization, are fundamental to its success as a practice and philosophy. As Robertson and Collinson (2011, p. 147) suggest, in the absence of these factors workers often feel isolated and unsupported in their attempts to utilize positive risk taking: some may 'see themselves as gambling' and others may seek security by resorting to conservative and procedurally bound responses, both of which can hinder therapeutic relationships and increase risks over a longer period of time (see Kirkley *et al.*, 2011). What is crucial here, as Munro (2010, p. 1135) has argued in the case of child protection services, is 'the need for feedback loops in the system where lower-level workers are not afraid to communicate honestly about their experiences, both good and bad, and senior managers treat their feedback as a valuable source of learning'. Excessive top-down control and proceduralization of human service work discourages learning, both in terms of analytic and intuitive reasoning and flexibility and, ironically, takes the focus away from 'the key quality aspects of a relationship-based service, that are at the heart of good practice' (Munro, 2010, p. 1148). The monitoring of procedural compliance remains important, but it must be combined with genuine support for the development of reflective frontline practice through clear risk policies, managerial support, and appropriate training and supervision (Titterton, 2011, pp. 33, 40).

Fourth, there is a need to educate the public about the nature of risk and risk taking in community care. While there is no agreement about an 'acceptable' level of risk taking, workers and organizations will remain vulnerable to unrealistic public and media expectations that risks can be kept in check through the actions of individual workers alone (Robertson & Collinson, 2011, p. 154). In summary, these key themes concerning positive risk taking encompass a focus on the centrality of relationship building between practitioner and service user; organizational risk cultures; and training and supervision. In order for practitioners to support service users' capacities for decision making, autonomy and social inclusion, they themselves must be supported and enabled by their employing organizations (Alban-Metcalfe & Black, 2013; Kirkley *et al.*, 2011, pp. 446–7; Yeatman, 2009, p. 19).

The imperatives of New Public Management and those of individualized service provision represent separate developments in the history of the human services, but they are brought together in everyday practice. Here practitioners have to bridge the worlds of service users and their families; the accountability regulations of their employing agencies, including risk management; government legislation; public policy imperatives of social justice; and the approaches of their particular disciplines. These responsibilities are often complicated, sometimes contradictory, and difficult to balance.

The study

Utilizing several interviews with practitioners and their managers from a recent Australian study, this chapter explores some of the ways frontline workers interpreted and negotiated the interface between managing risk and providing care that respects and enhances the human rights of service users. It is argued that as a practice, risk management can enhance service users' capacities for autonomy, freedom and social inclusion, but it can also work against these social justice ideals. The extent to which practitioners were able to successfully balance the delivery of human rights-based practice, alongside responsibly managing risk, seemed to depend primarily on their organization's risk culture and service goals, including the extent to which relationship building was valued as part of everyday practice, and whether they were able to approach the management of risk as part of, and integrated with, the practice of individualized care.

The interviews discussed here are drawn from a large qualitative study of the impacts of risk management on community-based care conducted in the Australian state of Victoria between 2006 and 2010. This study investigated the perceptions and experiences of risk management from the perspectives of a wide range of stakeholders: Chief executive officers and senior managers, programme managers, frontline workers, service users and family carers. This chapter focuses specifically on the interviews with the 19 programme managers and 40 frontline workers who participated in the study. These one-on-one, single-session interviews were semi-structured, and one to two hours in duration; workers and managers were asked about their interpretations and experiences of 'risk' in day-to-day practice, organizational responses to adverse incidents, occupational health and safety regulations, and the impact of risk management policies and procedures on their work with service users. Interviews were digitally recorded and transcribed, and pseudonyms were used to protect participants' identities. (For further details about methodology, data analysis and findings, see Green *et al.*, 2010; Green & Sawyer, 2010; Sawyer *et al.*, 2009; Sawyer & Green, 2013). Six scenarios have been selected to present a range of practice dilemmas. Each demonstrates the practitioner's complex reasoning in balancing the provision of care alongside the management of risk, together with expert 'insider' insights into the nature of systemic risks in frontline community care.

'Holding everyone's anxiety': positive risk taking as a whole-of-organization approach

Glenda, a programme manager of a large non-government community mental health agency, described how she and her staff had used a radical positive risk-taking approach with Robert, a 30-year old man, who, when referred to their programme, was designated as a 'very high-risk individual'. This scenario shows how risk management, as a practice, was utilized to enhance Robert's capabilities and autonomy – his needs as a self. It also shows the enabling influences on professional practice of organizational 'risk literacy' (Titterton, 2011, p. 35), and open and trusting relationships across different levels in the organization.

Robert had a long history of very serious self-harm, assaults to staff, and high use of emergency services (ambulance, police and short-term crisis admissions). These long-established crisis responses to his perceived riskiness had not improved his quality of life and coping behaviours or his relationships with service providers but, rather, seemed to imprison him in a negative, self-defeating cycle of dependence on services. Rather than continue this pattern of high service usage, because it was 'not going to contain or control the situation, anyway', Glenda decided to risk using a very different approach: to focus instead on building a 'therapeutic' relationship with Robert for the sake of long-term positive gains.

Looking back on their carefully reasoned plan, she explained that the aim was to try to 'sit with the client as much as possible [when he felt suicidal] … as uncomfortable and unpleasant for him as it is … [because] we can't actually fix [the problem]', adding that 'if we can … [maintain] a therapeutic relationship and ride through this with him, we actually think it's going to be more valuable' in the long run in that 'his self-harming behaviours will minimize over time. So, it's … balancing that but holding everyone's anxiety.'

Initially, the workers helped Robert to identify strategies that he might use 'so he didn't feel the need at that moment to self-harm' or, if he felt especially vulnerable, 'staff could assist him to self-soothe'. Through the process of relationship building, a plan evolved that was responsive both to his needs as a self and to the imperative for staff to protect his safety and their own under the given circumstances. In the first instance, to encourage self-empowerment and self-care, the worker would stay for him to 'care for' himself; but, as Glenda recalled, 'if you're going to choose to self-harm the staff are going to step back and you can talk to them on the phone and they'll assist you to get medical attention and you also know what you can do to get medical attention'. Working with and fostering Robert's self-knowledge and autonomy, she reasoned that: 'He's been self-harming for many years before he came to our programme and … I always held a belief … that he knew when he'd gone too far with his self-harming and actually did need to go to hospital to preserve his life.' Akin to the process of building a trusting and open relationship with the service user, the workers' selves were also respected:

> If he's not asking to go to hospital … and if you can sit with him in silence and hold that with him comfortably, that's Plan A. If it's really uncomfortable for you, Plan B is for you to leave and let him know that he can contact you … if he wants to talk.

Of critical importance, Glenda emphasized, was that staff be given access to 'the options they feel most comfortable with, so they can confidently ... translate them into a service [that] ... will work for the client'.

At the time I interviewed Glenda, five years had elapsed since Robert had become a recipient of their service. Only in the previous few months had any positive changes emerged, but they were 'valuable' ones: Robert's episodes of self-harm and his subsequent use of emergency services had decreased; he had sustained several brief periods of employment; and had reconnected with his family from whom he had been estranged for many years. He was more hopeful about his life, had developed some social connections, and felt optimistic about his achievements.

Reflecting on the use of risk as a 'lever of change' (Titterton, 2011, p. 39), Glenda argued that a commitment to looking for 'what will work for this person, not just for the organization' was fundamental, together with 'having a CEO who we keep informed, who's supportive of us ... and can trust us to actually do what we think is the way to go':

> I'm quite open saying, 'This is what I think, these are the positives; these are the negatives. We don't know which way it's going to go ... and this is what I'm recommending' and to have him say, 'Okay you're the practitioner, we'll go with what you do.'

Here a whole-of-organization approach is taken in the management of risk; open dialogue and trust between the CEO, programme manager and frontline workers parallels and reinforces the practice of developing recovery-oriented relationships between service users and workers (Alban-Metcalfe & Black, 2013). These conditions foster an organizational culture that is open to learning from mistakes and encourages rigorous thinking and skilled approaches to decision-making and risk taking.

Understanding systemic risk as a barrier to individualized care

As the dismantling of long-term inpatient care in stand-alone psychiatric hospitals came to an end, risks were transferred to general hospitals and community mental health teams but also increasingly to mainstream residential facilities, including private, often sub-standard, rooming houses; to the criminal justice system, and to families and service users themselves. Yet, scant attention has been paid in the literature to the far-reaching unintended consequences of deinstitutionalization. Issues of risk continue to be a common point of conflict between different service sectors and, with limited resources, this frequently creates barriers to the realization of sustained effective risk management and human rights-based practice.

In the following example, Julia, a senior case manager in a community mental health team, was deeply troubled by the predicament of Suzy, a young vulnerable woman in her care, for whom there was no appropriate accommodation.

Reflecting on the contemporary context of mental health practice, Julia felt caught between her obligation to manage the risks faced by Suzy 'in the community', and a range of systemic conditions, which intensified these risks: the early discharge practices of the inpatient unit together with pressure on beds, an increase in homelessness and a lack of 'secure accommodation' for people with severe and persistent mental illnesses, and increased illicit drug use. To Julia, these interrelated conditions had produced 'an increased tolerance of things' that would not have been accepted 20 years ago:

> So we've got a focus on risk but at the same time people aren't necessarily alarmed that their clients may be living in unsafe housing ... in our area we have a number of private rooming houses that people will be referred to and these ... can be awful environments, very unsafe ... it might be a four- or five-bedroom house; there might be four or five different people who are strangers living there, many of whom have drug and alcohol issues ... assaults occur, people's belongings are stolen, their medication may be stolen and they're really not conducive ... to good mental health and yet people will be living there because there's nowhere else for them to go ... But there's a real tolerance too and acceptance of that level of risk and that does have a risk to someone's mental health and sometimes to their physical safety and I guess many staff feel powerless about finding alternative accommodation because it's just not out there, so that's a significant problem but there's a level of acceptance of it.

Suzy had been living in one such unsupervised rooming house after a brief admission to hospital. While staying there, a male resident had assaulted her and stolen her money, mobile phone and psychiatric medications: she had 'noticeably been bashed, you could see a black eye and bruising' and she was 'too scared' to return. Julia spent half a day searching for more appropriate accommodation but the best she could find was another room in a similar facility in a different suburb. To Julia, this 'unacceptable scenario' would likely have a 'negative impact' on Suzy's mental state.

The heightened risks with which Julia must contend are, in some respects, outside the community mental health system but have been transferred into it because of inadequate resourcing in the housing sector. As Rogers and Pilgrim (2010, p. 209) claim, the 'three interweaving functions of care, control and accommodation' formerly provided by the old stand-alone psychiatric hospitals must be involved in any new reconfiguration of mental health work. 'Controversies', they argue, 'have tended to emerge for the very reason that critics ... have complained that government has still not delivered the correct blend of care, control and accommodation' (Rogers & Pilgrim, 2010, p. 209). Policies of mental health reform, including the provision of care and treatment in the 'least possible restrictive environment' often assume the capacity of professionals to establish and maintain the necessary, therapeutic relationships with service users, but their translation into practice remains contentious, at least in part, because of inadequate resources. This example demonstrates how the presence of systemic risks constrains the practitioner's capacities to deliver care that helps the service user realize her needs as a self: those of security, independence and social inclusion. It also underscores the need to educate the public about the uncontrollable and systemic dimensions of risk in community care.

Balancing the 'greatest benefit and least harm': positive risk taking in action

Ian, a team leader in an assessment and support programme for older people, spoke at length about the range of risks encountered in providing community care for the growing population of people with dementia. Public policy imperatives to support people at home for as long as possible often meant balancing two different alternative risk scenarios: supporting a 'normal' life with increasing but familiar risks, as opposed to a 'restricted' life with unfamiliar risks. For a person with dementia, living at home is inherently risky, but the familiarity of the home environment and neighbourhood provides a degree of security, autonomy and continuity, along with possibilities for social engagement. Conversely, transferring to the 'safety' of residential or hospital care could mean a range of new risks in an unfamiliar environment: sleep disturbances, infections, increased disorientation and increased risk of falls and, ultimately, reduced physical and mental wellbeing. Although a person with dementia living at home is 'exposed to risk', as Ian explained, one has to weigh up the course of 'greatest benefit and least harm'.

The process of navigating the interface between managing risk and providing care that respects and enhances the service user's human rights is clearly illustrated in a story he told about Lucy, a service user with 'moderate dementia'. She lived alone at home and 'had a routine of occasionally taking herself down to the McDonald's in the morning':

> She was getting daily nursing visits to provide her medication, and periodically the nurse would ring me and say, 'Look I can't find the client' and I'd say, 'Just go down to McDonald's'. By all accounts she was probably physically exposed

to risk, but what was working was that it was a routine that she knew, she could get there and back, she didn't have to cross a road which was the main thing, but yeah … she could have fallen and been out of range of support – but my view with that client was that if we had tried to circumvent that, she would have tried to circumvent our efforts, so working with the strength, working with the person's capacity – it's something she enjoys, so you're not going to take it away – the nurse would go down there and give her the medication in McDonald's.

This excerpt shows the very careful reasoning processes in which this worker has engaged to mount an argument for supporting Lucy at home. In recognizing her particular 'strength' and 'capacity' and the activities 'she enjoys', he demonstrated a positive risk-taking approach to her care, where her experience of autonomy and social participation were given centre-stage while, at the same time, he attended responsibly to her safety and security. Like other service users with cognitive impairments, she could 'quite successfully negotiate' her own local area, whereas placement in an aged care facility might generate 'a whole bunch of factors that when you look at it are of equal, if not greater, risk than crossing the road in her local community'.

At the same time, he was patently aware that, should an adverse event occur, the service could be seen as 'holding the client too long' at home. Like several other interviewees, this worker was concerned that there were no common community or political understandings regarding what constitutes 'acceptable' or 'unacceptable' risks in the home-based care of older people. He felt that 'a working agreement about risk in the community' was needed at a political level to 'validate what is occurring in terms of risk management and why it's occurring, but also to point out some challenges in improving risk management potentially'. Robertson and Collinson (2011, p. 160) also recognize the importance of educating the public about the way in which services support their service users, including the possibilities of 'positive risk taking occasionally failing'.

Using 'risk work' as a resource to enhance reflective practice

Several frontline practitioners felt that formal methods of risk assessment actually strengthened their professional practice. Steve, a case manager/social worker in a public mental health agency, regarded the risk assessment checklist as 'largely positive' and 'not constrictive'. In his workplace, case managers were required to complete this tool each time they had face-to-face contact with a service user. From

Steve's perspective, this requirement forced him to think more con-sciously about the different 'elements of risk' involved in service users' presentations:

> If you get to know a client ... well and you feel very comfortable ... some-times you can miss the cues because you're used to the conversation. Like I've got a fellow who says, 'Oh I just want to die, I feel like jumping off a bridge' – but he says that every single time and he has for the last 18 months and then in the next breath he'll say, 'Oh yeah, and what are we doing next week, are we going out for coffee?' ... But another person might say, 'I just feel really lousy' – and for them to say that when they haven't said it for six months means that they are really at risk, and having this framework that's in the back of your mind ... raises a level of consciousness towards risk issues ... I do need to take into account risk probably more than I would if I didn't have that as a constant reminder. Now because I come back to the office and I've got to read those questions, I've got to tick those boxes – and hang on a minute ... just because so and so said this every home visit for the last six months, should I just ignore it? I still need to think through and so I do think that the requirement to manage risk does shape the way I practise. And my experience in the organization is that it's been largely positive and not constrictive.

Steve observed that he was a more reflective practitioner as a result of using the risk assessment tool: 'Anything that makes a clinician think about their work and how they practise is ultimately a good thing ... and it gives a better chance for good outcomes'. In effect, he has taken what could be experienced as a routine compliance procedure and adapted it to enhance his own reflective practice as a professional.

Similarly, Jenny, a team leader in a non-government community support service, felt that the imperative to assess and manage risk actu-ally strengthened her relationship building with service users because it forced her to consider very carefully how she might raise potentially difficult risk issues with them sensitively and ethically. With risk as 'part of the everyday conversation', she felt she had become more self-conscious about her practice, thus enhancing her interpersonal skills and communication.

These two examples show how each worker has integrated the formal requirements to manage risk into the provision of individualized care. Here 'risk work' is used productively as a resource to advance the human rights of service users through heightening the practitioner's focus on the person's needs as a self, and on their own development as critically reflec-tive practitioners (Baker & Wilkinson, 2011, p. 22).

Countering the stigmatizing effects of 'high risk' classifications: A 'delicate balance'

The potentially stigmatizing effects that 'high risk' classifications exert over service users' lives was a strong theme in a number of interviews. A single assessment of 'high risk', whether to self and/or another, in an official file could produce a situation where a person is marked as a threat to society long after the assessment ceases to be relevant, especially if conducted following an isolated incident and in the absence of a subsequent review. Effectively, the 'high risk' classification may become the service user's major defining characteristic, prejudicing practitioners' perceptions across time, in spite of any positive changes in the person's life since the original assessment.

Jane, a senior support worker in a non-government community mental health agency, was troubled by the 'branding' effect that a significant risk history could have on a service user's future chances of recovery, noting the 'delicate balance' between perpetuating this effect as against supporting the person to focus on the progress they might have made:

> Once a client's been kind of branded as a significant risk to society ... It can be very often difficult for them to have any leeway to move out of that ... and the extent to which we perpetuate that inability to move ... I feel like that's always the really kind of delicate balance. And because ... places like X [forensic mental health service] to cover their arses ... will say, 'This client poses a long term threat and always will' ... if they don't say that and he ends up doing something, then it comes back to them ... So they will always err on that side. So there's not a lot of scope for people to feel like they're actually moving along and continuing and actually might be in quite a different place than they were five years ago ... And I think something that our service tries to do is really reflect that back to the person ... because it may not be being reflected back to them from any other places.

The persistent disadvantaging effects of 'high risk' labels can reduce the scope of human rights-based approaches that respect the service user's needs as a self. In such situations, the spectre of a documented episode of riskiness in the person's past is prioritized and presents a blanket barrier to socially just approaches even when, as another practitioner noted, the person has completed 'some education to learn about [the problem at hand] ... or they've grown'. Notwithstanding the need to manage risk responsibly, all-out conservative approaches often heighten people's isolation and dependence on the service system, and may generate negative outcomes in the long run (Robertson & Collinson, 2011, p. 161).

Prioritizing tool-based methods of risk assessment: An 'over-focus' on risk

Another strong theme emerging from the interviews was the constraining effects of 'risk thinking' (Rose, 1998) on interactions with service users. Julia, introduced above, observed that the dominance of risk had reduced opportunities for broader therapeutic interventions, arguing that 'it skews your mindset to focus on risk ... at times it's almost an over-focus on risk':

> Some case managers ... feel that their job has been almost reduced to monitoring someone's mental state, monitoring the compliance with medication and managing any potential risk ... and it doesn't leave a lot of room for them to do more therapeutic work ... and they feel that they would ignore those three issues ... at their peril or ... if something went wrong, then they'd be in deep water, so they feel a lot of pressure to pay attention to those issues and all the paperwork associated with that and therefore at times that means the exclusion of other things.

She also observed that the less experienced practitioners and those new to the mental health field were poorly equipped to resist the, often, overwhelming demands of procedural requirements in assessing and managing risk. This, in turn, limited development of their professional, clinical skills, *along with* limiting outcomes for service users. With an organizational emphasis on negative interpretations of risk, these workers were socialized into relying on actuarial, tool-based methods of risk assessment, at the expense of 'unstructured' professional and disciplinary knowledge:

> I think the less experienced people feel the need to routinely ask the client questions rather than making some judgements based on the way the person is presenting. For the client, they can often feel like ... they're being asked, 'Are you having suicidal thoughts?' and if the person says, 'Sometimes' – and some people have chronic suicidal thoughts - that's what gets explored and discussed at each appointment, rather than a whole range of other issues that might sit under that and might be contributing to them having a suicidal thought ...

> In fact, the less experienced staff ... often feel they can't ignore this stuff once a person maybe talked about having thoughts of deliberate self-harm or thoughts of suicide, they then feel obliged to explore that with the person and *maybe even at a level of depth that's not helpful* because it might be a chronic sort of risk and it might have been there for years. And it can take them a long time to feel confident enough and say, 'Okay, well we don't have to discuss this every fortnight.' (my emphasis)

Over recent years, mental health educators have identified 'structured professional judgement' (Robertson & Collinson, 2011, p. 161) as the best framework for assessing and managing risk. Here actuarial tools are used in combination with professional clinical skills, in order to make optimal use of all the available information. This is important, because, with reference to Munro's (2010, p. 1147) analysis of managing risk in child protection services, an organization that gives precedence to tool-based procedures 'runs the risk of undervaluing the professional skills needed to apply the procedures competently' and '[t]he more punitive the work culture and risk-averse the worker, the more practitioners will opt for the safer route of following procedures, however inappropriate they seem in a particular case'.

Reflections

Drawing on interviews with Australian mental health practitioners, this chapter has explored a range of practice issues at the interface between managing risk and providing care that enhances the service user's human rights and 'recovery'. The scenarios presented here illustrate the interpretive work engaged in by these practitioners as they enter into relationships with service users, reflect on the organizational contexts of their day-to-day practice, and encounter systemic constraints that shape the contemporary risk environment of mental health care. What stands out in their accounts is the 'delicate balance' and careful reasoning processes they must traverse in attempting to meet the challenges of providing care that fulfils the service user's needs as self, while responsibly managing risk.

Recovery-based practice has been enshrined in the Victorian Mental Health Act (State of Victoria, 2014), which came into operation on 1 July 2014. As in other Western democracies, including UK and US jurisdictions, 'recovery' is now the central tenet of mental health legislation and public policy. As a philosophy and practice, 'recovery' provides a framework for moving beyond traditional risk-dominated paradigms. In this context 'recovery' demands a positive view of risk and risk taking and, as for all iterations of individualized care, is realizable only through relationship building between worker and service user. At the organizational level, this means that the micro-social realm of practice, the minutiae of working with people, must be prioritized by making available the support and space for practitioners to engage in relationship building and to advance their professional skills and knowledge. In this regard, risk and recovery is everyone's business, the key 'going concern' of the organization. While tool-based methods of risk assessment remain important, professionals' analytical and intuitive reasoning must be accorded greater importance in decision making. Perhaps this will generate new and different standards of documentation in future mental health practice?

High workloads, administrative burdens and straitened resources often gravitate against reflective practice and cultural change in organizations. However, it is highly likely that recent policy initiatives of direct payments to mental health service users in Australia will intensify competition amongst services which may, in turn, generate incentives to establish high quality recovery-based programmes. These initiatives, along with the growing empowerment of mental health service users and the move to models of distributive leadership, themselves an expression of the ongoing democratization of society, may challenge the dominance of the risk paradigm in ways as yet unseen.

Acknowledgement: This chapter is based on research funded by an Australian Research Council Linkages Grant, no. LP0667485. I wish to thank the interviewees for generously giving up their time to participate in this research project.

References

Alban-Metcalfe, J. and Black, J. (2013) 'Mental Health: Making Leaders of Staff and Patients', *The Health Service Journal*, 123(6351), 26–7.

Baker, K. and Wilkinson, B. (2011) 'Professional Risk Taking and Defensible Decisions', in H. Kemshall and B. Wilkinson (eds), *Good Practice in Assessing Risk: Current Knowledge, Issues and Approaches* (London and Philadelphia: Jessica Kingsley Publishers), 13–29.

Barry, M. (2007) *Effective Approaches to Risk Assessment in Social Work: An International Literature Review* (Edinburgh: Scottish Executive).

Baxter, K. and Glendinning, C. (2013) 'The Role of Emotions in the Process of Making Choices about Welfare Services: The Experiences of Disabled People in England', *Social Policy and Society*, 12(3), 439–50.

Braithwaite, J. (1999) 'Accountability and Governance Under the New Regulatory State', *Australian Journal of Public Administration*, 58(1), 90–7.

Carey, M. (2007) 'White-Collar Proletariat? Braverman, the Deskilling/Upskilling of Social Work and the Paradoxical Life of the Agency Care Manager', *Journal of Social Work*, 7(1), 93–114.

Douglas, M. (1992) *Risk and Blame: Essays in Cultural Theory* (London: Routledge).

Ferguson, I. (2007) 'Increasing User Choice or Privatizing Risk? The Antinomies of Personalization', *British Journal of Social Work*, 37(3), 387–403.

Fine, M. (2005) 'Individualization, Risk and the Body: Sociology and Care', *Journal of Sociology*, 41(3), 249–68.

Green, D. (2007). 'Risk and Social Work Practice', *Australian Social Work*, 60(4), 395–409.

Green, D. and Sawyer, A. (2010) 'Managing Risk in Community Care of Older People: Perspectives from the Frontline', *Australian Social Work*, 63(4), 375–90.

Green, D., Sawyer, A., Moran, A. and Brett, J. (2010). *Managing Risk in Community Services: A Preliminary Study of the Impacts of Risk Management on Victorian Services and Clients*, Final Report to Industry Partners (unpublished; available from author).

Heller, N. R. (2014) 'Risk, Hope and Recovery: Converging Paradigms for Mental Health Approaches with Suicidal Clients', *British Journal of Social Work*, 45(6), 1788–1803.

Hood, C. (1995) 'Contemporary Public Management: A New Global Paradigm', *Public Policy and Administration*, 10(2), 104–17.

Kemshall, H. (2002) *Risk, Social Policy and Welfare*, (Buckingham: Open University Press).

Kirkley, C., Bamford, C., Poole, M., Arksey, H., Hughes, J. and Bond, J. (2011) 'The Impact of Organisational Culture on the Delivery of Person-Centred Care in Services Providing Respite Care and Short Breaks for People with Dementia', *Health and Social Care in the Community*, 19(4), 438–48.

McDonald, A., Postle, K. and Dawson, C. (2008) 'Barriers to Retaining and Using Professional Knowledge in Local Authority Social Work Practice with Adults in the UK', *British Journal of Social Work*, 38(7), 1370–87.

McDonald, C. and Chenoweth, L. (2009) '(Re)shaping Social Work: An Australian Case Study', *British Journal of Social Work*, 39(1), 144–60.

Munro, E. (2004) 'The Impact of Audit on Social Work Practice', *British Journal of Social Work*, 34(8), 1075–95.

Munro, E. (2010) 'Learning to Reduce Risk in Child Protection', *British Journal of Social Work*, 40(4), 1135–51.

Osborne, D. and Gaebler, T. (1992) *Reinventing Government: How the Entrepreneurial Spirit is Transforming the Public Sector* (Reading, MA: Addison-Wesley Publishing Company).

Robertson, J. P. and Collinson, C. (2011) 'Positive Risk Taking: Whose Risk is it? An Exploration in Community Outreach Teams in Adult Mental Health and Learning Disability Services', *Health, Risk and Society*, 13(2), 147–64.

Rogers, A. and Pilgrim, D. (2010) *A Sociology of Mental Health and Illness*, (Maidenhead: Open University Press).

Rose, N. (1998) 'Governing Risky Individuals: The Role of Psychiatry in New Regimes of Control', *Psychiatry, Psychology and Law*, 5(2), 177–95.

Sawyer, A. (2008) 'Risk and New Exclusions in Community Mental Health Practice', *Australian Social Work*, 61(4), 327–41.

Sawyer, A. and Green, D. (2013) 'Social Inclusion and Individualised Service Provision in High Risk Community Care: Balancing Regulation, Judgment and Discretion', *Social Policy and Society*, 12(2), 299–308.

Sawyer, A., Green, D., Moran, A. and Brett, J. (2009) 'Should the Nurse Change the Light Globe? Human Service Professionals Managing Risk on the Frontline', *Journal of Sociology*, 45(4), 361–81.

Stanford, S. (2010) 'Speaking Back to Fear: Responding to the Moral Dilemmas of Risk in Social Work Practice', *British Journal of Social Work*, 40(4), 1065–80.

Stanhope, V. and Solomon, P. (2008) 'Getting to the Heart of Recovery: Methods for Studying Recovery and their Implications for Evidence-Based Practice', *British Journal of Social Work*, 38(5), 885–99.

State of Victoria (2014) *Mental Health Act 2014* (Melbourne: Government Printer).

Taylor, B. J. (2006) 'Risk Management Paradigms in Health and Social Services for Professional Decision Making on the Long-Term Care of Older People', *British Journal of Social Work*, 36(8), 1411–29.

Titterton, M. (2005) *Risk and Risk Taking in Health and Social Welfare* (London: Jessica Kingsley Publishers).

Titterton, M. (2011). 'Positive Risk Taking with People at Risk of Harm', in H. Kemshall and B. Wilkinson (eds) *Good Practice in Assessing Risk: Current Knowledge, Issues and Approaches* (London: Jessica Kingsley Publishers), 30–47.

Webb, S. A. (2006) *Social Work in a Risk Society* (New York: Palgrave Macmillan).

Yeatman, A. (2009) *Individualisation and the Delivery of Welfare Services* (New York: Palgrave Macmillan).

9

LEADERSHIP, CRITICAL REFLECTION AND POLITICS: THE MANAGEMENT OF RISK IN MENTAL HEALTH ORGANIZATIONS

Catherine Hartley, Chris Lee and Jim Campbell

Introduction

This chapter is written from the perspective of three mental health social workers. The first two authors are mental health team managers working in the cash-starved and perennially restructuring National Health Service (NHS) in the UK (Lee, 2014). The third author is an academic who has explored the interface between mental ill-health of individuals, organizations and communities (Kapur & Campbell, 2005). In our own lives and practices, and in our relationships with colleagues and service users, we have experienced difficulties in managing our emotions when making decisions about risk. As managers, two of us attempted to use a number of strategies to manage intra- and interpersonal relationships when anxieties about risk emerged amongst colleagues. However, a broader political analysis was missing from our own understanding of what was wrong about how the organization, and how we as staff, approached issues of risk. We wondered if we had become intellectually atrophied, too exhausted by organizational demands, and limited by the ever-constricting spaces for professional judgement and organizational change. We now believe that leaders in a team should be able to talk back to power. This belief has helped us to reflect critically on the complex, interlocking processes whereby risk narratives are often unproblematically accepted and internalized by professionals. We found that we needed to strive towards facing up to and challenging the organizational and political processes that were constructing notions of risk in our work.

The chapter begins with a brief review of perspectives on risk and mental health and how these have become embedded in our everyday professional and managerial practices. It moves on to explain how we used a critical reflective approach with our colleagues to think about the complex nature of risk to both staff and service users. This approach is akin to that articulated by Fook and Askeland (2007), who highlight the importance of using critical reflection to better understand interpersonal communication and dialogue, and how to help others in workplace settings and culture, and ultimately to adopt novel learning approaches that attend to emotional needs. This form of reflection is illustrated through selected personal reflective logs (Thompson & Pascal, 2011) and what we call short 'critical propositions' that we wrote and used during periods of organizational change. These helped us to explore our own anger and frustration about organizational responses to what we viewed as narrow, uncritical and prescriptive social and political responses to issues of risk in mental health work. We conclude by exploring how we further developed this type of reflective process through arts-based approaches. This illustrates how we have moved from simply writing about our experiences towards different forms of praxis that challenge our own and others' views on risk and its management.

Discourses on risk

We assume that many mental health professionals reading this book expect that risk is recognizable, definable and has to be managed in the interests of clients, their families and the wider public. Such assumptions underpin important aspects of the management and delivery of mental health services. They tend to be reinforced by the notion of evidence-based practice, often expressed in actuarial terminologies (Kapur, 2000). Essentially, this implies that patterns of identity, thoughts and behaviours are identifiable and can be detected using technocratic approaches to risk assessment and management (Langan, 2010). A different, but arguably complementary, perspective tends to privilege the expertise of professionals and the way they use a range of knowledge and skills to make clinical assessments about risk. In our experience both approaches are usually enmeshed in professional practices and prioritized at different times and stages of organizational change.

However useful both actuarial and clinical approaches might appear to be – and we have found that they have indeed become normative in the organizations that we have worked in – the assumptions that underpin their use need to be interrogated. It has been argued, for example, that this binary approach does not capture the complexity of decision making by psychiatrists (Dixon & Oyebode, 2006). These ideas about risk and mental health are defined and reproduced in political and social mileux which create specific narratives about who is at risk and which agencies and professionals construct and manage notions of risk (Stanford, 2008). Thus notions of risk and dangerousness are often uncritically associated with the behaviour of mental health service users, despite the fact that, for example, people with mental health problems may be up to twice as likely to be the victims of homicide than the general population average (Rodway *et al.*, 2014). At the same time, risks associated with the iatrogenic harm caused by mental health regimes, social inequalities and stigma are often ignored (Warner, 2013). We therefore wish to develop alternative narratives that challenge risk orthodoxies, to create space for the mental health professionals better to understand risk to themselves and to service users, and to find ways of mediating the adverse effects of demands created by politics and organizational change.

Leadership, risk and politics

We now move on to reflect on our own leadership and management roles, as a way of reconsidering these alternative views on risk and mental health in practice. As with risk, leadership is a notoriously difficult concept to define, prompting debate about individual personality types and a variety of impediments to good leadership styles (Avolio *et al.*, 1999; Bass, 1990; Jackson & Parry, 2008; Maccoby, 2000). Foster (2013) has written extensively about management and leadership in mental health social work. He draws on the work of Huffington (2004) who stresses the importance of forming collaborative, rather than adversarial or hierarchical, relationships with 'followers' and stakeholders in modern organizations. 'Followers' is a term used to define those people who are led: the people whom managers manage. Our experience has been that when managers uncritically operationalize systems of risk assessment and assume the possibility that outcomes can usually be predicable, then another form of hidden risk emerges: risk to the professional. It is often then that the worker becomes:

> more inclined to see themselves as mistreated societal scapegoats, held almost wholly individually responsible and accountable and at risk of being professionally and publicly named, blamed and shamed when things go wrong with anyone with whom they have been working. (Foster, 2013, p. 120)

Of course such relationships are shaped by events that are external to the organization. As in other agencies in the UK, there has been constant reorganization of mental health services in attempts to save money. The consequence has been the downgrading of some frontline staff but the upgrading of some senior management posts (Unite, 2014). At the same time, budgets have been devolved to allow service users to pay for their own care, at a time when overall public spending was being drastically cut (Brookes *et al.*, 2015). The reduction in available resources to practitioners has meant that hospital and community-based mandated coercion has grown in the last two decades (Campbell, 2010; Campbell & Davidson, 2009), and with it increased pressures to understand and manage situations of elevated risk. At the same time, problematic stigmatizing narratives about the causes of mental ill-health, risk and dangerousness adversely affect the lives of service users and carers (Bogg, 2010).

As mental health team managers, the response of the first two authors, albeit without much sense of coherence, was that we agreed to do two things. The first was to make an effort to re-engage with academic social work, read journal articles and attend conferences. We discovered some solace in the work of two social work academics who challenged risk orthodoxies and focused on political dimensions of practice. Ferguson (2009), firstly, has written about the problems facing social workers when they are required to administer neoliberal polices. He claims:

> It is … policies which insist that the primary role of social workers is to 'manage' 'high risk' families or individuals, to ration increasingly meagre services, and to collude in the demonization of groups such as young people and asylum seekers which is giving rise to current discontent. (Ferguson, 2009, p. 4)

Ferguson argues for a holistic version of social work that can open up policies and procedures to critical scrutiny; by doing so, Ferguson argues social work can uncover and challenge simplistic narratives on community care. For example, we are concerned about the way that governments and agencies have uncritically espoused notions of personalization that privilege models of 'consumer-citizenship' and 'social entrepreneurship' at the expense of more collectivist approaches to dealing with need and risk (Carr, 2014). According to Ferguson (2012), this may actively efface, through organizational change and political campaigning, wider issues of inequality and deprivation that affect mental health service delivery. Tew (2014, pp. 45–6) further develops these ideas, using a strengths-based, post-Marxist perspective where different forms of capital (economic, social, relationship, identity and personal) are recognized and enhanced. Secondly, we were impressed by Garrett's (2013) approach to making social work theory relevant to the organization of social work and to social work practice. He asserts the continuing practicality of theory in social work, its vitality in bringing criticism to bear on how services are delivered and experienced and holding to account those who make policy. Garrett (2013, p. 15) unashamedly describes his own writing as 'a scholarly but still radical and disruptive read, situated among those books, actions, thoughts and dispositions that are irrevocably anti-capitalist'. Reinvigorated with a willingness to read, not just about the political world but about our world repoliticized, we wondered if we might be able to write something ourselves that would clarify our situation and help us to start thinking strategically about what we might do in terms of our views on risk and its management in mental health services. This brought us to our second strategy, of using reflective logs and 'critical propositions' to articulate ideas for change.

Using reflective logs and critical propositions

Our attempts to try and write something ourselves helped us to reflect upon these organizational changes that uncritically maintained and reproduced systems of risk assessment and that failed to acknowledge the relationships of power which existed between professionals and service users, and managers and staff. We found a number of theoretical positions on 'reflection' helpful in this respect (Fook, 2002). Fook and Gardner (2007) argue that critical reflection can be used to challenge common-sense views about power and society while also building theory-informed practices that promote social change. Fook and Askeland (2007) explain that critical reflection helps practitioners better to understand interpersonal communication and dialogue in a range of workplace settings and in the context of the wider cultural milieu. As a result, new learning approaches can be adapted that attend to social and emotional needs. Thus we sought to apply Fook's (2002) model by deconstructing practice assumptions (pp. 99–101) and then reconstructing more empowering knowledge (pp. 104–7). We determined that we could identify other ways to resist what we saw as the unethical and harmful impact of the risk mentality that was endemic to our organization's policy and practices and more broadly in the mental health sector. Fook (2002) states that such an approach can empower practitioners. However:

> Empowering people ... involves a complex (multi-layered) understanding (which includes their own perspective as well as those of other players) of how power is exercised and how it affects them, but also of how they exercise and create their own power. This includes an understanding of how they might participate in their own powerlessness as well as their own powerfulness. (Fook, 2002, pp. 103–4)

These indeed were the sentiments that encouraged us to write about our experiences. One of us created a brief diary of events of the sort that have been described in practice learning contexts as 'reflective logs' (Thompson & Pascal, 2011). This both enabled emotional reactions and pent up frustrations to be articulated, and helped us to make sense of the impact of organizational change. The other started to produce small paragraphs which we describe as 'critical propositions'. These are theorized reflections on the shifts in organizational practices, inspired by the work of the German cultural critic Walter Benjamin (1999). Both the logs and the propositions were written over a period of months while major changes were being experienced in the organization. We have edited them slightly for clarity of presentation here, but taking care that they remain true to, and retain the rawness of, the originals. The selection we present is expressive of our rage and hurt about the way that political and organizational changes tended to be informed by simplistic or common-sense notions of risk in mental health services.

Reflective logs

Paranoia

During restructuring we became aware of the organization's overriding concern with risk to its reputation. Harris (2014) argues that the application of neoliberal approaches to public sector organizations tends to commodify interventions and lead to ever-greater control over professional space. We believed that the organization reacted very negatively to criticism, and the following log illustrates how one of us struggled to understand how risk was being conceptualized in this way at that time:

> *The senior management group is perplexed as to why morale seems to be so low amongst frontline staff. We have 'improved' (that is reduced and repackaged) services after all, and some of the downgraded nurses still have jobs, so what could the problem be? External consultants have been brought in to investigate. No one cares about the risk to service users, and bizarrely even the risk some service users might pose to others if their service is cut; it doesn't compete as a concept with the main risk to the reputation of the organization. You would think we were a listed company: that our share price value had senior management in a sweat. The frustration and exasperation of the effect that the changes are having has made a colleague complain to senior management. The response is a demand for disciplinary action against that colleague. It seems extraordinary, given that our business is to provide a service to vulnerable, mentally ill service users, that there is such a lack of awareness of how people react when stressed or depressed. On the other hand, perhaps this isn't surprising at all, as*

public sector organizations recalibrate to focus solely on rationing resources and managing risk to themselves. There is no longer any room for compassion or reassurance for staff. **What about the risk to our mental health?**

Reorganization, redundancy and retirement

The following log reflects upon the sense of loss engendered by widespread redundancy and retirement that followed processes of organizational change. It also contemplates the failure of the organization to maintain a sense of 'relatedness', whereby interventions can encourage 'safe and respectful uncertainty of not knowing … and can contain the anxiety of emotionally charged human encounters and lived experiences' (Megele, 2015, p. 5).

> *I struggle to manage a new team, bring its members together and look after these stranded lost souls. There are so many endings that we have stopped writing cards or attending leaving drinks, so these endings go unmarked. None of us has the capacity to cope with all the loss. We stop reacting and we turn inwards. The Staff Survey results this year include a comment that the organization has lost its soul. We all have. Surely there is a great risk to the organization here? The loss of experience and knowledge, because it is too expensive, risks us all making more mistakes – doesn't it?*

The consequences were risks to health and wellbeing:

> *For an organization that provides a service to mentally ill people it seems to have no appreciation of the mental distress that this process causes. As a team manager I have to manage this distress and look after my staff. Any sense of achievement I might briefly have felt about being offered a job in this brave new world quickly dissipates into a mixture of survival guilt and the dawning realization of the unmanageable task that I have taken on.*

Where are the service users?

We tried to do our best to remember that we were employed to provide a mental health service. To keep the service users in mind, we had to find some ways to resist the storm of change that enveloped us. The following reflective log attempts to capture these ideas.

> *When an organization whose primary task is to work with vulnerable, mentally ill people becomes more insane than those it exists to help, what happens to the service users? Teams have become reactive. The quiet ones are forgotten. Some complain of course. I have had a raft of anonymous letters complaining about the cuts and the lack of care. I read the letters, looking for clues. And they are suffering: more than that I cannot tell. Others do use names. They tell me about the wonderful nurses and*

social workers they had and how lost they feel without them. One has killed himself. Others will follow. More are relapsing, their mental health unsettled by all the change. Perhaps increased risk to service users is a price worth paying for budget deficit reduction? The organization has forgotten its primary task. It has forgotten the service users. Out of sight out of mind. There are only financial risks now, not human ones.

In England, NHS trusts and social services departments claim to be putting service users first. But as NHS trusts behave more and more like businesses, they concentrate on their 'shareholders'. The latter are commissioners (the fund holders for NHS services), monitors (the regulators of NHS trusts), the Care Quality Commission (the inspection body for the NHS and social services departments) and other agencies that rely on targets. The result is that a plethora of performance indicators, used to judge the market value of organizations (Harris & Unwin, 2009), are now of paramount importance. This inevitably foregrounds risk to the sustainability of the organization as an ongoing concern, and one that is prioritized over risks to service quality and risks to or from service users. We believe that service managers must resist any trend to supplant the service user as the key focus of mental health service delivery.

Critical propositions

As an alternative, complementary way of trying to come to terms with what was happening in our organization, writing 'critical propositions' in a speculative way helped us to understand how ideas about risk were being articulated, and how these ideas could be challenged.

What is risk anyway?

It became apparent that the organization for which we were working was deeply concerned with risk. However, it was unclear what definition of risk was being used at any given point. The following critical proposition seeks to capture how this ambiguity was experienced in practice as a team leader.

Don't ask what risk is, we'll be here all day. Risk of what, risk to whom, risk from whom? Risk, danger, hazard, catastrophe – all the negatives. But also, following Titterton (2005), risk taking – positive risk, independence, empowerment. It's the same old whirl around: care and control, and empowerment and containment. Risk can mean anything – context defines risk. In these financially focused, austerity-driven times, we think of whole systems risk: the risk of credit default and the risk of spiralling debt. The result has been a transfer of responsibility as far down the hierarchy of power as possible. Banks create crisis and are rescued by the state, which in turn runs up a deficit, which leads to severe austerity measures whereby, in the end, the weakest and most vulnerable bear the consequences. And now even in social work we shake our personalized customers and shout 'pay up'. Risk is no longer from the dangerous schizophrenic to the innocent bystander; the triple dip recession has seen to that. The risk is now to a whole glorious way of life. Lapavitsas et al. (2012) present three options for economies trying to emerge from recession: more austerity, a change in economic policy to stimulate growth via public sector investment, or default on debts. How might our customers default? How might we help them? But stop, for a form is already being drafted deep in the fortress of the state's conscience – a risk assessment for the likelihood of customer default!

The desirable risk of failure

Leys and Player (2011) and Mandelstam (2011) have demonstrated how the NHS has become a battleground for England's politicians, its failings highlighted by the parties not currently in power, and its achievements undermined by political bickering over the validity of statistics that suggest systemic improvement. The critical proposition below takes an apocalyptic approach to this concern:

We begin with what some might view as a startling assumption: the NHS and social services in the UK exist to fail. They grant both government and opposition parties an endless permission to castigate and taunt each other. In a violent flurry of teleological cant of modernization, improvement, flexibility and (most loathsome of all) choice, the ritual of denouncement prevents any attempt at a more objective process of change and development that would cherish the institutions and nurture them towards better ways of working. The psychological damage that has been inflicted on the workforce by this permanent war has been so serious that recovery, if possible, would take years. In the meantime the political parties are agreed that their mutual hatred of the NHS and social services will eventually be satisfied by the erasure of both, in an absolute privatization. And yet the final execution of these universal scapegoats would be so intolerable that the governmental psyche could not complete the act. We are on a never-ending journey where we are always heading closer to abolition in the name of private enterprise, but never actually arriving at the destination. The failure, the castigation and the taunts must continue forever.

Risk to the share price: Targets and performance

The proposition below uses Seddon's (2008) critique of the target culture of the public sector as a springboard for examining personal rage:

Seddon (2008) has argued that targets, performance indicators and outcome measures are all the same. They serve not to improve services, but to act as a pseudo currency for the public sector, as the justification for making comparisons between NHS trusts and local authorities, and for the bonuses and pay rises of chief executives and board members. They make services worse, as everyone knows. They force workers to lie and to cheat, they make organizations 'game the system'; they provide no useful information about the reality of receiving services or about the actual performance of employees. Seddon's outrage is comforting: his analysis is irrefutable. But he does seem to believe that the point of public services is to provide a service to the public, when surely we all realize by now that the point of public services is to fail to provide adequate services. This is because the threat of privatization must be permanent and in any case those who need public services are by definition undeserving. All risk is business risk, and business risk can be managed by targets. There are no people anymore.

Art, innovation and change

By writing reflective logs and critical propositions we were able to express our anger and reflexively to relate it to the social work literature we had begun to read. Through this process we began to connect to our own power, and in doing so it became possible to recognize how pervasive were the various notions of risk that informed our practices and the ethos of our organization. This approach helped us to deconstruct simplistic notions of risk and to consider their impact on the lives of colleagues and clients. But we also wanted to be able to do something real to help our staff to resist, where possible, the worst aspects of a pervasive risk mentality. We established what we called 'micro-strategies' for enabling 'good enough practice' to continue in the face of the pressures we have outlined. Our attempts to implement these, with greater and lesser degrees of success, gave us the confidence in the potential importance of our service manager roles.

Drawing on the work of Halton (2004), we wondered if we could use art to help colleagues reflect on the process of change in the organization and on any action that we could take from within. For example, in two team meetings and one open presentation to team members, we presented slides of some famous and some not-so-famous paintings, to help colleagues to vent and explore their own feelings about their experiences. We have described this process in detail elsewhere (Hartley & Lee, 2013), but broadly speaking we used pictures to enable colleagues to express their views about personal, organizational and political change. These sessions successfully started our analysis of the change process.

In one of these team meetings we began by showing the picture *Waterfall* by the artist M. C. Escher and asked our colleagues what it made them think about. We were careful not to ask leading questions although our selection of pictures was inevitably partial. *Waterfall* shows a strange watermill, where the water drops down from a height, is turned by a wheel and then flows along until it is at the drop point again. At each point the picture seems to represent water flowing normally and yet, taken as whole, what is represented is impossible – that is, water flowing uphill and downhill at the same time. Without any prompting several people in the team immediately associated the apparent paradox at the core of the picture with their own jobs. We asked them to elaborate and they told us how they felt that their task as mental health practitioners was impossible as they could not both genuinely give their attention to service users and meet the performance agenda of their employers. Another picture we discussed was Francisco de Goya's *The Third of May 1808*, which shows a man about to be shot by a firing squad. It is a painting that is famous for depicting the reality of the Napoleonic wars in Spain. This picture provoked debate among the team as to whether practitioners were more like the firing squad, hurting their service users through coercive interventions and helping to implement the policies of austerity, or whether they were more like the victim, horror struck at being the target for destruction.

Although we were initially quite worried about the intensity of the thoughts and feelings that we had encouraged our team members to express, our presentation and meetings helped to rekindle a wider reclaiming of the right to criticize, debate and put comments in writing to the organization. We had a real sense that the vocation of mental health work was being seriously undermined, or placed at risk, by the priorities of our organization. After writing our reflective logs and critical propositions, and holding our art-inspired team discussions, we realized that we had been reactive in our day-to-day practices, always responding to what we were told to do, rather than trying to develop the service ourselves on the ground. As a consequence of this critical realization, we have since been able to set up new groups, meetings and 'clinics' in our teams, deploying our practitioners' own skills and training in different approaches ranging from mindfulness to family therapy. We now understand the value of reflective writing, of using visual aids to help others explore their own responses to conflicting and challenging demands, of trying to uphold practitioner values, and of connecting with theory and critical literature about and around our profession. This has enabled us further to recognize and critique normative ideas of risk and to defend the concept of the therapeutic alliance between service users and frontline workers.

Conclusion

In this chapter we have explored the negative ramifications of an unproblematic risk focus in mental health and service delivery. In particular, we have been critical of how organizational priorities have been shaped by defensive strategies to manage perceptions of risk to the agency. We have illustrated how our leadership in the context of managing mental health teams has necessitated our re-engaging with literature on politics, social policy and social work in order to develop critical perspectives on the realities of frontline management. Venting frustration through the use of reflective writing full of emotional content was a starting point for us to redevelop our ideas about our own effectiveness as leaders. We realize that such processes must also lead to strategies not just for enduring but resisting the stresses of organizational change and unpalatable policy implementation. By enabling ourselves and our teams to 'speak back to power', and by trying to take some initiative for developing caring services at the local level, we have been able to move beyond focusing on managerial concerns about risks to the organization, and risk to and from service users. Instead we have moved towards giving greater consideration to risks that are posed to public service values and to social work itself.

The approaches we have presented indicate that we have consciously and sometimes unconsciously departed from conventional approaches to leadership. Our aspiration had been to challenge the orthodoxy and limitations of organizational ideologies and populist expectations about mental health services. By using reflective logs and critical propositions, along with art and critical literature, in order to engage with organizations, colleagues and service users, we realize that we feel freer to express our thoughts and feelings. This in turn has led to new behaviours. We believe that once practitioners and managers are encouraged to think together then it is possible to take action, no matter how small, to move beyond constraining risk paradigms in mental health services.

References

Avolio, B. L., Bass, B. M. and Jung, D. J. (1999) 'Re-examining the Components of Transformational and Transactional Leadership using the Multi-factor Leadership Questionnaire', *Journal of Occupational and Organizational Psychology*, 72, 441–62.

Bass, B. M. (1990) 'Concepts of Leadership', in B. M. Bass and R. M. Stodgill (eds) *Handbook of Leadership: Theory Research and Managerial Applications* (New York: Free Press), 3–20.

Benjamin, W. (1999) *Illuminations* (London: Pimlico).

Bogg, D. (2010) *Values and Ethics in Mental Health Practice* (Exeter: Learning Matters).

Brookes, N., Callaghan, L., Netten, A. and Fox, D. (2015) 'Personalisation and Innovation in a Cold Climate', *British Journal of Social Work*, 45(1), 86–103.

Campbell, J. (2010) 'Deciding to Detain: The Use of Compulsory Mental Health Law by Social Workers', *British Journal of Social Work*, 40(1), 328–34.

Campbell, J. and Davidson, G. (2009) 'Coercion in the Community: A Situated Approach to the Examination of Ethical Challenges for Mental Health Social Workers', *Ethics and Social Welfare*, 3, 249–63.

Carr, S. (2014) 'Personalisation, Participation and Policy Construction: A Critique of Influences and Understandings', in P. Beresford (ed.) *Personalisation: Critical and Radical Debates in Social Work* (Bristol: Policy Press), 27–32.

Dixon, M. and Oyebode, F. (2006) 'Uncertainty and Risk Assessment', *Advances in Psychiatric Treatment*, 13(1), 70–8.

Ferguson, I. (2009) *Reclaiming Social Work* (London: Sage).

Ferguson, I. (2012) 'Personalisation, Social Justice and Social Work: A Reply to Simon Duffy', *Journal of Social Work Practice*, 26, 55–74.

Fook, J. (2002) *Social Work: Critical Theory and Practice* (London: Sage).

Fook. J. and Askeland, G. A. (2007) 'Challenges of Critical Reflection: "Nothing Ventured, Nothing Gained"', *Social Work Education*, 26(5), 520–33.

Fook, J. and Gardner, F. (2007) *Practising Critical Reflection: A Resource Handbook* (Maidenhead: Open University Books).

Foster, A. (2013) 'The Challenge of Leadership in Frontline Clinical Teams Struggling to meet Current Policy Demands', *Journal of Social Work Practice*, 27, 119–31.

Garrett, P. M. (2013) *Social Work and Social Theory* (Bristol: Policy Press).

Halton, W. (2004) 'By what Authority? Psychoanalytical Reflections on Creativity and Change in Relation to Organisational Life', in C. Huffington, D. Armstrong, W. Halton, L. Hoyle and J. Pooley (eds) *Working Below the Surface: The Emotional Life of Contemporary Organizations* (London: Karnac), 107–24.

Harris, J. (2014) '(Against) Neoliberal Social Work', *Critical and Radical Social Work*, 2(1), 7–22.

Harris, J. and Unwin, P. (2009) 'Performance Management in Modernised Social Work', in J. Harris and V. White (eds) *Modernising Social Work: Critical Considerations* (Bristol: Policy Press), 9–30.

Hartley, C. and Lee, C. (2013) 'Can Art Based Reflection Help us Cope with Organisational Change in the Public Sector?', *Journal of Social Work Practice*, 27(4), 441–53.

Huffington, C. (2004) 'What Women Leaders can Tell us', in C. Huffington, D. Armstrong, W. Halton, J. Hoyle and J. Pooley (eds) *Working Below the Surface: The Emotional Life of Contemporary Organisations* (London: Karnac), 49–66.

Jackson, B. and Parry, K. (2008) *A Very Short, Fairly Interesting and Reasonably Cheap Book About Studying Leadership* (London: Sage).

Kapur, N. (2000) 'Evaluating Risks', *Advances in Psychiatric Treatment*, 6, 399–406.

Kapur, R. and Campbell, J. (2005) *The Troubled Mind of Northern Ireland* (London: Karnac Books).

Megele, C. (2015) *Psychosocial and Relationship-based Practice* (Northwich: Critical).

Langan, J. (2010) 'Challenging Assumptions about Risk Factors and the Role of Screening for Violence Risk in the Field of Mental Health', *Health, Risk and Society*, 12(2), 85–100.

Lapavitsas, C., Kaltenbrunner, A., Labrindis, G., Lindo, D., Meadway, J., Michell, J., Painceira, J. P., Pires, E., Powell, J., Stenfors, A., Teles, N. and Vatikiotis, L. (2012) *Crisis in the Euro Zone* (London: Verso).

Lee, C. (2014), 'Conservative Comforts: Some Philosophical Crumbs for Social Work', *British Journal of Social Work*, 44(3), 2135–44.

Leys, C. and Player S. (2011) *The Plot Against the NHS* (Pontypool: Merlin).

Maccoby, M. (2000) 'Narcissistic: The Incredible Pros, the Inevitable Cons', *Harvard Business Review*, 78(1), 68–77.

Mandelstam, M. (2011) *How We Treat the Sick: Neglect and Abuse in our Health Services* (London: Jessica Kingsley).

Rodway, C., Flynn, S., While, D., Rahman, M. S., Kapur, N., Appleby, L. and Shaw, J. (2014) 'Patients with Mental Illness as Victims of Homicide: A National Consecutive Case Series', *Lancet Psychiatry*, June 2014.

Seddon, J. (2008) *Systems Thinking in the Public Sector* (Axminster: Triarchy).

Stanford, S. (2008) '"Speaking Back" to Fear: Responding to the Moral Dilemmas of Risk in Social Work Practice', *British Journal of Social Work*, 40(4), 1065–80.

Tew, J. (2014) 'Agents of Change? Social work for Well-being and Mental Health', in J. Weinstein (ed.) *Mental Health: Critical and Radical Debates in Social Work* (Bristol: Policy Press), 39–48.

Thompson, N. and Pascal, J. (2011). 'Reflective Practice: An Existentialist Perspective', *Reflective Practice*, 12(1), 15–26.

Titterton, M. (2005) *Risk and Risk Taking in Health and Social Welfare* (London: Jessica Kingsley).

Unite (2014) *Briefing Document on NHS Pay* (London: Unite Union).

Warner, J. (2013) 'Social Work, Class, Politics and Risk in the Moral Panic over Baby P', *Health, Risk and Society*, 15(3), 217–33.

10

BEYOND SOCIAL MEDIA PANICS FOR 'AT RISK' YOUTH IN MENTAL HEALTH PRACTICE

Natalie Ann Hendry, Brady Robards and Sonya Stanford

Introduction

It has been argued that 'self harm hashtags may be driving [an] increase of cutting in young people' (Chang, 2014). These discourses frame self-harm, suicidal or eating disorder content that circulates across online sites – such as Instagram, Tumblr, Facebook and Snapchat – as seductive and powerful, posing a significant risk to young people with mental health problems. Young people in recovery from mental illness have conveyed similar concerns, as expressed in these television and radio accounts (*ABC 7:30* and *ABC Radio* respectively):

> It's a really big subculture on Tumblr, especially, the self-harming websites and taking photos of them and all of that and that's sort of where I learnt a lot of different ways to do it ... you just get consumed by it. Sometimes I'd be cutting just so I could have a photo to put up there ... now that I look back at it, it was like how could I have been doing that? (Cooper, 2013)

> Sometimes it can have a very ugly impact and actually be really triggering for you and make you want to self-harm or make you feel even worse than you did when you initially went out maybe seeking help. There are some sites in particular that would glorify it or support it and say, you know, 'this is my body I can do whatever I want'. And when you're in that mind frame when you're depressed, vulnerable, using a maladaptive coping mechanism to deal with your issues, going to websites like that and making friends with people like that on the internet is probably the worst thing that you could do for yourself. (Rice, 2013)

Personal accounts like these suggest that viewing distressing online images automatically and negatively affects young people with mental health problems. Being reliant on social media is perceived as a risk to recovery as it distances them from 'appropriate' (face-to-face, adult, professional), support and care (Cooper, 2013).

Community and professional 'panic' concerning young people's online vulnerability is not new: it reflects ongoing public anxiety about young people's behaviour within a history of broader social and cultural concerns about both youth cultures and technologies (Ferreday, 2010; Holmes, 2009; Marwick, 2008; Phillipov, 2009). Such concerns are often framed as 'moral panics'; however, McRobbie and Thornton (1995) argue that 'media panic' more precisely conveys the moral anxiety that news media specifically incites about 'risky' youth cultures that are supported by new 'niche- and micro-media'. Livingstone (2008, p. 396) explains that 'media panics amplify the public anxieties associated with social networking services', which Phillipov (2009) argues manifests in the regulation of young people's behaviour in the name of protection. Extending this view, Marwick (2008) suggests that 'technopanics' link new technologies to risk but, like moral panics, these risks are not proportionate to the levels of harm actually experienced by young people. As disciplinary tactics, technopanics curtail the exploration of how and why young people engage with social media.

In this chapter we argue the need to look beyond simplistic or alarmist analyses of social media use by young people experiencing mental health problems promoted by news media and other concerned stakeholders. We suggest that the sensationalization of online activities, such as self-harming blogs and pictures, by news media shifts the focus away from young people's experiences of social suffering. This diminishes recognition of 'the lived experience of the social damage inflicted in late capitalist societies on the least powerful and the intra-psychic and relational wounds that result' (Frost & Hoggett, 2008, p. 440). Instead, attention is drawn to the 'spectacular performance of despairing' that is afforded by the social media in question (Ferreday, 2010, p. 424). At the same time, news media also warps the actual nature of young people's lived experiences of social suffering that results from mental illness. Media panics over young people's use of social media obscure the complex human rights issues faced by young people with mental illness. The many social injustices young people face are also muted amidst the noise of alarmist social media discourses. This means that young people's online expression of their experiences of mental illness is framed as a distortion in mental health policy and practice contexts. Their accounts of suffering injustices and restricted or denied human rights are at risk of being invalidated by policymakers and practitioners.

We acknowledge that young people *do* post and share emotionally distressing content online; however, news media accounts that create technopanics pathologize young people's use of social media. As Slavtcheva-Petkova *et al.* (2015) argue, harm cannot be directly implied from content without understanding how young people experience risk. While journalists may have the dubious 'bad news sells' excuse for their framing of social media (Clark *et al.*, 2008, p. 17), we argue that mental health practitioners working with young people have a greater responsibility to adopt more critical perspectives when engaging with risk discourses that falsely frame young people's online social practices as *necessarily* negative.

Positive accounts about social media use in news media and research emphasize its transformative potential to prevent and treat mental illness through mental health e-therapies, health literacy apps and social media-based campaigns. Yet even this more optimistic perspective is troubled by a lack of understanding of *how* young people use and understand social media. Without this understanding social media campaigns that aim to destigmatize mental illness create irreconcilable contradictions over the risks of online media use. For example, such campaigns ask young people to share their experiences of mental illness. This places them in a contradictory position: in speaking back to stigma, they are required to be open and honest about their lived experiences, but they are also cautioned to not expose personal information online (Phillipov, 2009). In addition, young people are encouraged to disclose their mental illness stories in adult-moderated spaces (such as mental health clinics, at school or the family home), but at the same time they are censured for being inappropriate or excessive in disclosures in spaces beyond adult surveillance.

Keeping in mind that social media affords 'a heterogeneous bundle of practices' (Couldry, 2012, p. 29), we argue the need to develop a more nuanced understanding about how social media can enhance young people's lived experience of mental illness. The dramatization of young people's postings by news media erases an appreciation of social media as a place that has capacity for supporting the development of diverse, complex and empathetic narratives. Such narratives can enable mental health and other practitioners to respond more meaningfully to young people's experiences of social suffering. It is this alternative perspective of the affordances of social media that can support young people's recovery that we draw attention to in this chapter.

We begin with an historical account of the theoretical controversies surrounding the social web where the digital world is envisaged as a haven from 'real world' concerns and events (utopic vision) and, dichotomously, as a world gone wrong in which moral structures have disintegrated (dystopic vision). Next, we examine the particular affordances of Facebook and Tumblr in relation to young people's experiences of mental illness, these being control, immediacy and telling stories of the self. We conclude by suggesting that mental health practitioners can better support and strengthen young people's recovery by focusing on the affordances of social media, and taking into account young people's own attitudes, practices and experiences of sites such as Facebook and Tumblr.

Utopic and dystopic visions of the social web

The 'World Wide Web' (what we 'surf' in browsers and apps) was depicted as a social and political utopia in early scholarship on the social web. It was seen as a democratic space where individuals could cast off their faulty bodies and escape the social, economic and political oppression of their everyday, 'real world' lives (McRae, 1997). Reflecting on the profound importance of the internet, Weinberger (2002, p. xii) notes that 'the Web gives us an opportunity to rethink many of our presuppositions about our nature and our world's nature'. The internet challenges fundamental notions about knowledge, space, power, time, self and belonging.

Contributors to the scholarship on the internet in the early 1990s highlighted the radical potential of 'cyberspace' to transform the cultural stereotypes of people with mental illness, allowing movement away from damaging, negative labels of people such as 'mad', 'insane' or 'crazy'. This optimism reflects how, as a medium, the internet was often positively framed as an 'identity laboratory' (Wallace, cited in Jordon, 2005, p. 203) where the individual experimented with aspects of their 'self'. McRae (1997), for example, asserted that online, individuals can remake themselves according to their choosing. Her research indicated a 'freedom of expression, of physical presentation and of experimentation beyond one's own real-life limits' (McRae, 1997, p. 75) that could enhance the wellbeing of users. McRae (1997, p. 79) notes that when markers of identity become an option or a point of description rather than a strictly defined biological or social construct, they can (and will) be subverted.

Turkle (1995, 1996) also understood the internet to be a place of identity-play where users could experiment with and perform different versions of self. One of Turkle's interviewees described online identity play as a 'chance for all of us who aren't actors to play (with) masks ... and think about the masks we wear every day' (1995, p. 256). Over the past two decades, however, the rapid expansion of the user base of the social web and the integration of social media into everyday public and private practices has produced new, pessimistic discourses and 'risks' associated with the web. These dystopic counter-arguments frame the internet as 'the destroyer of identity and community ... (where) critics wonder if relation-ships between people who never see, smell and hear each other could be the basis for true community' (Wellman, 2004, p. 26). A clear example of this utopic/dystopic divide in research literature is evident in the juxta-position between the 'identity laboratory' understanding of the internet from Turkle (1995), and to some extent McRae (1997), and the 'identity crisis' scenario described by Gergen (1991, p. 7):

> Under postmodern conditions, persons exist in a state of continuous con-struction and reconstruction; it is a world where anything goes that can be negotiated. Each reality of self gives way to reflexive questioning, irony and ultimately the playful probing of yet another reality. The center fails to hold.

This tension between the utopic and the dystopic still maintains some impetus (see Jordon, 2005) and is at the heart of a series of concerns that have sprung up around social network sites, particularly in terms of issues to do with trust and authenticity. Indeed, in her more recent work, Turkle (2011) has moved towards a more pessimistic reading of the influence technology has on our experience of the social world. She argues that 'digital connections ... offer the illusion of companionship without the demands of friendship ... (and) allow us to hide from each other, even as we are tethered to each other' (Turkle, 2011, p. 1). Despite her early utopic visions, 16 years later Turkle now insists that we are 'alone together', and 'literally at war with ourselves' (2011, p. 296).

A recent trend in internet studies moves beyond the utopic/dystopic and online/offline dichotomies towards the role of the internet as embed-ded in everyday life, broadly described as domestication theory (Baym 2010). Baym (2012) explains, 'domestication focuses on the processes through which technological devices move from being viewed as danger-ous objects we may allow on the outskirts of our lives, to being acceptable and harmless – how they become part of the family'. For Wellman (2004, p. 29), the internet should not be understood in dystopian terms as being associated with a 'loss of community' and loss of identity, nor should it be seen in utopic terms in which a significant gain in community is visible. Instances of both the positive and negative effects of the internet on iden-tity and on community are numerous, but reproducing the utopic/dystopic dichotomy only serves to frame the internet as separate from everyday life. Wellman (2004) contends the internet should not be understood as a unique medium that exists external to the everyday, lived reality of the individuals who use and thus constitute the internet. Rather, the internet makes the everyday lives of its users visible, though variably depending on the site being used; it is a social utility upon which systems of belonging can (for better or worse) be produced, articulated and acted upon.

It is our argument that a utopian viewpoint of social media is unhelpful: it belies the many contradictions and risks that arise in the complex interplay that occurs between users, technology and broader sociocultural and political structures. However, by simply highlighting the risks of social media for young people it is possible to negate the affordances of such technology, including those that can support mental health. Facebook and Tumblr are commonly used social media sites. In this next section of the chapter we explain their affordances. We do this as a means of moving beyond risk as the dominant paradigm for framing young people's use of social media. Hutchby's (2001) definition of affordances has focused our analysis. He states that:

> [A]ffordances are functional and relational aspects which frame, while not determining, the possibilities for agentic action in relation to an object. In this way, technologies can be understood as artefacts which may be both shaped by and shaping of the practices humans use in interaction with, around and through them. (Hutchby, 2001, p. 144)

Three of Facebook's key affordances are reviewed in the context of young people experiencing mental health problems; a similar exercise is then applied to Tumblr.

What are the affordances of Facebook?

Facebook is the most widely used online social network site. At the end of 2014 there were 1.39 billion active monthly users, and 890 million of those accessed the site daily (Facebook.com, 2015). Since its inception in 2004, the people behind Facebook – most notably its co-founder and current CEO Mark Zuckerberg – have framed the site as concerned with 'caring', 'empowerment', 'community', 'connecting', and 'sharing' (Lincoln & Robards 2014a, p. 1047). While Facebook is undeniably a tool for connecting and communicating, it has also been critiqued for: its revenue model (user behaviours contribute to a marketing profile that allows for targeted advertising); its involvement in government surveillance schemes (Rushe, 2013); and even for contributing to a broader cultural shift towards a greater reliance on technology at the expense of 'real' connections (Turkle, 2011). Despite the deterministic arguments about the damage Facebook might be having on our society, empirical research paints a different picture: Facebook users are more trusting, have more close relationships, get more social support, and are more politically engaged than non-Facebook users. Facebook revives 'dormant' relationships and is used to keep up with close social ties (Hampton *et al.*, 2011). In this section, we take an optimistic approach to Facebook by presenting three affordances of Facebook: control, immediacy and storying self. The section primarily draws on eight years (2007 to current) of qualitative research undertaken by one of the authors, Brady, with young social media users (from their mid-teens through to their late twenties) in Australia. The names of participants have been changed to protect their anonymity.

Control

Facebook users are able to exercise control over their presence on the site in two distinct but related ways: practically and symbolically (Hodkinson & Lincoln, 2008; Lincoln & Robards, 2014b). Practical control describes the user's capacity to make, accept, reject, or ignore 'friend' requests, thus determining who can and cannot access their profile and the disclosures that constitute that profile. The extent to which users exercise practical control on Facebook varies from users who: will initiate and accept friend requests from just about anyone; have completely public profiles; are very selective with who they 'let in' and accept or initiate requests from only close friends (Robards, 2010). This enables young people experiencing mental illness to disclose elements of their lives to select audiences. They may choose to write about their emotional state, treatment or recovery with trusting friends who they feel will support them.

Consider 20-year-old Eric. He saw Facebook as 'documenting real life' rather than as a tool to be used to meet new people, and so his friending strategies mirror that approach. Of the 500 or so 'friends' Eric has on Facebook, there are only five he has not met before and a further 25 to 50 he has only met once or twice. Eighteen-year-old Tim also prefers to keep his profile just for friends he knows offline, but he has also been open to meeting new people online, contingent on the potential for an offline meeting. When Tim is added by 'randoms' he first initiates contact with them by way of private messages to determine whether or not he wants to add them as 'friends' and eventually meet them offline. Through these practices, young people with mental illness are able to share their lived experiences with people they consider friends, enabling them to elicit support when it is needed. These practices represent reasonably high and common levels of practical control.

On the other hand, 21-year-old Debra has an unusual approach to friending, which serves as a useful demonstration of the messiness of any kind of attempt to frame friending practices into a neat spectrum. Debra has an open (public) profile, but she is highly restrictive when it comes to adding 'friends' or accepting 'friend' requests: 'When it was set to private I got lots of add requests, so I just made it public so all those people from high school could have a snoop.' Her justification for this unusual strategy is that people are simply curious about other people's lives, and she has no problem allowing them to indulge their curiosity. However, for Debra, adding someone as a friend on Facebook is an important act that she doesn't undertake lightly, friending only people she thinks of as real friends. While Debra didn't disclose experiencing mental ill health, her friending practices illustrate the potential affordance of Facebook to help educate the curious viewer about the lived experience of mental illness.

This brings us to symbolic control. Symbolic control describes the user's capacity to shape their profile, and their 'presentation of self' through selecting profile pictures, determining what kind of disclosures to include in status updates, curating (or not) images uploaded and tagged, and providing biographical data relating to employment, education, family, religion, sexuality, and so on. As with practical control, the extent to which symbolic control is exercised on Facebook varies from user to user. Some users populate their profiles with as little content as possible (a performance of identity in itself) and don't think of their Facebook use as actively managing an impression. Other users regularly update and manage their profile, ensuring they can't be tagged in images or posts without their direct consent. For example, Eric (introduced above) is fairly lax when it comes to autobiographical data, but he regularly oscillates between two profile pictures to reflect his different 'sides' – one, a fun, music-festival-going guy, and the other, a more conservative, suit-wearing young adult. Symbolic control is crucial for young people experiencing mental illness over different stages of their recovery. By regularly updating their profile, young people may create a hopeful or positive impression of their lives that may help them avoid harassment or ridicule from peers, or, equally, they may choose to post about emotionally complex or challenging moments.

Having considered the ways Facebook affords users a sense of practical and symbolic control over their profiles, we now turn to the affordance of immediacy.

Immediacy

While social interactions on Facebook have previously been described largely as asynchronous (Hull *et al.*, 2010; Quan-Haase & Young, 2010), participants in Brady's studies have described their social interactions on Facebook as often synchronous or 'real-time', especially at certain times during the day.

Nineteen-year-old Charlotte, for instance, tends to spend more time on Facebook between 4pm and 9pm, interacting with friends via IM (Instant

Messenger) or comment threads (on status updates, pictures, or other posts). Outside these times, Charlotte explained that 'usually people aren't on then, so I don't go on then'. Twenty-year-old Brad has synchronous chats that last between 30 minutes and two hours in the evenings. Twenty-year-old Bree distinguishes between who she prefers to interact with synchronously, and who she prefers to interact with asynchronously:

> If it's closer friends I'm talking to them on Instant Messenger, if it's just people I'm associated with who I'm like checking up on – well, not checking up on – getting in contact with again, it's just a comment.

Twenty-four-year-old Camilla disabled Facebook's IM function (set herself to always be 'offline' or 'unavailable', and thus invisible to others) as she found synchronous interaction 'annoying' and potentially disruptive. Thus, Facebook affords immediacy through IM and synchronous comment threads, and it also affords the capacity to withdraw from that immediacy. Whereas offline or during a phone call it can be difficult to 'slip away' discretely, Facebook users are able to easily move between synchronous immediacy and asynchronous modes of interaction (or not). The affordance of immediacy enables young people with mental illness to control their sociality depending on their needs for connection.

Storying self

One of Facebook's most valuable, long-term affordances is its capacity to tell stories. In 2014, Facebook celebrated 10 years in operation by allowing users to generate one-minute personalized 'look back' videos for themselves, where key images and status updates (selected by algorithm) were pieced together and set to nostalgic music (for more on these videos, see Robards, 2014). Along with other features Facebook has begun rolling out, such as the year in review and 'friendship summaries', these videos represent the value of Facebook as a storytelling device. Facebook affords users with a space to present stories of self with others and serves as a site for self-reflection. The current iteration of Facebook's profile – the 'timeline' – allows users to quickly 'scroll back' to previous disclosures, see 'highlights' from each year of use, and even 'resurface' old images or posts into newsfeeds. One example of resurfacing is occurring at the time of writing this chapter (early 2015) as people in our own networks participate in a phenomenon whereby users re-post their first profile pictures. Just like looking through old photo albums, or coming across old diaries, the longitudinal depth of disclosures made on and retained by Facebook evoke reflections on progress, change and identity-work, which is particularly important developmentally for adolescents and young adults.

This affordance can be both positive and negative, especially for young users experiencing mental health challenges. As much as Facebook is about connecting people and presenting 'real life', it's also very much a space for the presentation of an 'idealized self' (Goffman, 1959) where vulnerability, turmoil and listlessness can be obscured or erased in favour of positive stories of achievement and 'good times'. For example, Katie, a young woman surviving depression and who participated in a study on social media practices conducted by another of the authors, Natalie, explained:

> Facebook portrays like, happy shiny bubble people like in their bubble world ... for most people you don't see they're upset or when they're just being ordinary. You see it when they're outside having a good time, having fun, having awesome breakfasts, having awesome lunches, and all that. So if you read, if you compare your life (as someone with depression) to their life, of course your life isn't going to look as good as theirs on Facebook.

For another of Brady's participants, 22-year-old Mark, a female-to-male transman, Facebook's storytelling capacity was a double-edged sword. When he transitioned, Mark created a new profile on Facebook in order to craft a new story to align with his real gender identity after coming out as trans to his friends and family. However, before transitioning, Mark had carefully documented his life on Facebook, and he was especially hesitant to lose that digital trace, especially his overseas travel photos. Mark explained how he went about selecting elements from his old profile to 'reload' on his new profile:

> When I created my new profile ... I made a Facebook folder on my laptop hard drive, downloaded the photos I wanted to keep off my old profile, then uploaded photos again into different albums on Facebook ... I reloaded my life ... I reloaded all the photos ... I did it over a couple of days, then just made everything seeable to everyone ... For all my old photos, I didn't put up many photos of myself. I put up a couple of photos of myself, where I was rugged up (wearing lots of warm layers of clothing) ... like you couldn't see me much ... I didn't feel too dysphoric.

This is an explicit example of how Facebook figured into Mark's story of self. It served as a site for private reflexive identity work, but also, when he was ready, as a platform for communicating his story to a very tightly controlled networked public. Thus, Mark was able to draw on Facebook's storytelling affordances in order to shape a narrative that he felt comfortable with, bringing us back to the first affordance – control.

In this section we have explored just three interrelated affordances of Facebook in order to assert the need to move beyond a risk focus to better understand the role of social media in young people's recovery processes. In the following section, we consider these affordances in relation to a different and less-researched form of social media – Tumblr.

What are the affordances of Tumblr?

Tumblr is a micro-blogging site that allows users to create their own user-designed blogs to share content including images, text, music and videos. When users join Tumblr they create a primary, public tumble-blog attached to a single username. The site allows for multiple tumblrs (a user's personal tumble blog) to be established from one account, including private or group blogs. In February 2015, the site hosted over 220 million of these blogs, consisting of almost 105 billion posts, in 13 languages (Tumblr, 2015a).

When users log into the site they are presented with their 'feed', a continuous stream of content posted by blogs they follow, organized chronologically, with the most recent post at the top of the feed. Users can 'like' a post by clicking a heart-shaped icon, comment on the blog (dependent on its settings), or 'reblog' content. Unique to Tumblr, reblogging shifts the context and meanings associated with content as it 'tumbles' and reproduces posts over many tumblrs, linking the original poster under the post.

In this section we draw on research to focus on how Tumblr affords young people control, immediacy and storying of the self, albeit through distinct affordances to Facebook. We also draw on workshops facilitated by one of the authors, Natalie, with young people under 18 years engaged with Australian mental health services (for more detail see Hendry, 2017). Identifying information has been removed to ensure anonymity.

Control

Tumblr allows users both practical and symbolic control over their blogs. Unlike Facebook, Tumblr is predominantly public and affords limited practical control over who can see and follow a user's tumblr and the content they share, reblog, like and comment on. Although users may create private, password-protected secondary blogs, most of Tumblr's social features are restricted to the user's primary, public username and blog. Thus initiating social features, such as liking or reblogging content, posting comments on posts, following other tumblrs, or submitting content to other blogs, are all linked to a public username. Users can follow blogs without seeking approval from blog owners, and are unable to follow blogs or comment on posts anonymously. As Tumblr describes, a user's primary, public blog is required to be visible and open, 'where you live large and in-charge' (Tumblr, 2015b).

Even as Tumblr affords limited practical control, participants in workshops facilitated by Natalie considered Tumblr to be a 'safe' space for sharing personal, often taboo, thoughts, images and other content. Unlike Facebook, young people are unable to adjust most of the privacy settings on Tumblr, yet still felt that it provided them with control over their public presence and their represented interests. In common with boyd's (2014) research on social media use of young Americans, workshop participants described Tumblr as a place to avoid adult surveillance.

'Liv(ing) large and in-charge' is less about practical control on Tumblr and more about the extensive symbolic control users have over their blogs. Renninger (2014, p. 11) describes identity on Tumblr to be 'often closeted, collective, obscured, or evanescent'. This affords marginalized communities the capacity to engage in 'public anonymity' (Cho, 2011) thereby potentially avoiding the risk of harassment, exclusion or ridicule. As one example of this, an Australian study investigating technology in youth health services demonstrated that Tumblr afforded publicly anonymous connections:

> When I was very ill, I was on my computer and the computer became my life. And it was kind of almost like a 'kill or cure' thing for me. I was lucky because I found support groups online ... I was on Tumblr a lot and you kind of develop a network of Tumblr friends. There's a lot of support there. Because no one actually knows what you look like, kind of thing, there's no judgment based on – it's all just about your mental health. (Montague *et al.*, 2014, p. 31)

Just as users on Facebook vary in how they exercise symbolic control, Tumblr users vary in how much and what they present on the platform. For example, one of Natalie's participants established two different Tumblr accounts, using two different email addresses to log in, and subsequently maintained two distinct primary blogs. Her primary blog focused on inspirational and motivational art, quotes and music, while the second focused on mental health-related content, including self-injury and depression. The blogs she followed on each account reflected the content posted on each of her blogs. Tumblr allowed this young woman to choose which blog and dashboard of followers she wanted to view, depending on how she felt. Another participant maintained two Tumblr blogs: her primary blog shared recipes and food information, and her secondary blog shared and reblogged her consumer 'tastes' including musicians, art and beauty how-to videos. Her food tumblr included a small profile sharing her age, city of residence, and information about her mental illness diagnosis. While Tumblr affords less practical control in comparison to Facebook, it affords diverse strategies for users to exercise symbolic control through the creation of personally controlled, 'safe' spaces for identity-work and connection.

Immediacy

Immediacy on Tumblr does not involve synchronous conversations or connecting through networked 'friend' lists. Users often reblog their own content to comment on, add extra content, or respond to others' comments through chains of comments attached to posts. In this way posts act as asynchronous threads of public conversation as users initially connect through shared content rather than private conversation. Like Twitter, Tumblr may 'contribute to a conversational ecology in which conversations are composed of a public interplay of voices that give rise to an emotional sense of shared conversational context' (boyd et al., 2010). Asynchronous communication on Tumblr is also possible through comments and messages sent via Tumblr's inbox function.

In her workshops, Natalie asked participants to dress up as social media sites or draw them as people. Participants used these 'social media bodies' to represent the sites in a number of ways including visualizing who they perceived to be the main users, or expressing their relationships with social media and how it made them feel. For all examples of 'Tumblr bodies', participants drew people that were almost invisible in comparison to accessories or objects surrounding these bodies. Sketches of marginalized, subcultural or taboo interests and practices were foregrounded in these representations, such as bongs, make-up bags, rainbow flags, self-injury markings, and anti-depressant medications. Tumblr afforded participants authenticity related to substance use, beauty and fashion practices, sexuality and mental illness. Participants agreed that these interests and attitudes were often inappropriate or 'too personal' for other social media. The *Tumblr Community Guidelines* affirm this perspective: 'We want you to express yourself freely and use Tumblr to reflect who you are, and what you love, think, and stand for' (Tumblr, 2014).

Who a user is on Tumblr was considered less important for workshop participants than the interests they shared on the platform. Young people felt a sense of connection and co-presence with others through the familiar and affirming content others posted (Hjorth & Hendry, 2015). Immediacy is therefore difficult to determine on Tumblr as it affords a feeling of being there for and with others, rather than directly speaking to them. In this way, Tumblr 'creates its own publics' based on shared content rather than drawing on a user's existing connections (Renninger, 2014, p. 7). This blurs the distinction between following *people* and following *blogs*: the adaptability of the platform affords both. Young people feel a sense of emotional connection when engaging with content that relates to their lives. Lasén (2013, p. 95) explains:

> distant and asynchronous modes of communication help to avoid some of the risks and embarrassing consequences of emotionally charged exchanges, so that the apparent lower affective bandwidth appears to be an advantage for the display, expression and performance of more intense emotions.

Tumblr affords emotionally connecting with content (and subsequently, the users that posted it) as opposed to directly engaging in conversation about confronting or overwhelming topics. Thus Tumblr affords a protective strategy of self-expression for these young people, without requiring them to manage the complex emotional terrain of direct relationships.

Storying self

Finally, as a 'network of digital self-representation', Tumblr champions representations of identity that are adaptable and emotionally authentic (Fink & Miller, 2014, p. 611). *Who* people are on Tumblr is not anchored to their 'passport' identity as it tends to be on Facebook: Tumblr users are not required to use their 'real' names or demographic information. Instead, users can shape stories about who they are by how they customize their blog design and the content they select to create, upload or reblog. For Cho (2015, p. 45) stories of self are constructed through *curation* as users become 'the sum of (their) posts ... a visualization of (their) connections to others – a porous, living assemblage'.

For some young people experiencing mental illness, Tumblr supports stories and expressions that perpetuate emotional distress. For others, the adaptability of the site (in comparison to other social media such as Instagram or Facebook) and its focus on creativity means that Tumblr provides a productive space for identity-work and recovery. The affordances of anonymity and symbolic control provide users with the opportunity to disclose personal stories about challenging experiences of frustration, fear, distress and hope. These stories might be anecdotes about waiting at health clinics, their opinions on medication or experiences of stigma related to self-injury. These stories may be shared alongside seemingly contradictory personal and reblogged content such as text sharing praise for their treatment, images from a popular television series, videos featuring cute animals, or other non-health related content. As such, Tumblr affords young people a space to curate a non-linear story of the self to disclose their lives beyond diagnoses, symptoms or treatment regimes. Hester

Parr (2008, p. 17) emphasizes the importance of these 'disclosive identities as ones containing both fluid and stable properties' that may counter more reductive, 'singular enclosed identit[ies] implicated in the mental patient label', such as those that are frequently absent from mainstream media.

Stories are also shared visually through images and videos, as young people use Tumblr to share, curate and reblog visual content that affectively resonates with their own complex experiences, both distressing and hopeful. Keeping in mind that the representation of mental ill-health is always partial, visual content allows users to begin to tell stories about their feelings, moods and affect without needing to find the 'right' words. Tumblr affords visual representations to describe mental illness, with evidence suggesting image-based posts to convey more emotional sentiment than those with only text (Bourlai & Herring, 2014). For Cho (2015, p. 43), Tumblr users sharing LGBT and queer-related content 'relied less on text and more on the felt register of suggestive imagery, one of intimation, assemblage, intensity, and aesthetic'. For young people experiencing mental health challenges, Tumblr allows them to share affective stories of self without disclosing too much or being perceived as 'too emotional'.

Conclusion

The 'logic' of risk thinking has become institutionalized across all aspects of the health and welfare sectors (Stanford & Taylor, 2013; Webb, 2006). In turn, a risk focus preoccupies practitioners in these services (including mental health services), such that practitioners – social workers, nurses and psychologists – are referred to as 'risk professions' (Horlick-Jones, 2005; Stanford, 2012). The mentality of risk is generative of powerful identity-defining categories applied to people who access these services: they are denoted as 'at risk' and 'a risk'. In the mental health context, these categorizations reflect systemic concerns about people's vulnerability (at risk of harm from others or self-harm) and dangerousness (a risk to the safety of others). These risk identities can operate as totalizing problem-focused identities limiting a strengths-focused approach, which is a feature of the recovery model.

These problematic risk identities are in operation in mental health settings (Heller, 2015; Sawyer, 2009). For example, research by one of the authors, Sonya, found that 'recovery identities' (Scott & Wilson, 2011; Yanos et al., 2010) of people with severe mental health problems were compromised when mental health practitioners emphasized how risk was a part of their everyday lives (non-crisis periods). In other research

(Lemon *et al.*, 2016; Stanford, 2012), Sonya has illustrated the interpretative dimensions of risks and the need to ensure this more interpretative space is managed carefully in alignment with recovery policy, mental health legislation and professional ethics. We have raised a similar problem in this chapter in the context of social media panics about young people with mental illness. Relying on linear and uncomplicated media effects *thinking* – that when young people see distressing images or read suicidal remarks online that they will immediately self-harm – emphasizes young people's risk identities and de-emphasizes their recovery identities.

Resisting accounts that theorize social media in a technological dystopia acknowledges that young people's digital lives are intertwined with their media practices: the relationship between social media and mental illness cannot be simply understood as unidirectional or linear. We do not argue that social media is a problem-free utopia that shields young people from bullying, 'triggers' or discrimination; however, we do think it is important to recognize that academic and practice research that focuses on social media panic at the expense of productive youth practices can reinforce public and professional anxieties. The exaggeration of young people's vulnerability, located in social media panics that in turn influence mental health practice, ignores the ways young people do safely negotiate distressing content online (Holmes, 2009). Social media does make social problems, such as depression and addiction, visible in a very personal way and this can prove confronting. Suggesting that social media is causative (as claimed by O'Keeffe & Clarke-Pearson, 2011) of these problems makes the medium (social media) the primary focus of scrutiny. This contrasts with critically examining those social, cultural, economic and political factors that give rise to and exacerbate the experience of mental illness for young people and that, in turn, are generative of individual and social risks of living with a mental illness.

It has been our argument that there is a need to critically review how a risk focus distorts the productive ways young people use social media to enhance their recovery, and when they are unwell to communicate their distress to others. This means that mental health and other practitioners need to find ways to explore how younger clients use social media. Focusing on the specific affordances of social media, rather than simply assessing for risk online, may better place mental health practitioners and policymakers to understand young people's experiences of mental illness. In doing so, they may work towards the transformation of media panics to better support young people's recovery and wellbeing.

References

Baym, N. K. (2010) *Personal Connections in the Digital Age* (Cambridge: Polity).

Baym, N. K. (2012) '4 Media Theories: Domestication of Technology', https://4mediatheories.wordpress.com/2012/10/29/domestication-of-technology/, date accessed 8 September 2015.

Bourlai, E. and Herring, S. C. (2014) 'Multimodal Communication on Tumblr: i have so many feels!', *Proceedings of the 2014 ACM Conference on Web Science* (Indiana University, Bloomington), http://dl.acm.org/citation.cfm?id=2615697, date accessed 8 September 2015.

boyd, danah (2014) *It's Complicated: The Social Lives of Networked Teens* (New Haven: Yale University Press).

boyd, danah, Golder, S. and Lotan, G. (2010) 'Tweet, Tweet, Retweet: Conversational Aspects of Retweeting on Twitter', 10 Proceedings of the 2010 43rd Hawaii International Conference on System Sciences (Kauai, Hawaii).

Chang, C. (2014) 'Self Harm Hashtags may be Driving Increase of Cutting in Young People', *News.com.au*, www.news.com.au/lifestyle/health/self-harm-hashtags-may-be-driving-increase-of-cutting-in-young-people/story-fniym874-1227056210456, date accessed 8 September 2015.

Cho, A. (2011) 'Queer Tumblrs, Networked Counterpublics', *Annual Meeting of the International Communication Association* (Boston, MA), http://citation.allacademic.com/meta/p_mla_apa_research_citation/4/8/8/8/4/p488843_index.html, date accessed 8 September 2015.

Cho, A. (2015) 'Queer Reverb: Tumblr, Affect, Time', in K. Hillis, S. Paasonen and M. Petit (eds), *Networked Affect* (Cambridge: MIT Press).

Clark, C., Ghosh, A., Green, E. and Shariff, N. (2008) *Media Portrayal of Young People: Impact and Influences* (London: Young Researcher Network, National Children's Bureau), www.open.ac.uk/researchprojects/childrens-research-centre/sites/www.open.ac.uk.researchprojects.childrens-research-centre/files/files/ecms/web-content/clarke.pdf, date accessed 8 September 2015.

Cooper, H. (2013) 'Alarming Rise of Self Harm by Teenagers', *7.30 Report* (television programme), Australian Broadcasting Corporation, www.abc.net.au/7.30/content/2013/s3845800.htm, date accessed 8 September 2015.

Couldry, N. (2012) *Media, Society, World: Social Theory and Digital Media Practice* (Cambridge: Polity Press).

Facebook.com (2015) 'Company info: Facebook', http://newsroom.fb.com/company-info/, date accessed 9 April 2015.

Ferreday, D. (2010) 'Reading Disorders: Online Suicide and the Death of Hope, *Journal for Cultural Research*, 14(4), 409–26.

Fink, M. and Miller, Q. (2014) 'Trans Media Moments: Tumblr, 2011–2013', *Television & New Media*, 15(1), 1–16.

Frost, L. and Hoggett, P. (2008) 'Human Agency and Social Suffering', *Critical Social Policy*, 28(4), 438–60.

Gergen, K. (1991) *The Saturated Self: Dilemmas of Identity in Contemporary Life* (New York: Basic Books).

Goffman, E. (1959) *The Presentation of Self in Everyday Life* (London: Penguin).

Hampton, K., Goulet, L. S., Rainie, L. and Purcell, K. (2011) 'Social Networking Sites and our Lives', *Pew Research Centre*, www.pewinternet.org/2011/06/16/social-networking-sites-and-our-lives/, date accessed 8 September 2015.

Heller, N. R. (2015) 'Risk, Hope and Recovery: Converging Paradigms for Mental Health Approaches with Suicidal Clients', *British Journal of Social Work*, 45(6), 1788–1803.

Hendry, N. A. (2017) '"Social Media Bodies": Revealing the Entanglement of Sexual Wellbeing, Mental Health and Social Media in Education', in L. Allen and M. L. Rasmussen (eds), *Palgrave Handbook of Sex Education* (New York: Palgrave Macmillan).

Hjorth, L. and Hendry, N. A. (2015) 'A Snapshot of Social Media: Camera Phone Practices', *Social Media + Society*, April–June, 1–3.

Hodkinson, P. and Lincoln, S. (2008) 'Online Journals as Virtual Bedrooms?: Young People, Identity and Personal Space', *Young*, 16(1), 27–46.

Holmes, J. (2009) 'Myths and Missed Opportunities: Young People's Not So Risky Use of Online Communication', *Information, Communication & Society*, 12(8), 1174–96.

Horlick-Jones, T. (2005) 'On "Risk Work": Professional Discourse, Accountability, and Everyday Action', *Health, Risk & Society*, 7(3), 293–307.

Hull, G., Lipford, H. R. and Latulipe, C. (2010) 'Contextual Gaps: Privacy Issues on Facebook', *Ethics and Information Technology*, 13(4), 441–56.

Hutchby, I. (2001) 'Technologies, Texts and Affordances', *Sociology*, 35(2), 441–56.

Jordon, J. W. (2005) 'A Virtual Death and a Real Dilemma: Identity, Trust and Community in Cyberspace', *The Southern Communication Journal*, 70(3), 200–18.

O'Keefe, G. S. and Clarke-Pearson, K. (2011) 'The Impact of Social Media on Children, Adolescents and Families', *Pediatrics*, 127(4), 800–4.

Lasén, A. (2013) 'Digital Inscriptions and Loss of Embarrassment: Some Thoughts about the Technological Mediations of Affectivity', *Intervalla*, 1, 85–100.

Lemon, G., Stanford, S. and Sawyer, A-M. (2016) 'Trust and the Dilemmas of Suicide Risk Assessment in Non-government Mental Health Services', *Australian Social Work*, 69(2), 145–59.

Lincoln, S. and Robards, B. (2014a) '10 Years of Facebook', *New Media & Society*, 16(7), 1047–57.

Lincoln, S. and Robards, B. (2014b) 'Being Strategic and Taking Control: Bedrooms, Social Network Sites and the Narratives of Growing Up', *New Media & Society*, online first: http://nms.sagepub.com/content/early/2014/10/07/1461444814554065.abstract, date accessed 8 September 2015.

Livingstone, S. (2008) 'Taking Risky Opportunities in Youthful Content Creation: Teenagers' Use of Social Networking Sites for Intimacy, Privacy and Self-expression', *New Media & Society*, 10(3), 393–411.

Marwick, A. E. (2008) 'To Catch a Predator? The MySpace Moral Panic', *First Monday*, 13(6), http://firstmonday.org/article/view/2152/1966, date accessed 1 January 2015.

McRae, S. (1997) 'Flesh Made Word: Sex, Text and the Virtual Body', in D. Porter (ed.) *Internet Culture* (New York: Routledge).

McRobbie, A. and Thornton, S. L. (1995) 'Rethinking "Moral Panic" for Multi-Mediated Social Worlds', *The British Journal of Sociology*, 46(4), 559–74.

Montague, A. E., Varcin, K. J. and Parker, A. G. (2014) *Putting Technology into Practice: Evidence and Opinions on Integrating Technology with Youth Health Services* (Melbourne, Australia: Young and Well Cooperative Research Centre).

Parr, H. (2008) *Mental Health and Social Space: Towards Inclusionary Geographies* (Malden: Blackwell Publishing).

Phillipov, M. (2009) '"Just Emotional People"? Emo Culture and the Anxieties of Disclosure', *M/C Journal*, 12(5), http://journal.media-culture.org.au/index.php/mcjournal/article/view/181, date accessed 8 September 2015.

Quan-Haase, A. and Young, A. (2010) 'Uses and Gratifications of Social Media: A Comparison of Facebook and Instant Messaging', *Bulletin of Science, Technology & Society*, 30(5), 350–61.

Renninger, B. J. (2014) '"Where I can be myself … where I can speak my mind": Networked Counterpublics in a Polymedia Environment', *New Media & Society*, 1–17.

Rice, D. (2013) 'Spike in Self-harm Behaviour among Girls and Women', *PM* (radio programme), ABC Radio, 23 August 2013, www.abc.net.au/pm/content/2013/s3832623.htm, date accessed 8 September 2015.

Robards, B. (2010) 'Randoms in my Bedroom: Negotiating Privacy and Unsolicited Contact on Social Network Sites', *PRism*, 7(3), www.prismjournal.org/fileadmin/Social_media/Robards.pdf, date accessed 8 September 2015.

Robards, B. (2014) 'Digital Traces of the Persona through Ten Years of Facebook', *M/C Journal*, 17(3), http://journal.media-culture.org.au/index.php/mcjournal/article/viewArticle/818, date accessed 8 September 2015.

Rushe, D. (2013) 'Facebook and Google Insist they did not know of Prism Surveillance Program', *Guardian Online*, www.theguardian.com/world/2013/jun/07/google-facebook-prism-surveillance-program, date accessed 10 August 2014.

Sawyer, A-M. (2009) 'Mental Health Workers Negotiating Risk on the Frontline', *Australian Social Work*, 62(4), 447–59.

Scott, A. and Wilson, L. (2011) 'Valued Identities and Deficit Identities: Wellness Recovery Action Planning and Self-management in Mental Health', *Nursing Inquiry*, 18(1), 40–9.

Slavtcheva-Petkova, V., Nash, V. J. and Bulger, M. (2015) 'Evidence on the Extent of Harms Experienced by Children as a Result of Online Risks: Implications for Policy and Research', *Information, Communication & Society*, 18(1), 48–62.

Stanford, S. (2012) 'Critically Reflecting on being "at Risk" and "a Risk" in Vulnerable People Policing', in I. Bartkowiak-Théron and N. L. Asquith, *Policing Vulnerability* (Sydney: The Federation Press), 20–32.

Stanford, S. N. and Taylor, S. (2013) 'Welfare Dependence or Enforced Deprivation? A Critical Examination of White Neoliberal Welfare and Risk', *Australian Social Work*, 66(4), 476–94.

Tumblr (2014) *Tumblr Community Guidelines*, www.tumblr.com/policy/en/community, date accessed 28 October 2014.

Tumblr (2015a) *Tumblr About*, www.tumblr.com/about, date accessed 28 October 2014.

Tumblr (2015b) *Blog Management*, www.tumblr.com/docs/en/blog_management, date accessed 28 October 2014.

Turkle, S. (1995) *Life on the Screen: Identity in the Age of the Internet* (New York: Touchstone).

Turkle, S. (1996) 'Who Am We?', *Wired*, January, 149–99.

Turkle, S. (2011) *Alone Together: Why we Expect more from Technology and Less from Each Other* (New York: Basic Books).

Webb, S. A. (2006) *Social Work in a Risk Society* (Houndsmills and Basingstoke: ounPalgrave Macmillan).

Weinberger, D. (2002) *Small Pieces Loosely Joined* (New York: Basic Books).

Wellman, B. (2004) 'The Glocal Village: Internet and Community', *idea&s*, 1(1), 26–9.

Yanos, P. T., Roe, D. and Lysaker, P. H. (2010) 'The Impact of Illness Identity on Recovery from Severe Mental Illness', *American Journal of Psychiatric Rehabilitation*, 13(2), 73–93.

11

MENTAL HEALTH RISK, POLITICAL CONFLICT AND ASYLUM: A HUMAN RIGHTS AND SOCIAL JUSTICE ISSUE

Shepard Masocha and Kim Robinson

Introduction

This chapter examines the dominant discourses concerning asylum seekers and refugees and the intersection of these with human rights in social work practice. The term discourse is used in a 'more open sense to uncover all forms of spoken interaction, formal and informal, and written texts of all kinds' (Potter & Wetherell, 1987, p. 7) that are used to talk about asylum seekers. The chapter problematizes the notion of risk and in particular how asylum seekers and refugees are framed in a binary position as a risk *to* the host society or at risk *of* poor mental health. It also explores the concept of 'othering' in relation to the experience of discrimination faced by asylum seekers and the complex relationship between poor mental health outcomes and the experience of migration. There are wider implications of these processes in terms of their influence on other practice domains, where 'othering' and racism are thrown into even sharper relief. The racist demand to 'go back where you came from' is directed at third and fourth generation citizens as much as the newly arrived. Our discussion provides insights into how contemporary social work practice can challenge and disrupt the dominant risk paradigm in this field.

Psychological stress, mental health difficulties and asylum seekers' migration

Asylum seekers are a particularly vulnerable social group within the Western world. Porter and Haslam's (2005) meta-analysis of studies that investigate the mental health of asylum seekers, displaced persons and refugees found a high prevalence of mental illness in this group of migrants. It also concluded that there was a strong correlation between the socio-political context of the refugee/asylum-seeking experience and the prevalence of mental health difficulties in this group. Evidence also strongly indicates that within the developed Western world the levels of mental illness amongst asylum seekers are significantly higher than those usually found in their respective host nations (Robjant et al., 2009). Research in the UK (Chantler, 2011; Robjant et al., 2009; Summerfield, 2000; Tribe, 2002; Watters, 2001;), Australia (Silove et al., 1999; Silove et al., 2007a), and the US (Human Rights Watch, 2010; Welch & Schuster, 2005) demonstrate the extent to which asylum seekers experience significant threats to their psychological and mental wellbeing.

Early studies (Carpenter & Brockington, 1980; Hemsi, 1967) have pointed out the vulnerabilities of immigrants to mental illness. With reference to migrant Norwegians in the US, for example, Odegaard (1932) suggested that there was a strong link between migration and mental illness. However, this supposed link should not be accepted uncritically, particularly as it has informed many misconceptions about mental health difficulties that are experienced by immigrants including asylum seekers. In the UK, for a considerable time, the dominant view was that immigrants' countries of origin had high incidences of mental illness attributable to innate biological vulnerability (Bhugra & Bhui, 2001). It was suggested that particular populations had a biological predisposition to mental illness. This argument has been refuted by findings from studies by Jablensky et al. (1992), as well as studies from Jamaica (Hickling & Rodgers-Johnson, 1995), Trinidad (Bhugra et al., 1996), and Barbados (Mahy et al., 1999). Such studies found that the incidence of mental illness in these countries was not as high as previously suggested and inferred from the populations who had migrated. We argue in this chapter that discourses about the mental health of asylum seekers need to be critically examined. It is important that mental health problems are not 'indigenized': they must be located in sociocultural, political and legal contexts, which we now examine.

The experience of trauma and the mental health of asylum seekers

Longitudinal studies involving the follow up of refugees who experience severe trauma have demonstrated that mental health symptoms are long lasting, even after many years in a new country (Carlsson et al., 2006; Silove et al., 2007b). The literature identifies three key phases: first, increasing political repression and violence in their home country; second, major traumatic experience, frequently involving torture and loss; and third, the phase of exile and adapting to a new cultural environment (Watters, 2001). A comprehensive understanding of the mental health difficulties experienced by immigrants such as asylum seekers should not be only limited to biological causation. Research highlights that the experience of having to leave one's home and family, coupled with a difficult journey to a new country, is in itself a stressful experience (Ager, 1999; Castles & Loughna, 2004; Grove & Zwi, 2006). Refugees and asylum seekers may also have experienced torture and trauma: some studies suggest a wide range of estimates between 20 per cent of male migrants (Gupta et al., 2009) to 69 per cent of refugee populations depending on the ethnicity and gender of the population (Jaranson et al., 2004). The effects of war and torture are far-reaching and vary according to each person's psychological make-up and protective factors (Fernando, 2010). Therefore, there are several exogenous factors that specifically impact on the mental health of asylum seekers. These factors include the conditions of conflict and political upheaval in their countries of origin; the perilous journey to the host countries; and the hostile climate in host countries characterized by racism, immigration detention, significant difficulties in dealing with immigration authorities, economic instability and an uncertain future. We now focus on the specific impact of detention on asylum seekers' mental health.

Detention and the mental health of asylum seekers

Western governments are imposing tight legislation and interpretation of Human Rights Conventions to restrict asylum applications. Some of the measures to restrict access have been labelled 'state crime' and have positioned the asylum seekers as 'deviant' on the basis of challenges to the Western systems seeking to exclude them (Grewcock, 2010). The policies of deterrence have resulted in restrictions on asylum seekers seeking to gain access to Australia, the UK and the US to claim asylum including stringent border controls. In Australia there is the widespread use of mandatory detention and blanket interdiction or removal. These strategies constitute a hostile approach by these states towards asylum leading to the alienation, criminalization and abuse of asylum seekers (Dauvergne, 2008; Grewcock, 2010). During the time when they are being processed, asylum seekers' lives are characterized by low income, poor housing, limited access to health care and social isolation: a situation where 'illness exacerbates marginalisation and marginalisation exacerbates illness, creating a downward cycle' (Ingleby, 2005, p. 101). It is this complex set of circumstances that can contribute to a range of physical and mental health issues.

There is a strong body of international research that highlights the psychological hardship immigration detention causes to asylum seekers, and provides evidence of an increase in depression and PTSD (post-traumatic stress disorder) (Robjant et al., 2009; Steel, 2006). Research in Australia investigating the psychological effects of detention used mixed methods and interviewed detainees on average three to four years after release from detention. Results show enduring harm to asylum seekers who were subject to prolonged detention, and demonstrate the erosion of 'asylum seekers' sense of self, to their relationships, and their core values' (Coffey et al., 2010, p. 2078). In addition, research done with refugees on temporary protection visas in Australia has provided insight into the psychological damage caused by uncertainty and the limited access to resources such as housing, education and employment (Moorehead, 2005; Steel, 2006). Similar research in the UK also found that this 'dark period of uncertainty' (Masocha & Simpson, 2011a) impacts negatively on asylum seekers' mental health. Recent research in the US highlights an alarming number of people in detention with severe mental health issues, identified as 'disabilities', who are unable to access appropriate care and legal representation (Human Rights Watch, 2010).

A survey by the National Institute for Mental Health in England (2006) found that asylum seekers generally felt that their mental health had deteriorated since arriving in the UK. Without exception, those interviewed in the survey felt that the cloud of uncertainty regarding their future and the difficulties they experienced daily placed an unbearable psychological burden on them (Dumper et al., 2006). Research by Fazel et al. (2012) concurs with these findings and in addition emphasizes the importance of longitudinal investigation of individual, community and societal contexts. Mental distress in varying degrees is therefore a common experience and manifestation amongst asylum seekers. The appropriateness of medicalizing asylum seekers' experiences has also been questioned, which is the focus of the next section.

Cultural and political concerns about the use of mental illness diagnosis

Researchers have emphasized that not all asylum seekers and refugees are traumatized and that appropriate tools for assessment and care are needed to respond to individual needs. Research has increasingly identified that arrival in the host country and the subsequent settlement period have a major impact on the mental health and wellbeing of refugees and asylum seekers (Watters, 2001). Studies have identified the lack of social support, racism, lower proficiency in the language of the host country and unemployment with higher levels of poor mental health (Carlsson et al., 2006). Importantly, practitioners have emphasized understanding the meaning of distress in a cultural context (Fernando, 2010), along with the need to recognize the way in which distress manifests as an appropriate reaction to grief, despair and loss (Summerfield, 2008). Kleinman (1980) raised concerns about the appropriateness of applying diagnostic categorizations such as PTSD in cultural settings where symptoms may be understood and interpreted very differently from the Western consulting room. Increasingly academics have argued that the field has become dominated with an emphasis on PTSD, which was evidenced by the dramatic increase in the literature focusing on trauma (Ager, 1999).

Ingleby (2005, p.9), in his analysis of the development of services, notes it is 'trauma researchers who become interested in refugees, rather than refugee researchers becoming interested in trauma', suggesting research in this area has been 'theory-driven' in the psychological and psychiatric literature rather than 'problem-driven' by a concern for the person's wellbeing. This has resulted in trauma being conflated to describe both the causation and the disturbance of poor mental health, and a series of unexplained variations of symptoms of PTSD. Many researchers and practitioners working with refugees are critical of the individual mental health model and argue that it pathologizes refugees with damaging effects (Harrel-Bond, 1999; Summerfield, 1999). There is also criticism of the acceptance of the *Diagnostic and Statistical Manual of Mental Disorders* (DSM) definitions in relation to their cultural appropriateness and relevance (Bracken et al., 1995). Researchers and social workers are concerned about applying psychotherapeutic language to describe behaviour and experiences that may be understood as an appropriate and adaptive response to violence and oppression and human rights violations (Ife, 2012). For example, Summerfield notes (1999, p. 132):

> For the vast majority of survivors 'traumatisation' is a pseudo-condition, a reframing of the ordinary distress and suffering engendered by war as a technical problem to which technical solutions (like 'counselling') are supposedly applicable.

Researchers have also identified how trauma has increasingly become the mechanism for recognition of human rights abuses, and that biolegitimacy (the physical manifestation of trauma) forms part of the social and political context of health (Fassin & d'Halluin, 2005). This can be linked to what Foucault (1991) describes as governmentality being the convergence of power and knowledge, with both positive and negative connotations. He used the term 'bio-power' (power over life and the body) to describe the way the body is the place where social practices are located and embodied (Foucault, 1998). Bio-power refers to the mechanisms that are utilized to manage the population and to discipline individuals. The body is seen as the place of social practices of power. Validating social needs based on a medical diagnosis of psychiatric disorder has become a key mechanism for refugees to obtain support and recognition. This is not to suggest that those suffering from distress ought not to be supported medically: needs must be seen in a broader social and human rights context.

If trauma and distress are not addressed, they may manifest themselves in a variety of ways, as Adamson (2005, pp. 67–8) notes:

> What begins as a unique individual or community response to experience may be laid down over time as a series of behavioural and social responses, created by traumatic experience but now masked by other descriptive labels of violence, addiction, loss of values and beliefs, and depression etc.

Some researchers and practitioners suggest cultural bereavement is a more appropriate term to describe the loss associated with the experience of survival, and the feelings of despair and isolation that are so present in many refugee populations. This acknowledges the complex relationship between the person and their environment and community, and enables a wider exploration of the issues that may contribute to their recovery.

Our review of the mental health of asylum seekers raises the need to consider how various contexts impact how mental illness is understood. This is also the case in terms of how asylum seekers are positioned in discourses about their 'risk status'.

Being 'at risk' as an asylum seeker

The various risk factors that impinge on asylum seekers' mental wellbeing have a complex relationship with one another and are interlinked. Risk factors can interact to exacerbate mental health problems, and psychological adaptation will be affected by the extent to which asylum seekers have experienced and coped with previous risk factors (Masocha & Simpson, 2011a). The risk factors inherent in migration, such as sexual abuse, may trigger mental health problems associated with the original human rights abuse (for example rape and torture), thereby minimizing capacity to cope. Trying to deal with these experiences, along with the anxieties of the immigration system and associated uncertainty about the likelihood of future protection, adds increasing layers of psychological pressure. The legacy of traumatic experiences can persist long after the initial causes. More significant is the fact that some risk factors, such as separation from home and family, may never disappear. Dealing with immediate risk factors, such as access to health, housing and employment, may be essential before dealing with problems resulting from earlier traumas. Research by Robinson (2013) has highlighted the impact of the demands facing frontline workers and advocates in securing these rights with and for service users.

Significantly, the vulnerability of asylum seekers in terms of their exposure to the risk factors identified above, which would clearly cast them as *at* risk, is not readily acknowledged and/or responded to within the developed Western world. This is exemplified by the ways Western countries respond to people that seek sanctuary from political conflict and persecution. In spite of the evident vulnerability of asylum seekers to mental health difficulties in the US, UK and Australia, there is not a general rejection of the ways asylum seekers are treated in government policy. Asylum seekers are not seen in dominant discourses as deserving sympathy, rather they are treated with suspicion and hostility. With reference to the UK, Lynn and Lea (2003, p. 433) note the dominant view is that 'many asylum-seekers are not fleeing persecution from oppressive and hostile conditions in their home country'. It is accepted as 'common sense' that asylum seekers are in fact economic migrants taking advantage of the asylum route to circumvent border controls. In the post 9/11 era in the US, the dominant discourses cast asylum seekers as a risk, often linking them to the threats of terrorism (Human Rights Watch, 2002; Welch & Schuster, 2005). In this context, asylum seekers are seen as posing a credible risk to nation states rather than them being a vulnerable social group. That is, their *'a* risk' status, as opposed to their *'at* risk' status, is emphasized. The risks to asylum seekers' mental wellbeing are not foregrounded in the dominant discourses that oppose asylum seeking. As such the vulnerabilities of asylum seekers are far from what might be regarded as common-sense understandings. In the next section of the chapter we use risk theory to highlight the social and political processes that are used to influence dominant discourses about the asylum seekers as a risk.

How asylum seekers are constructed as 'a risk'

Risk, as a construct, is a politically contested notion. Who or what gets 'attached' to ideas about risk reflects political contexts. Risk theory can help, as a first step, to disrupt taken-for-granted negative constructions of asylum seekers that predominantly cast them as a credible risk to host nations. This is important as asylum seekers are seen as an embodiment of risk in dominant anti-asylum-seeking discourses across the developed Western world. We present a poststructural perspective of risk in order to explain how risk discourses affect understanding about asylum seekers.

Risk theory

Discourses are constitutive because they contribute to the production, transformation and reproduction of what is known about people, events and the world. Hence discourses constitute our understanding about asylum seekers. What and who is categorized as *risky* or *at risk* is mediated and accomplished through the rhetorical practices and substance of discourses. Given that ideas about risk are socially constructed, ideas about what constitutes risk reflects power relations (Foucault, 1972). Unlike the Marxist view of power as sovereign and the preserve of a powerful minority, Foucault treats power as present in all forms of social interaction and therefore power is everywhere (Minson, 1980). Power does not operate through force or consent, instead discourses both reflect the operations of power and they shape how power is exercised. Thus dominant discourses of risk are perceived as playing a significant role in terms of influencing people's belief systems and ideas: they normalize belief systems and the ways in which ideas about individuals are constituted. Dominant discourses play a key role in 'shaping grids and hierarchies for institutional categorization and treatment of people who are the subject of the discourses' (Luke, 1995, p. 8). Influence is exercised through established systems and methods of surveillance, which include internalized or inner surveillance of conduct.

Stanford (2012, p. 21) argues that risk needs to be understood as socially constructed given that 'what or who is defined as "a risk" or "at risk" bears the markings of a complex interplay of competing claims, interests, politics, ideologies, technologies, emotions, and moralities'. Prevailing discourses can be viewed as part of a coherent system of meanings that are in competition with each other, with discursive ascendancy, or predominant view, manifesting itself in the corridors of political power (Tuffin, 2005). Thus contemporary notions of risk are products of different competing discourses in which the influential or dominant discourses play a decisive role in shaping the prevailing notions of risk. The discursive acts that prevail will succeed in transforming risk as it is known. As such, risk is a historically contingent construct that is in a state of flux as it is dependent on the prevailing discourses. Webb (2006), Beck (2003) and Kemshall (2002) illustrate how notions and meanings of risk have changed over time. The ways in which risk is conceptualized and understood depends on the prevailing social relationships, specific cultural contexts, knowledge, and discursive practices.

Furthermore, it is important to pay attention to the ideological nature of risk. Ideology can be understood as shared beliefs or social representations that are used to accomplish everyday social practices. Briskman (2013) identifies 'wicked policies' in the risk society as requiring attention of critical social workers in order not to collude with controlling powerful practices. Foucault (1972) views ideology as forms of power/knowledge justifying the actions of *all* groups. These social beliefs are organized into systems, which are deployed, by social classes and other groups, in order to make sense of, figure out and render intelligible the way society works.

Framing asylum seekers as a risk

In spite of being identified and accepted as a particularly vulnerable group that are at high risk of experiencing mental health and psychological difficulties, asylum seekers are instead constructed as *a risk* to their respective host nations. Research studies illustrate how media accounts and politicians contribute to parliamentary debates that are replete with negative representations of asylum seekers where the spectre of asylum seekers as dangerous is foregrounded. For instance, asylum seekers are portrayed in dominant anti-asylum seeking discourses as: taking advantage and abusing the generosity of host nations (Every & Augoustinos, 2008); and posing a significant threat to the host nations' values and cultures (Capdevila & Callaghan, 2008) as they could potentially dilute (and contaminate) Western values. Asylum seekers are also portrayed as overwhelming in their numbers and presenting significant risk of overrunning the entire country (Buchanan, 2001). They are seen to pose a significant threat to an already overburdened welfare system: they are a diseased social group that poses a significant threat to the social body of the host nation and they are a threat to national security (Klocker & Dunn, 2003; Masocha & Simpson, 2011b; Pickering, 2001; Welch & Schuster, 2005).

The formulation of asylum seekers as *a risk* rather than *at risk* needs to be understood in the context of governmentality and neoliberalism. The notion of governmentality is associated with the work of Foucault (1991), which focuses on the practices of liberal governments. The eighteenth century saw the emergence of a new way of governing populations where governments increasingly deployed strategies that enabled them 'to govern at a distance' (Rose, 1996, p. 42). The governmentality risk thesis (Garland, 2003; O'Malley, 2008; Rose, 2000) focuses on how advanced liberal governments conceptualize, articulate and manage risk.

Researchers have noted how asylum seekers are described as a dangerous social group that poses a credible threat to the security of nations through making links to extremism and terrorism (for a detailed analysis of these negative representations see: Every & Augoustinos, 2008; Lynn & Lea, 2003; Masocha & Simpson, 2011b; Pickering, 2001). These negative representations of asylum seekers are drawn on to rationalize the deployment of specific governmental technologies and practices of securitization. Casting asylum seekers as a risk places them outside the moral order, which provides justification for their segregation, marginalization, exclusion and banishment. A core aspect of liberalism is the affirmation of people's freedom, but one that is a 'well-regulated and "responsibilized" liberty' (Barry et al., 1996, p. 8). However, contradictory practices exist in liberal regimes. According to Christie and Sidhu (2006, p. 451) 'what distinguishes liberal from despotic regimes is the forms of rationality justifying illiberal action'.

Liberal governments have long histories of subjecting sections of their society to 'all sorts of disciplinary, biopolitical and even sovereign interventions' (Dean, 1999, p. 134). As Dean (2002, p. 38) argues, 'governing liberally does not entail governing *through* freedoms or even governing in a manner that respects liberty' (emphasis in the original). As such, the kinds of treatment that asylum seekers receive in the advanced liberal countries are not necessarily incompatible with neoliberal governmentality. In fact, such treatments are important practices for managing those who are deemed as falling outside the realm of mainstream society and against whom liberal governmentality strategies of self-responsibility, accountability, and prudentialism are difficult to apply. The constitution of asylum seekers as a risk and the institution of restrictive legislative regimes that result in asylum seekers' human rights being undermined are, as Rose (2000, p. 330) argues, part of the strategies instituted 'to manage these anti-citizens' and the marginal spaces they occupy 'through measures which seek to neutralize the dangers they pose'.

The constitution of asylum seekers as a risk has significant implications for the ways in which asylum seekers as a social group are understood and subsequently treated. For instance, it justifies government policy responses to the perceived threat. The US, Australia and the UK governments have responded to the arrival of asylum seekers and refugees by focusing on their perceived threat to: the nation state, cultural identity, the labour market, welfare, and security. Zetter et al. (2005, pp. 9–10) argue that the governmental response in the UK, and we would argue similarly in Australia, has shifted decisively towards deterrence and 'restrictionism, prompted by media generated panic about abuse of the asylum system and political manipulation of the asylum issue'.

In the case of the US, the government's response to the perceived risks to national security posed by asylum seekers was the institution of the Operation Liberty Shield (2003) and the Blanket Detention Order (2003), which resulted in widespread detention of asylum seekers (Welch & Schuster, 2005).

Research illustrates how in both Australia and the UK successive governments have responded to asylum seeker risks through restricting and excluding them from mainstream welfare provisions (Klocker & Dunn, 2003; Neumann, 2004; Sales, 2007). A key theme in this research is the manner in which asylum seekers have been demonized and arbitrarily detained: this is largely a response to the perceived risks associated with the claimants. The systems in Australia differ significantly from Europe. For example, here refugees have been processed and approved prior to arrival 'offshore', and consequently they enter into a clearly systemized process under the 'Australian Humanitarian Assistance Program'. Asylum seekers have not engaged with that process for various reasons, however, and they apply for asylum 'onshore'. This effectively has cast them as the 'bad refugees' and 'queue jumpers' who take the place of the 'good refugees' who patiently wait in refugee camps. In both the UK and Australia, asylum seekers are demonized for: paying for their journey (being seen as rich and/or corrupt); and being 'forum shoppers' who select the most affluent countries. Most recently, they are portrayed as 'terrorists' and a danger to society (Crawley, 2010; Gale, 2004). The Liberal government in Australia, and indeed the populist press, often refer to asylum seekers as 'illegals', which is technically an incorrect term because Australia has ratified the 1951 Convention which specifically recognizes that refugees are not obliged to have documents in order to claim asylum (Moorehead, 2005, p. 104).

Problematizing the notion of asylum seekers as a risk

As noted above, notions about who and what are risks are socially constructed and these ideas are reinforced in risk discourses. As such, notions of risk relating to asylum seekers are socio-political products and reflect prevailing asylum seeker risk discourses. The presentation of asylum seekers as *a risk* is part of a discourse that constructs and positions asylum seekers as the Other. As a social group, asylum seekers exist on the borders/margins of society and are generally perceived as highly risky by those that occupy the centre of mainstream society (Douglas, 1966). As a consequence of their liminality, asylum seekers are constructed and treated as the Other, necessitating the need for containment and control. As this chapter illustrates, asylum seekers are seen as 'the repository for fears not simply about risk but about the breakdown of social order and the need to maintain social boundaries and divisions' (Tulloch & Lupton, 2003, p. 7). The process of Othering (Riggins, 1997) involves the negative representation of asylum seekers. The representation of asylum seekers as the Other is achieved through the attribution of negative characteristics, in particular the categorization of asylum seekers as a subversive, dangerous and illegitimate social group that poses a credible risk to the host nations. Asylum seekers are depicted negatively in anti-asylum seeking discourses as 'bogus', economic migrants, a burden on the public purse, taking advantage of British/Australian generosity, a threat to the social body, and deviant (Masocha & Simpson, 2011b). Various studies (Baker *et al.*, 2008; Gabrielatos & Baker, 2008; Goodman, 2007; Jones, 2000; Lynn & Lea, 2003; van Dijk, 1997) have analysed how asylum seekers are constructed as the Other in the dominant anti-asylum seeking discourses. These studies explore the various linguistic strategies that are deployed to negatively portray asylum seekers while at the same time performing the important ideological function of denying, protecting and perpetuating racism and discriminatory practices.

In the mental health context, the effect of such negative formulations is that asylum seekers' individual vulnerabilities are ignored and their mental health needs are not adequately nor sensitively responded to. Asylum seekers' mental health needs are rendered problematic in risk discourses that emphasize their vulnerability: their vulnerability to mental illness reinforces the risks they pose to the host society. Asylum seekers are often depicted as mentally unstable, lacking the ability to integrate in mainstream society, and being prone to crime and social disorder. Therefore, in this context, the use of vulnerability as a category for constructing asylum seekers accomplishes important *moral* work (Edwards, 1991). The category is used to great effect in stripping asylum seekers of their humanity, individuality, strengths and weaknesses by building a picture of a homogeneous group that poses a credible threat to the host nations. This harsh and restrictive legislative provisions enacted by Western governments is therefore presented as a reasonable response to these identified threats.

Adopting a human rights perspective that emphasizes social work's commitment to social justice has potential to challenge and deconstruct these negative constructs (Robinson, 2013). A starting point towards achieving this is to engage in counter discourses that foreground the numerous threats to asylum seekers' psychological and mental wellbeing. By doing this the '*at risk*' identities of asylum seekers can be emphasized, as opposed to their '*a risk*' identities, which in turn can enable social workers and other mental health practitioners to, in Stanford's (2010) terms, 'speak back to fear'.

Moving beyond the risk paradigm

Clearly, there is a need to move beyond essentialized constructs of risk towards understanding risk as a fluid concept that is ideologically patterned as ideas about risk reflect the ways in which society responds to perceived threats at a given time. According to Cameron (2001, p. 124), ideologies serve to naturalize and legitimate 'particular social arrangements which serve particular interests, so that in time they may seem like the only possible and rational arrangements.'

Understanding that risk is ideologically patterned can help disrupt the taken-for-granted notions of asylum seekers as 'a risk'. Instead, the prevailing negative constructs of asylum seekers can be understood as reflecting the different vested interests of various stakeholders participating in those discursive acts that construct this social group as risky. Thus ideas about risk 'serve to advance the interests of some whilst concomitantly interfering, undermining or disadvantaging the interests of others' (Stanford, 2012, pp. 20–1). The risk that asylum seekers pose needs to be understood as a highly contextual 'manufactured' concept (Adam & Van Loon, 2000). By investigating the discursive practices that are used to define the riskiness of asylum seekers it is possible to identify the underpinning ideologies of the negative ways in which asylum seekers are constructed, and how the construction of asylum seekers as posing a credible risk to host nations is rendered acceptable and understandable. Significantly, this view foregrounds the instability of meanings of risk. This provides opportunities to consider alternative (multiple) viewpoints and identities of asylum seekers that are otherwise silenced by the dominant majority who project them as a risk.

A paradigmatic shift in the conceptualization of risk is likely to have fundamental impacts on responses to vulnerable service user groups such as asylum seekers. A shift from the spectre of asylum seekers towards constructs of asylum seekers as '*at risk*' aligns social work and other mental health professions towards a social justice agenda. It brings into focus the various significant current threats to asylum seekers' psychological and mental wellbeing. It will also result in a shift in practice from a focus on control and surveillance towards an interest in upholding the human rights of asylum seekers to meet their mental health needs. A social justice agenda has to be at the centre of any psychosocial work with this service user group.

We have argued that risk is a socially constructed concept as is the very notion of an asylum seeker. As part of their advocacy role, social work and other mental health professions need to become more active and vocal in public and policy debates and to articulate the multiple challenges that asylum seekers face in host countries. Through participating in such discursive acts that construct hegemonic notions of risk, mental health practitioners can occupy specific subject positions that would enable them to influence the ways in which risk is conceptualized and operationalized in practice. As Stanford (2012, p. 21) notes, 'it means that professions can have an impact on how ideas about risk, and in turn vulnerability, are recognized and implemented in practice'. Doing this will result in a politically transformative practice, but this requires mental health professionals to find their voice and speak for this socially marginalized group.

Conclusion

Social work and other mental health professions have to adapt to the ever-changing nature of discourses of exclusion, which in this case are articulated through taken-for-granted notions of risk and reasoned arguments about the dangers that asylum seekers pose to host nations. The importance of practitioners being both critically reflective and reflexive must be understood. Mental health practice, such as social work practice, is a socially constructed activity (Garrett, 2003; Parton & O'Byrne, 2000) and as such is both exposed to and shaped by dominant discourses. There is a key role for mental health practitioners to challenge these discourses, and to find a language of support and care within a human rights framework. This is challenging work particularly in a sector that is deeply embedded in a moral conundrum of care and control. An uncritical acceptance and application of notions of risks relating to the negative ways in which asylum seekers are constructed in dominant anti-asylum-seeking discourses may have the unintended consequences of oppressing the very people mental health professions endeavour to empower.

References

Adam, B. and Van Loon, J. (2000) 'Introduction: Repositioning Risk: The Challenge for Social Theory', in B. Adams and J. Van Loon (eds) *The Risk Society and Beyond: Critical Issues for Social Theory* (London: Sage),1–13.

Adamson, C. (2005) 'Complexity and Context: An Ecological Understanding of Trauma Practice', in M. Nash, R. Munford and K. O'Donoghue (eds) *Social Work Theories in Action* (London: Jessica Kingsley), 64–80.

Ager, A. (1999). (ed.) *Refugees: Perspectives on the Experience of Forced Migration* (London: Continuum).

Baker, P., Gabrielatos, C., Khosravinik, M., Krzyzanowski, M., McEnery, T. and Wodak, R. (2008) 'A Useful Methodological Synergy? Combining Critical

Discourse Analysis and Corpus Linguistics to Examine Discourses of Refugees
and Asylum Seekers in the UK Press', *Discourse & Society*, 19, 273–306.

Barry, A., Osborne, T. and Rose, N. (1996) 'Introduction', in A. Barry, T. Osborne
and N. Rose (eds), *Foucault and Political Reason: Liberalism, Neo-liberalism and
Rationalities of Government*. (London: Taylor & Francis Group), 1–19.

Beck, U. (2003) *World Risk Society* (Cambridge: Polity Press).

Bhugra, D. & Bhui, K. (2001) 'African-Caribbeans and Schizophrenia:
Contributing Factors', *Advances in Psychiatric Treatment*, 7, 283–91.

Bhugra, D., Hilwig, M., Hossein, B., Marceau, H., Neehall, J., Leff, J., Mallett, R. and
Der, G. (1996) 'First-contact Incidence Rates of Schizophrenia in Trinidad and
One-year Follow-up', *The British Journal of Psychiatry*, 169, 587–92.

Bracken, P., Giller, J. E. and Summerfield, D. (1995) 'Psychological Responses to
War and Atrocity: The Limitations of Current Concepts', *Social Science and
Medicine*, 40, 1073–82.

Briskman, L. (2013) 'Courageous Ethnographers or Agent of the State: Challenges
for Social Work', *Critical and Radical Social Work: An International Journal*, 1,
51–66.

Buchanan, S. (2001) *What's the Story? Sangatte: A Case of Media Coverage of
Asylum and Refugee Issues*, London, Article 19.

Cameron, D. (2001) *Working with Spoken Discourse* (London: Sage).

Capdevila, R. and Callaghan, J. E. M. (2008) '"It's not Racist. It's Common Sense".
A Critical Analysis of Political Discourse around Asylum and Immigration in
the UK', *Journal of Community & Applied Social Psychology*, 18, 1–16.

Carlsson, J. M., Olsen, D. R., Mortensen, E. L. and Kastrup, M. (2006) 'Mental
Health and Health-Related Quality of Life: A 10-Year Follow-Up of Tortured
Refugees', *The Journal of Nervous and Mental Disease*, 194, 725–31. DOI:
10.1097/01.nmd.0000243079.52138.b7, date accessed 15 September 2015.

Carpenter, L. and Brockington, I. F. (1980) 'A Study of Mental Illness in Asians,
West Indians and Africans Living in Manchester', *The British Journal of
Psychiatry*, 137, 201–5.

Castles, S. and Loughna, S. (2004) 'Globalization, Migration and Asylum', in
V. George and R. Page (eds) *Global Social Problems and Global Social Policy*
(Cambridge: Polity), 177–200.

Chantler, K. (2011) 'Gender, Asylum Seekers and Mental Distress: Challenges for
Mental Health Social Work', *British Journal of Social Work*, 42, 318–34.

Christie, P. and Sidhu, R. (2006) 'Governmentality and "Fearless Speech":
Framing the Education of Asylum Seeker and Refugee Children in Australia',
Oxford Review of Education, 32, 449–65.

Coffey, G. J., Kaplan, I., Sampson, R. C. and Tucci, M. M. (2010) 'The Meaning and
Mental Health Consequences of Long-term Immigration Detention for People
Seeking Asylum', *Social Science and Medicine. [Online]* 70(12), 2070–2079,
www.ncbi.nlm.nih.gov/pubmed/20378223, date accessed 8 June 2014.

Crawley, H. (2010) *Chance or Choice? Understanding why Asylum Seekers Come to
the UK* (London: Refugee Council).

Dauvergne, C. (2008) *Making People Illegal. What Globalization Means for Migration
and Law* (New York: Cambridge University Press).

Dean, M. (1999) *Governmentality: Power and Rule in Modern Society* (London: Sage).

Dean, M. (2002) 'Liberal Government and Authoritarianism', *Economy and Society,* 31, 37–61.

Douglas, M. (1966) *Purity and Danger: Analysis of Concepts of Pollution and Taboo,* (London: Routledge & Kegan Paul).

Dumper, H., Malfait, R. and Scott-Flynn, N. (2006) *Mental Heath, Destitution and Asylum Seekers – A Study of Destitute Asylum Seekers in the Dispersal Areas of the South East of England* (London: National Institute of Mental Health in England).

Edwards, D. (1991) 'Categories Are for Talking: On the Cognitive and Discursive Bases of Categorization', *Theory & Psychology,* 1, 515–542.

Every, D. and Augoustinos, M. (2008) 'Constructions of Australia in Pro- and Anti-Asylum Seeker Political Discourse', *Nations and Nationalism,* 14, 562–580.

Fassin, D. and d'Halluin, E. (2005) 'The Truth from the Body: Medical Certificates as Ultimate Evidence for Asylum Seekers', *American Anthropologist,* 107, 597–608.

Fazel, M., Reed, R. V., Panter-Brick, C. and Stein, A. (2012) 'Mental Health of Displaced and Refugee Children Resettled in High-income Countries: Risk and Protective Factors', *The Lancet,* 379, 266–82.

Fernando, S. (2010) *Mental Health, Race and Culture* (London: Palgrave Macmillan).

Foucault, M. (1972) *The Archaeology of Knowledge* (London: Tavistock Publications).

Foucault, M. (1991) 'On Governmentality', in G. Burchell, C. Gordon and P. Miller (eds) *The Foucault Effect: Studies in Governmentality* (Brighton: Harvester Wheatsheaf), 87–105.

Foucault, M. (1998) *The Will to Knowledge: The History of Sexuality Volume 1,* (London: Penguin Books).

Gabrielatos, C. and Baker, P. (2008) 'Fleeing, Sneaking, Flooding: A Corpus Analysis of Discursive Constructions of Refugees and Asylum Seekers in the UK Press, 1996–2005', *Journal of English Linguistics,* 36, 5–38.

Gale, P. (2004) 'The Refugee Crisis and Fear: Populist Politics and Media Discourse', *Journal of Sociology,* 40, 321–40.

Garland, D. (2003) 'The Rise of Risk', in R. V. Ericson and A. Doyle (eds) *Risk and Morality* (Toronto: University of Toronto Press), 48–87.

Garrett, P. M. (2003) *Remaking Social Work with Children and Families: A Critical Discussion on the 'Modernisation' of Social Care* (London, New York: Routledge).

Goodman, S. (2007) 'Constructing Asylum Seeking Families', *Critical Approaches to Discourse Analysis Across Disciplines,* 1, 36–50.

Grewcock, M. (2010) *Border Crimes. Australia's War on Illicit Migrants* (Annandale: Federation Press).

Grove, N. J. and Zwi, A. B. (2006) 'Our Health and Theirs: Forced Migration, Othering and Public Health', *Social Science and Medicine,* 62, 1931–1942.

Gupta, J., Acevedo-Garcia, D., Hemenway, D., Decker, M. R., Raj, A. and Silverman, J. G. (2009) 'Premigration Exposure to Political Violence and Perpetration of Intimate Partner Violence Among Immigrant Men in Boston', *American Journal of Public Health,* 99, 462–9.

Harrel-Bond, B. (1999) 'The Experience of Refugees as Recipients of Aid', in Ager, A. (ed.) *Refugees. Perspectives on the Experience of Forced Migration* (London: Continuum).

Hemsi, L. K. (1967) 'Psychiatric Morbidity of West Indian Immigrants', *Social Psychiatry* 2, 96–100.

Hickling, F. W. and Rodgers-Johnson, P. (1995) 'The Incidence of First Contact Schizophrenia in Jamaica', *The British Journal of Psychiatry*, 167, 193–6.

Human Rights Watch (2002) *Presumption of Guilt: Human Rights Abuses Post-September 11*, 14(4)(G), August (Washington: Human Rights Watch).

Human Rights Watch (2010) *Deportation by Default: Mental Disability, Unfair Hearings, and Indefinite Detention in the US Immigration System* (New York: Human Rights Watch).

Ife, J. (2012) *Human Rights and Social Work. Towards Rights-Based Practice*, (Cambridge: Cambridge University Press).

Ingleby, D. (2005) *Forced Migration and Mental Health: Rethinking the Care of Refugees and Displaced Persons* (New York: Springer).

Jablensky, A., Sartorius, N. and Ernberg, G. (1992) 'Schizophrenia: Manifestations, Incidence and Course in Different Cultures', *Psychological Medicine*, Supplementary 20, 1–97.

Jaranson, J. M., Butcher, J., Halcon, L., Johnson, D. R., Robertson, C., Savik, K., Spring, M. and Westermeyer, J. (2004) 'Somali and Oromo Refugees: Correlates of Torture and Trauma History', *American Journal of Public Health*, 94, 591–8.

Jones, J. (2000) 'Asylum Seekers in UK Receive Poor Health Care', *British Medical Journal*, 320, (7248): 1492.

Kemshall, H. (2002) *Risk, Social Policy and Welfare* (Buckingham: Open University Press).

Kleinman, A. (1980) *Patients and Healers in the Context of Culture: An Exploration of the Borderland between Anthropology, Medicine and Psychiatry* (California: University Press).

Klocker, N. and Dunn, K. M. (2003) 'Who's Driving the Asylum Debate? Newspaper and Government Representations of Asylum Seekers', *Media International Australia Incorporating Culture and Policy*, 71–92.

Luke, A. (1995) 'Text in Discourse in Education: An Introduction to Critical Discourse Analysis', in D. W. Apple (ed.) *Review of Research in Education* (Washington DC: American Educational Research Association), 3–48.

Lynn, N. and Lea, S. (2003) '"A Phantom Menace and the New Apartheid": The Social Construction of Asylum-seekers in the United Kingdom', *Discourse and Society*, 14, 425–52.

Mahy, G. E., Mallett, R., Leff, J. and Bhugra, D. (1999) 'First-contact Incidence Rate of Schizophrenia on Barbados', *The British Journal of Psychiatry*, 175, 28–33.

Masocha, S. and Simpson, M. K. (2011a) 'Developing Mental Health Social Work for Asylum Seekers: A Proposed Model for Practice', *Journal of Social Work*, 12, 423–43.

Masocha, S. and Simpson, M. K. (2011b) 'Xenoracism: Towards a Critical Understanding of the Construction of Asylum Seekers and its Implications for Social Work Practice', *Practice*, 23, 5–18.

Minson, J. (1980) 'Strategies for Socialists? Foucault's Conception of Power', *Economy and Society*, 9, 1–43.

Moorehead, C. (2005) *Human Cargo. A Journey Among Refugees* (London: Chatto and Windus).

Neumann, K. (2004) *Refuge Australia. Australia's Humanitarian Record* (Sydney: University of New South Wales Press Limited).

O'Malley, P. (2008) 'Neoliberalism and Risk in Criminology', in T. Anthony and C. Cunneen (eds) *The Critical Criminology Companion*. (Leichhardt: Federation Press), 55–68.

Odegaard, O. (1932) 'Immigration and Insanity: A Study of Mental Disease Among the Norwegian-born Population in Minnesota', *Acta Psychiatrica Scandinavica*, 7, 9–209.

Parton, N. and O'Byrne, P. (2000) *Constructive Social Work: Towards a New Practice* (London: Macmillan).

Pickering, S. (2001) 'Common Sense and Original Deviancy: News Discourses and Asylum Seekers in Australia', *Journal of Refugee Studies*, 14, 169–86.

Porter, M. and Haslam, N. (2005) 'Predisplacement and Postdisplacement Factors Associated with Mental Health of Refugees and Internally Displaced Persons', *Journal of the American Medical Association*, 294, 602–12.

Potter, J. and Wetherell, M. (1987) *Discourse and Social Psychology: Beyond Attitudes and Behaviour* (London: Sage).

Riggins, S. H. (1997) 'The Rhetoric of Othering', in S. H. Riggins (ed.) *The Language and Politics of Exclusion: Others in Discourse* (London: Sage), 1–31.

Robinson, K. (2013) 'Voices from the Front Line: Social Work with Refugees and Asylum Seekers in Australia and the UK', *British Journal of Social Work*, 44(6), 1602–20.

Robjant, K., Hassan, R. and Katona, C. (2009) 'Mental Health Implications of Detaining Asylum Seekers: Systematic Review', *The British Journal of Psychiatry*, 194, 306–12.

Rose, N. (1996) 'Governing "Advanced" Liberal Democracies', in A. Barry, T. Osborne and N. Rose (eds) *Foucault and Political Reason: Liberalism, Neo-liberalism and Rationalities of Government* (London: UCL Press), 37–64.

Rose, N. (2000) 'Government and Control', *British Journal of Criminology*, 40, 321–39.

Sales, R. (2007) *Understanding Immigration and Refugee Policy: Contradictions and Continuities* (Bristol: Policy Press).

Silove, D., Austin, P. and Steel, Z. (2007a) 'No Refuge from Terror: The Impact of Detention on the Mental Health of Trauma-affected Refugees Seeking Asylum in Australia', *Transcultural Psychiatry*, 44, 359–93.

Silove, D., Steel, Z., McGorry, P. and Drobny, J. (1999) 'Problems Tamil Asylum Seekers Encounter in Accessing Health and Welfare Services in Australia', *Social Science & Medicine*, 49, 951–6.

Silove, D., Steel, Z., Susljik, I., Frommer, N., Loneragan, C., Chey, T., Brooks, R., Le Touze, D., Ceollo, M., Smith, M., Harris, E. and Bryant, R. (2007b) 'The Impact of the Refugee Decision on the Trajectory of PTSD, Anxiety, and Depressive Symptoms Among Asylum Seekers: A Longitudinal Study', *American Journal of Disaster Medicine*, 2, 321.

Stanford, S. (2010) '"Speaking Back" to Fear: Responding to the Moral Dilemmas of Risk in Social Work Practice', *British Journal of Social Work*, 40, 1065–80.

Stanford, S. (2012) 'Critically Reflecting on Being "at Risk" and "a Risk" in Vulnerable People Policing', in I. Bartkowiak-Théron and N. L. Asquith (eds) *Policing Vulnerability* (Annandale: Federation Press), 20–32.

Steel, Z. (2006) 'Impact of Immigration Detention and Temporary Protection on the Mental Health of Refugees', *British Journal of Psychiatry*, 188.

Summerfield, D. (1999) 'Sociocultural Dimensions of War, Conflict and Displacement', in A. Ager (ed.) *Refugees. Perspectives on the Experience of Forced Migration* (London: Continuum), 111–135.

Summerfield, D. (2000) 'Conflict and Health: War and Mental Health: A Brief Overview', *British Medical Journal*, 321, 232–5.

Summerfield, D. (2008) 'How Scientifically Valid is the Knowledge Base of Global Mental Health?', *British Medical Journal*, 336(7651), 992–4.

Tribe, R. (2002) 'Mental Health of Refugees and Asylum Seekers', *Advances in Psychiatric Treatment*, 8, 240–248.

Tuffin, K. (2005) *Understanding Critical Psychology* (London: Sage).

Tulloch, J. and Lupton, D. (2003) *Risk and Everyday Life* (London: Sage).

Van Dijk, T. A. (1997) 'Political Discourses and Racism: Describing Others in Western Parliaments', in S. H. Higgins (ed.) *The Language and Politics of Exclusion. Others in Discourse* (CA: Sage), 31–64.

Watters, C. (2001) 'Emerging Paradigms in the Mental Health Care of Refugees', *Social Science & Medicine*, 52, 1709–18.

Webb, S. A. (2006) *Social Work in a Risk Society: Social and Political Perspectives* (New York: Palgrave Macmillan).

Welch, M. and Schuster, L. (2005) 'Detention of Asylum Seekers in the UK and USA: Deciphering Noisy and Quiet Constructions', *Punishment and Society*, 7, 397–417.

Zetter, R., Griffiths, D. and Sigona, N. (2005) *Refugee Community Organisations and Dispersal: Networks, Resources and Social Capital* (Bristol: Policy Press).

12

CONCLUSION: REMORALIZING RISK IN MENTAL HEALTH POLICY AND PRACTICE

Elaine Sharland, Nina Rovinelli Heller, Sonya Stanford
and Joanne Warner

Introduction

This book started life when a group of like-minded colleagues from across the world came together at a conference in Prato, Italy, in May 2012 and again in 2013. We were animated by a shared interest in *'Moving beyond the risk paradigm'*, taking the latter to mean the predominant neoliberal discourse that overdetermines public and professional thinking, practice and policies in human services. We recognized that much has already been said and written about the architecture of the risk paradigm, its discourse and operations. But our core focus was different. True, we wanted to develop a shared understanding of how the paradigm works, and indeed our debates about, for example, the functions and value of contemporary Western approaches to risk assessment and management were lively, not to say heated at times. But our core purpose, through critical engagement with what the risk paradigm is and what it does, was to challenge it and to identify how it might be – perhaps already is being – resisted, or more radically, transcended.

From our enlivening conversations in Prato grew the proposal for the three-part book series of which this volume is one. We four editors began in earnest to consider what it was we wanted to achieve through our own and others' contributions to a volume dedicated to *'Moving beyond the risk paradigm in mental health policy and practice'*. At the point of concluding, it is as intriguing to us as we hope it is to our readers to look back at our original aspirations, both by way of reflexive critique and to situate our concluding thoughts.

We identified early on that we wanted the volume to have three distinctive features. The first was *'speaking back to the risk paradigm in critical and practical terms'.* By this we meant developing a critical understanding of the limits and possibilities of the paradigm in the context of mental health policy and practice, and through this to reach towards ways of moving beyond them. Key to this would be exploring how the 'mentality of risk' and 'risk thinking' (Beck, 2003; Rose 1998) underpin and are deployed by the risk paradigm that has become institutionalized in mental health services and culture (Stanford & Taylor, 2013; Webb, 2006). In particular, we wanted to shed light on what the paradigm can obscure. We were keen to expose how, as the risk paradigm hides and distorts the experience of living with mental health difficulties, it can reinforce the structural disadvantages that people with mental illness suffer. This in turn encouraged us to expose the connections between lived experiences of mental ill-health that are situated and local, and the underpinning relationships of power that are societal and global. Complementing this aim, we were keen to highlight the dilemmas that the risk paradigm can generate for mental health service leaders and for frontline practitioners. To 'speak back' (Stanford, 2010) to these occlusions and distortions, we wanted to explore how they may be resisted and resolved in practical, grounded ways that accord with professional ethics and goals, and benefit mental health service users. This is not to suggest that the precarious balance between Kantian and utilitarian ethics (respectively privileging autonomy/respect for the individual and 'best interests'/the greater good) can ever be avoided (Banks, 2006). But we wished to show how critical understanding of this sort can help practitioners and managers at micro and meso levels, and also policymakers and others at macro levels, to 'speak back' to the constraining theoretical, substantive and technical logic of the risk paradigm (Stanford & Taylor, 2013).

To do this, we planned to foreground mental health risks not – as the risk paradigm would have them – as calculable probabilities, nor as economic threats, or individualized responsibilities, or as the product of fixed identities (see, for example, Culpitt 1999; Kemshall, 2010; Rose 2000), but instead as issues of human rights and social justice (see, for example, Allan *et al.*, 2009; Craig *et al.*, 2008) that deserve professional and public recognition and response. In particular, we anticipated that a focus on human rights and social justice may throw into relief the locally situated lived experiences so often obscured by the risk paradigm. Most important, it may also expose how these profoundly personal experiences are expressions not just of individual but of social suffering – that is, of suffering produced and reproduced by the relations of power embedded in our social institutions and culture (Kleinman, 1988; Wilkinson, 2005).

The second distinctive feature of our book was to be *'integrating theoretical knowledge, practice knowledge and lived experience knowledge'.* As Miles (2001), among others, acknowledges, critical theories of risk are often accused of resting too safely within the world of academic argument; they can seem all too distant from the 'real world' concerns of practice and human lives. In social work, for example, the gap between the broader worlds of theory and academic research on the one hand, and practice on the other, is well documented, with only mixed success in interrupting the 'circle of resistance' between the two (Orme & Powell, 2008). Distinctively, our intention was to bring both critical/theoretical and practical/applied approaches to the subject of risk in mental health. In our view, what theory offers is of fundamental importance for good practice; in turn, practice and lived experiences throw up challenges that theory must tackle. By integrating theoretical, practice and lived experience perspectives, we intended our volume to stimulate reflective and proactive responses on the part of policymakers, managers and practitioners to the challenges and demands of the risk paradigm in mental health.

Third, we were committed from the outset to taking *'a partnership approach to the co-production of knowledge for practice'*. To achieve critically informed practical responses *'speaking back to'* the risk paradigm we were keen to bring together different perspectives – from people who live with, or are close to, mental distress, from mental health service managers and practitioners, and from academic researchers and educators. Through doing this, our aim was to co-produce diverse and nuanced knowledge of risk-related issues and possibilities, across a spectrum of mental health problems and settings.

These three aspirations were of course interwoven. Together they are threaded throughout the discussion that follows, as we reflect on what our book has achieved and the challenges that remain. We begin with some reflections on the representation of diverse voices, the extent to which this has been achieved and what this adds to our vision for 'moving beyond' the risk paradigm. Next we turn to the key insights that emerge from our collective critical scrutiny of the paradigm, and we present our case that the process of critical reflection itself provides the platform for 'speaking back to' and 'moving beyond' the risk paradigm. Central to this, we argue, is to re-vision and remoralize mental health and risk, as questions of social justice and human rights. Reflecting through this lens, we look first at how our contributors have illuminated what the risk paradigm obscures, and, second, at the possibilities they open up for resisting, challenging, even transcending what the risk paradigm does to those who live, work and suffer within it. Finally, we offer some thoughts about where we believe we have reached, the distance yet to travel and directions for the way ahead.

Representing diverse voices

Bringing together the voices of contributors from different backgrounds to co-produce knowledge inevitably involves challenges. First among these is balancing the requirements of academic convention with those of practice relevance and accessibility. Our book is intended to stimulate and inform academics and researchers, advanced level students and, most important, professionals engaged in mental health and risk work. The challenge of doing so is accentuated by our commitment to integrating theoretical with practical and user knowledges.

We have tried to achieve this in ways that lend coherence to the book as a whole and allow the distinctive perspectives of our authors to come through. For some chapters we worked in co-writing partnerships between service users, practitioners or managers, and researchers (Bennison & Talbot (Chapter 5), Hartley *et al.* (Chapter 9), Lee *et al.* (Chapter 3)). One of us (Heller) brought to Chapter 6 her insights as both an academic and a continuing practitioner. Throughout all chapters, we played a close but not heavy-handed editorial role. Hence, for example, we resisted taking a standardized approach to risk-related language as it is used throughout the text. We are all too aware of the 'wicked problem' of terminology when it comes to risk. The frequent temptation is to use the word 'risk' just as the paradigm we are trying to unsettle encourages us to do – as a shorthand that objectifies risk as something discrete that can be seen and known, rather than an idea that is constructed, often unknowable and uncertain. While we recognize this dilemma, we also accept that different authors among us are accustomed to different idioms. So, for example, as editors we have outlined in Chapter 4 what we see as the distinctions between risk thinking, risk mentalities, risk rationalities, risk logic and the risk paradigm itself. At the same time, we accept that these terms are used differently, at times interchangeably, through the course of the book, but we are confident that their meanings in each case are made clear and their critical edge is not lost.

There has also been a balance to be struck between pursuing the themes that we were keen to see threaded through the volume and those to which our authors directly spoke. We encouraged our contributors throughout to hold in mind the core aspirations and themes that we wanted the book to address. But we did not impose our own frame of reference. As a result, the themes of human rights and social justice in particular are more explicit in some chapters (for example Chapters 2, 5 and 8) and more implicit in others. Likewise our interest in illuminating the connections between the local and the global emerge more powerfully in some chapters (such as Masocha and Robinson's on asylum seekers and mental health (Chapter 11)) than in others that are more locally situated.

There have been two further challenges to including diverse voices that we have met in part, not in whole. There are slightly fewer service user or practitioner perspectives brought directly to the volume than we had hoped. Nonetheless, in addition to the chapters to which Bennison and Talbot contributed as service users, Lee and Hartley as service managers, and Heller as a practitioner/academic (Chapters 5, 3, 9 and 6 respectively), the perspectives of service users and of frontline practitioners are strongly represented through empirical material offered, for example, by Bland and Wyder, Sawyer, Hartley *et al.* and Lee *et al.* (Chapters 7, 8, 9 and 3 respectively).

The second challenge and limitation is that our perspectives as editors, and those of most our contributors, are drawn from the United Kingdom, United States and Australia, and this bias is doubtless reflected in our thinking. There is no question that the risk paradigm we confront is institutionalized at the heart of neoliberal governance in contemporary Western societies; so an obvious next step will be to draw into the conversation voices from other Western democracies where the same paradigm is endemic. Still more important, in the context of globalization, it is clear that the logic and operations of the risk paradigm are far wider in their colonizing reach. Chapter 11 by Masocha and Robinson demonstrates this in a manner all too raw at the time of writing, as desperate migrants fleeing conflict in the Middle East and Africa are confronted by European states too fearful of risk to their own economic security to offer humane and safe haven. In future work, we need to pay more heed to the social suffering perpetrated worldwide by the risk paradigm, and to the opportunities to resist and overcome these injustices.

Our discussion turns now to our reflections on the key insights arising from the volume as whole. Here we have taken the liberty of highlighting from our contributors' chapters what we see as the critical understandings they bring to our core themes, and the messages that emerge most powerfully across the piece.

Critical scrutiny of the risk paradigm in mental health

We are impressed by the range and sophistication with which our contributors have integrated theory within their narrative critiques. Several have drawn on societal level theory, including of risk society (Beck 2003, 2004; Giddens 2003a, 2003b) and of governmentality (Rose 1996, 2000) to expose how the preoccupation with risk in neoliberal society overdetermines how mental illness is configured, regulated and lived. In addition, for example, as editors in Chapter 1 we have drawn on cultural theory, using Douglas's work (1992) to explain how the concept of risk allows us to respond to anxiety by invoking blame, and on Lupton's work (1999) to highlight how the idea of risk underpins the cultural process of 'othering' and the stigmatization that follows. Distinct from, but complementing this, in Chapter 3 Lee *et al.* have turned to Klein's (1975) psychodynamic theory to explore how risk anxiety within mental health service organizations leads to defensive professional practice and 'splitting' that is characteristic of Klein's 'paranoid schizoid position'. Turning to the ethical dimensions of risk, Masocha and Robinson (Chapter 11) have drawn on Edwards' work (1991) to explain how the use of risk as a category accomplishes the 'moral work' of stripping asylum seekers of their individuality and humanity.

We are confident that our contributors have collectively offered a resounding and nuanced critique of the risk paradigm in mental health. To summarize, they have highlighted how risk thinking and rationalities are pervasive in contemporary Western societies, that these are ideologically patterned, and they have shaped how mental health is understood and responses to it configured. While the meanings of risk and risk rationalities are fluid, their travel over time reflects the power and influence of those who deploy them to legitimate particular social arrangements, serving particular interests, at particular times. In contemporary neoliberal welfare regimes, distinctive risk rationalities, institutionalized through law, policy and practice, have come to colonize the site of mental health. Their logic is driven by the market, and their value base by the notion of security. On the surface, security is framed as 'safety' – for those who suffer mental illness from risk to themselves, and for others from the risks they pose. Fundamentally, however, within the neoliberal risk paradigm security equates to economic security. Those with mental health problems are costly, so as 'customers' of mental health services we require them to 'recover' capacity for economic prudence and responsibility. For their part, mental health services work to a business model driven by performance and efficiency. This propels their preoccupation with the forensic functions of risk management, and their faith in technocratic, actuarial solutions to the problems of mental health and risk.

Configured this way, not only risk but also people themselves become objectified. Those with mental illness are ascribed essentialized risk identities – as 'a risk' or 'at risk'. Worse, these categories are moralized and responsibility for occupying them is privatized. So people with mental health needs become designated either as good/responsible or deviant/irresponsible. This invokes the cultural process of 'othering' them, and legitimates the blame, stigmatization and marginalization that compound their suffering.

For those in positions of power and accountability, it is not difficult to see what may be seductive about these risk rationalities. They offer the promise of certainty – that risks can be known, predicted, controlled, even eradicated if the correct formulae are applied. Where failures to manage risk happen, service organizations can defend themselves by showing they have followed procedures. Those not on the front line (and sometimes even those who are) can protect themselves from the emotional pain of recognizing suffering, through recourse to bureaucratic procedures and technocratic solutions. Above all, attributing responsibility for mental illness and recovery to individual sufferers and those close to them rids the rest of us, societally and professionally, of the duty to look to our own moral responsibility for generating and exacerbating mental health risk and suffering.

Nonetheless, even for those who espouse this logic, its seductive promise is not borne out. The economic cost of mental illness does not abate, and the market economics of welfare have come under increasing strain. Mental health risk 'failures' still occur and recourse to technocratic solutions does not make the problem go away. Also, and increasingly troubling for those who do 'risk work', the culture of blame has intensified, fanned by the media and shored up by our professional and public regulatory systems. Totalizing, moralizing and responsibilizing risk identities are not reserved for mental health sufferers. Individual practitioners and organizations may, with a following wind, be judged good or effective, but they live under constant threat of being condemned as bad or failing, and suffering the penalties.

In all these ways, contributors to this book – like others – have demonstrated that the contemporary risk paradigm does not hold up to scrutiny. But where we believe their individual and collective contributions distinctively take us forward is in the direction that this discussion now turns. As we have outlined in Chapter 4, core to our case is that the power of critical reflection lies in its potential to open up the space for 'speaking back to' and 'moving beyond' the risk paradigm in mental health, through exposing not just what the risk paradigm does, but what it obscures. Most important, we argue that this exposure becomes all the sharper when mental health and risk are scrutinized through the lens of human rights and social justice. This is where we believe the distinctive contribution of the book comes into its own.

Illuminating lived experience through the lens of human rights and social justice

True to its aims, this book has brought to light the contextualized lived experience of people with mental illness and those who work with them. More than this, our contributors have shown how the operations of the risk paradigm do not simply obscure the lived experience of mental suffering; they also generate and reproduce it. The compromise to service users' human rights and social justice brings shame and loss of dignity, stigma and social exclusion, to compound distress. In our view, the experience is not just one of individual suffering, still less one of individual pathology or culpability as the neoliberal risk paradigm suggests. Instead, it is one of social suffering – an expression of the hurts we inflict on one another (Frost & Hoggett, 2008; Kleinman *et al.*, 1997; Wilkinson 2005) as a consequence of our use and misuse of power. This is why as editors we have argued (in Chapters 1 and 4) for a shift away from conceiving mental health as a question of risk, towards recognizing both mental health and risk as questions of human rights and social justice.

Upholding human rights – to dignity and respect; to protection; to self-determination, participation and choice; to non-discrimination, fairness and equality – is after all fundamental to the espoused goals of the core social and health care professions. So too are the moral principles of social justice that are intended to guide our professional and public institutions' actions in order to uphold human rights. These principles – of humanity, fairness and equity; of reciprocity in the distribution of social goods; of inclusivity and solidarity – come sharply into relief in the field of mental health. In part (as Campbell and Davidson, Bland and Wyder, Heller, Hendry *et al.*, and Sawyer respectively highlight in Chapters 2, 7, 6, 10 and 8) this is for the obvious reason that rights to liberty, self-determination and autonomy can be called into question when a person lacks the capacity to ensure that they are safe, and others safe from them. But the case goes deeper than that. We argue that principles of human rights and social justice deserve prominence in the mental health field precisely because they are so often compromised by the risk paradigm itself, and because the social suffering this causes is so profound. Campbell and Davidson, for example, draw attention on the one hand to the injustice of excessive use of coercive community-based legal powers, where lack of capacity among mental health service users deemed to be 'high risk' is assumed, rather than carefully situated judgements made. On the other hand, along with Bland and Wyder these authors point to the social injustice of under-intervention perpetrated by a paradigm fixated on high risk. This leaves those deemed 'low risk' insufficiently supported; it diminishes their wellbeing and compromises their rights to inclusion in the worlds of community and work. Heller, writing about suicide, highlights the human rights dilemma facing those with disabilities in light of 'euthanasia' legislation. Disability advocates have raised the alarm at the vulnerability they experience in the face of able-bodied people's projection of the 'miserableness of their lives'. They demand the right to be seen as vital human beings who also deserve suicide prevention efforts, rather than a tacit societal acceptance of the 'right to die'.

Among the many contributions to this book that demonstrate the value of re-visioning mental health and risk as questions of social justice and human rights, some convey this intimately through accounts of lived experience. Bennison and Talbot (in Chapter 5), for example, tell of their confusion, distress and sense of isolation on the receiving end of pathologizing and insensitive professional risk thinking. Striking in their narrative is not just the impact on their personal wellbeing, but their overwhelming sense that this treatment was wrongful and denied them their human rights to personhood, dignity and autonomy. It also compounded the wider social injustices of stigmatization, marginalization and exclusion, done to them as a consequence of their diagnoses. Lee *et al.*'s case example (in Chapter 3) of mental health service user Mr J is similarly powerful. Reluctantly responsibilized to manage his own 'personalized' care package, he found himself harried as a debtor following an organizational policy shift. His resulting distress, deteriorated mental health and hospitalization (ironically at increased cost to the public purse) were felt as profoundly personal lived experiences; but what they embodied too was social suffering. At the hands of a market-driven risk regime, Mr J's dignity was demeaned, his right to make genuine choices not respected, with the stigma of debt adding social to personal injury.

Drawing on empirical evidence from practitioners, Sawyer (in Chapter 8) highlights how corporate-oriented risk management strategies, overly focused on the possibility of harm or danger, obscure the value of risk-taking activities. Such negative 'risk thinking' sets the stage for narrow and defensive practice, reduces opportunities for therapeutic intervention and privileges meeting service (rather than service users') goals. All this comes at a cost – not just to fulfilling service users' needs, but also to enhancing their capacities for autonomy, along with their freedom and social inclusion. Along with Sawyer, Lee *et al.* and Hartley *et al.* (in Chapter 9) also draw attention to the challenges for practitioners trapped within such a risk regime. The personal pain of this could hardly be more poignantly evoked than by Hartley and Lee's colleagues, who, when confronted with Goya's painting *The Third of May 1808*, were unable to decide whether they identified more with the firing squad (destroying their service users' lives) or with the victim (targeted and horror-struck). However, the metaphor is all the more profound because the suffering they describe is shared. Not individual collectively these practitioners found themselves embedded within an organizational risk paradigm that denies them the right to exercise their professional values and judgement, while simultaneously threatening them with blame and shame should they 'fail'. Heller (in Chapter 6) addresses the challenges faced in 'high-stakes' work with the suicidal client and the ways in which the practitioner's own fears about the consequences of failure (the client's death by suicide) can obscure the thoughtful and realistic assessment of actual risk. Noting that prediction of rare events such as suicide is difficult, Heller discusses the importance of engaging the client in the assessment, a form of validating their very humanity. This offers the client the opportunity for self-agency in the direction of life, not death – and simultaneously provides a critical human connection when it is most needed.

Three sets of contributors turn their attention to wider mental health sites, to expose how the risk paradigm both obscures and generates social suffering and injustice. Two of these have already been noted: Masocha and Robinson (in Chapter 11) reflect on the denial of citizenship and basic human rights to asylum seekers who are 'othered' as 'a risk' to host society or 'at risk' of mental illness, and Campbell and Davidson (in Chapter 2) offer a nuanced critique of excessive use of legal coercion, denying to 'high risk' service users recognition of their capacity, the right to participate in decision making, and freedom of lifestyle choice. In the third example, Hendry *et al.* (in Chapter 9) draw on their empirical research with young people to challenge the moral anxiety that underpins 'social media panic' about 'risky youth'. Such risk thinking, they argue, assumes that young people will be harmed, or driven to self-harm, or that social media will endanger their recovery from mental illness. It ignores the ways that young people with mental health needs may use social media productively, to enhance their recovery when well, or to communicate their distress when unwell. Worse, it takes their online expressions to be distorted and so invalidates their accounts of suffering. This perpetrates not just individual but social suffering. It exaggerates young people's risk identities, de-emphasizes their recovery identities and disempowers them from helping themselves. It also denies them the right to participate in the community and youth cultures where digital and non-digital lives are intertwined.

Bringing to light, as our contributors have done, both the individual and the social suffering that the risk paradigm obscures is not an end in itself. Beyond this, as the remainder of this discussion intends to show, we believe that critical reflection through the lens of human rights and social justice offers us the platform to 'speak back to' and to begin to 'move beyond' the risk paradigm itself in mental health.

'Speaking back to' and 'moving beyond' the risk paradigm in mental health

The impulse to create this book, and the series of which it is part, sprang from the conviction that through changed thinking we can change practice and change lives. This is ambitious, but we think not a naive aspiration. As our discussion has shown, we are all too aware of the structures and relations of power that bolster and are bolstered by the neoliberal risk paradigm. Nonetheless, we have taken courage from, for example, Lupton

(2006) and Mythen and Walklate (2006) whose work highlights that there is nothing static or immutable about the concept of risk, nor indeed about risk society itself. Neither is there anything fundamental that should stop us as social actors (whether researchers, practitioners or service users) from contesting and resisting the practices and injustices that the risk paradigm perpetuates. We have also taken encouragement in this from several commentators within the social work field. Ferguson (2009), Garrett (2013) and Tew (2014), for example, all point to the imperative and the potential for bringing to bear theory-informed critique on how services are configured and experienced, holding to account policymakers, challenging and transforming the power inequities on which they rest. In particular too, we have borrowed from Fook (2002) and Fook and Askeland (2007) to inform our understanding that the power of the risk paradigm in mental health rests on the extent to which it goes unquestioned. Critical reflection gives us the chance both to unsettle the paradigm and to develop practices that are underpinned by principles of human rights and social justice, and are grounded in lived individual and social experience. Lastly, drawing on Frost and Hoggett (2008), among others, we have been encouraged to take the 'affective turn', to allow ourselves to connect the emotional with the political and moral dimensions of suffering, in order to harness the impetus for change. Put simply, whether at the micro level of interpersonal relationships and dialogue, or through resisting and reshaping workplace culture and practice, or through wider, macro level efforts to reframe public understanding and policies, we believe it becomes possible to change the way we recognize, feel, live with and respond to mental illness and risk.

We have been struck by the diversity of the strategies identified by contributors to this book, both for 'speaking back to' and for 'moving beyond' the risk paradigm in mental health. In some cases, these strategies are based on descriptive (rather than prescriptive) accounts, grounded in direct experience or empirical research in practice settings. Both Sawyer (in Chapter 8), and Bland and Wyder (in Chapter 7), for example, show how the recovery model in mental health practice can work in ways very different from the neoliberal construction of recovery as the mark of return to economically responsible citizenship. Frontline practitioners and managers interviewed by Sawyer demonstrated the potential of an individualized and relationship-based recovery model that 'negotiates the interface between risk management and human rights-based care', transforming the asymmetries of power between professionals and service users. This approach does not reject the options of risk calculation, nor the use of risk assessment tools so favoured within the dominant risk paradigm. However, it also privileges positive risk taking and principles of social justice in ways that balance service users' rights to participation and inclusion with attention to safety and risk management. Complementing this, Bland and Wyder's empirical research shows how a 'recovery-focused approach to risk assessment' – one that does not reject the concept of risk, but recognizes its complexities and conceives of risk in terms of recovery and empowerment – can promote more socially just outcomes for those people and their families whose lives are impacted by psychotic illness. Bennison and Talbot, sadly, did not experience practice of this sort. As service users, in Chapter 5 they make the plea for professional responses that are more humane, more enabling and more respectful of their person-hood. For them, mental health risk is not just a question of safety, nor just of recovery; fundamentally, it is a question of social justice and human rights. They argue passionately for mental health policy and practices that are mindful of social suffering. These approaches would both recognize and tackle the stigma and poverty, the denial of lifestyle choice and rel-egation to the margins of community, that mental illness diagnosis brings with it and that the risk paradigm amplifies through and through.

Returning to direct experience of clinical practice, Heller argues (in Chapter 6) that in work with suicidal clients it is imperative that practi-tioners examine both their internalized fear and their intolerance of sitting with uncertainty when the stakes are so high. The client who has suicidal thoughts, feelings or actions invariably feels helpless, worthless, bereft and alone. Any action on the part of the therapist that either reinforces or negates those feelings exacts its own risks. The person who feels suicidal needs to be seen and to have their humanity confirmed. Heller cautions that an exclusive reliance upon standardized predictive instruments in the absence of a relational context is inherently problematic. At the same time, standards of good practice require that mental health professionals make use of all the best knowledge available and that we have a responsibility to develop comprehensive holistic ways of engaging clients in the joint assess-ment of suicidal risk, which includes the examination of reasons for living.

Also grounded in direct experience and in practice settings, service man-agers Hartley and Lee (in Chapter 9) illustrate the creative 'micro-strategies' they have developed to enable themselves and their colleagues to resist the destructive impact of risk rationalities within their own organization's cul-ture. Interestingly, these mirror in lived professional practice the process we have proposed in this book, of moving from critical reflection to action in 'speaking back to' and, to some degree at least, 'moving beyond' the risk paradigm. Through writing their own 'reflective logs' and 'critical proposi-tions' and through shared arts-based activities, they have found forms of reflexive expression that help them to cope with their anger and anxiety – enough to find 'breathing room' to resist the some of the practice dis-tortions of the risk regime in which they work. Their strategies for 'revival' and 'creative renewal' have reduced their own individual and collective suffering. This of course is not an end in itself – the purpose is to enable their return to compassionate, direct work with service users, where neither party feels themselves on the shooting or receiving end of the firing squad.

Where our contributors turn to wider sites of professional and societal response to mental health and risk, their models for challenging and transcending the dominant risk paradigm are offered more by way of proposal than description at this stage. Nonetheless, they are powerful and illuminating. Hendry *et al.*, firstly, propose (in Chapter 10) that in place of the distortions and disabling impulse of social media panic, mental health professionals and policymakers develop more nuanced understandings that can enhance young people's lived experience of mental illness and their recovery. This approach does not sidestep the dangers of online bullying, 'triggering' or discrimination. But it focuses on the productive use and 'affordances' of social media, among them control and immediacy, the opportunity to speak with authenticity but anonymity about one's own lived experience, to make emotional connections with others without emotional charge or embarrassment, and to receive and offer information and support. All these, of course, can be understood as matters of social justice and of rights – to self-expression, to personhood and autonomy, and to participate in community and culture.

Secondly, Campbell and Davidson (in Chapter 2) turn their attention to specific, legally mandated professional practices that may constrain the lives and choices of mental health service users in the community. They argue for a holistic, reflexive and rights-based approach to risk decision making, in place of the excessive use of legal coercion with people deemed 'high mental health risk'. Like Sawyer, and Bland and Wyder, their 'situated ethical stance' acknowledges the complexity and ambiguities faced when making such decisions, and their approach maintains the commitment to ensuring safety. But their proposal also embodies a shift towards a capacity and strengths-, rather than deficits-, based approach to service users, and with this more reciprocal exchange of expertise and some redistribution of power. More broadly, as a matter of social justice, they also make the case for investment in community-based resources that mitigate, rather than confound, the everyday risks that mental health service users experience.

Lastly, Masocha and Robinson (in Chapter 11) speak to the profound and pressing need to disrupt the ideological construction of asylum seekers as 'a risk' to the host society. They point to the clear imperative to recognize and respond humanely to the mental distress that follows from trauma and violence, political oppression, separation, loss and exile, compounded by the migrant experience of uncertainty, danger, destitution, detention, racism and rejection. But they highlight too how damaging it can be to ascribe to asylum seekers the essentialized identity of 'at risk' – this all too easily casts them as mentally unstable, and thereby incapable of integrating into civil society, prone to social disorder and to crime. So

there is a fine balance to be struck, in the midst of highly charged political and ideological environments. Here Masocha and Robinson envisage a
crucial advocacy role for mental health professions. We need to be active
in public and policy arenas, to speak up loud and clear for the human
rights of asylum seekers, and to pursue socially just responses to their
mental health needs and suffering.

Reflecting on the strategies suggested by our contributors for 'speaking
back to' and 'moving beyond' the risk paradigm in mental health, as editors we are struck not only by their range and diversity but by a distinctive quality that unifies them. All are characterized by the call for what
we can describe as 'remoralizing' risk in mental health practice and policy.
Technically, we might more accurately refer to this as 're-remoralizing',
since, as Webb (2006) reminds us, it is the risk paradigm itself that has
already 'remoralized' risk and need as matters of individual responsibility
and individual failure. But by reclaiming the less clumsy term 'remoralizing', what we intend to capture is the urge towards reframing risk itself,
risk thinking and risk practice in mental health, as a matter of moral
imperative. This demands a turn towards a value-based and ethical, rather
than a technical and instrumental, stance taken to those who live with
mental illness. It involves engaging emotionally as well as rationally (Frost
& Hoggett, 2008) with the social relationships that underpin our responses
to mental health and risk. It means taking an holistic approach to mental
health risk prevention, assessment and management, one that pays heed
to safety while at the same time recognizing and respecting individual
personhood (rather than risk identity), agency and lived experience. At
the heart of this, if we are to 'speak back to' and 'move beyond' the risk
paradigm, we need to recognize the intimate relationship between the
individual and the social. Holding up the lens of human rights and social
justice allows us to see how the logic and operations of the risk paradigm
commonly do damage to, and inflict social suffering upon, those who live
with mental illness. Challenging this demands remoralizing mental health
and risk, both in principle and in practice. As Williams and Briskman
(2008, p. 8) go as far as to describe it, this means reviving our practice
through '"moral outrage" as a positive sentiment for change and action'.

Continuing challenges and opportunities for moving beyond the risk paradigm

Promising as they are, we are not suggesting that the strategies put forward in this book provide the 'solution to risk and mental health'. Not
least, our contributors' critical observations throughout the volume cast

light on some of the key challenges still faced in 'moving beyond' the risk paradigm. Our closing reflections turn briefly towards these challenges, and onwards to the opportunities we may take.

For all of us, especially those charged with preventing, managing and reducing mental health risks, troubling the rationalities and workings of the risk paradigm unsettles us too. First, it denies us the tidy understandings of mental health and risk categories that the paradigm so seductively offers, and it deprives us of the technical and instrumental formulae for deciding what to do and doing it. Confronting and disrupting the risk paradigm exposes complexity and uncertainties, and these displace all of us from our comfort zone. Second, these complexities and uncertainties become still more acute once we re-vision mental health and risk as questions of human rights and social justice. Mental health is inescapably a site of tension for human rights. There is no avoiding the dilemma that the rights of people with serious mental illness to liberty, freedom of choice and self-determination may conflict not just with the rights of others to protection from harm, but also with service users' own rights to protection from themselves. Exposing this dilemma is nothing new. Still, our call for more situated, more holistic, more capacity and recovery-oriented decision making may make our practice more moral, but this does not make our judgements any easier to reach. Neither, unless we can simultaneously dislodge the institutional and public risk rationalities that responsibilize professionals for their 'failures', will it relieve us of the threat of blame and shame.

There are also tactical and strategic challenges. We have argued strongly for critical reflection that is mindful of human rights and social justice, as the key prerequisite for 'speaking back to' and 'moving beyond' the risk paradigm. Such critical reflection, and the clear vision that can follow from it, takes sustained reflexivity to achieve. For all of us trained and socialized within the contemporary risk culture, not only are many of its assumptions (not to mention its language) ingrained in the worlds we inhabit, but we ourselves have to greater or lesser degrees internalized them. Here a couple of illustrations can show the tactical need for reflexivity and vigilance to accompany our sense of purpose. Sawyer (in Chapter 8), for example, advocates for a sensitively calibrated individualized approach to supporting service users to recover from mental illness. If we follow this course, we need to take care to avoid the organizational risk rationality that also foregrounds the individual not the social, but in this case responsibilizes service users for their own suffering and their recovery. Likewise, if in our practice we bring to the fore service users' human rights, we need to beware how, as Lee *et al.* show (in Chapter 3), the language of rights (to 'personalized' choice) has been co-opted by marketized risk regimes, and we must take care to avoid the same trap.

Above and beyond these tactical considerations, we are all too aware of the strategic scale of challenging a paradigm that is embedded throughout our political, social and welfare institutions, and of doing so under conditions of austerity. Marketized solutions to the distribution of social goods are becoming more, not less, endemic, with the rights to these goods – social justice among them – increasingly conditional on being 'deserving' by virtue of being economically prudent and non-risky. This brings us, in turn, to what is probably the greatest challenge of all for resisting and transcending the risk paradigm in mental health. Entrenched neoliberal risk rationalities do not just allow but also encourage us, professionally and societally, to overlook our own roles in contributing to personal suffering and perpetrating social suffering. Remoralizing risk exposes our own culpability for social injustice; it means remoralizing ourselves, within a policy and resource environment that is distinctly amoral.

Against such obstacles, what are the chances for 'moving beyond' the risk paradigm in mental health? We are under no illusion that the challenge is simple or straightforward to meet. Nonetheless, along with our contributors, as editors we are convinced that the opportunities exist, and in some cases we can see they are already being taken. We also believe that this book has opened up the space for critical reflection, and with it the opportunity to offer clear messages for the way forward. Critically reflective risk thinking and risk practice in mental health need to be contextual and dialogic. They need directly to engage with the deeply personal, situated and lived experience of mental health service users and their families, while also being alert to their commonalities and distinctions across global contexts. Whether locally or globally, as practitioners, educators and researchers it is our responsibility to nurture strategies of resistance to the relationships of power and privilege that sustain the neoliberal risk paradigm to the advantage of some and the harm of many. In their place, we need to strive to reinstate principles the of human rights and social justice, on policy and practice agendas that presently serve to reproduce, rather than mitigate, human and social suffering. Remoralizing mental health and risk will take honesty with ourselves, bravery, persistence and pragmatism. Above all, it will take continued willingness to engage with complexity, while holding fast to our commitment to humane and just outcomes for those who experience mental illness.

References

Allan, J., Briskman, L. and Pease, B. (eds) (2009) *Critical Social Work: Theories and Practices for a Socially Just World* (2nd edition) (Crows Nest, New South Wales: Allen & Unwin).

Banks, S. (2006) *Ethics and Values in Social Work* (3rd edition) (London: Palgrave Macmillan).

Beck, U. (2003) *World Risk Society* (Cambridge: Polity Press).

Beck, U. (2004) *Risk Society: Toward a New Modernity* (London: Sage).

Craig, G., Burchardt, T. and Gordon, D. (2008) (eds) *Social Justice and Public Policy: Seeking Fairness in Diverse Societies* (Bristol: Policy Press).

Culpitt, I. (1999) *Social Policy and Risk* (London: Sage).

Douglas, M. (1992) *Risk and Blame: Essays in Cultural Theory* (London and New York: Routledge).

Edwards, D. (1991) 'Categories are for Talking: On the Cognitive and Discursive Bases of Categorization', *Theory & Psychology*, 1(4), 515–42.

Ferguson, I. (2009) *Reclaiming Social Work: Challenging Neo-liberalism and Promoting Social Justice* (London: Sage).

Fook, J. (2002) *Social Work: Critical Theory and Practice* (London, California and New Delhi: Sage).

Fook. J. and Askeland, G. (2007) 'Challenges of Critical Reflection: Nothing Ventured, Nothing Gained', *Social Work Education*, 26(5), 520–33.

Frost, L. and Hoggett, P. (2008) 'Human Agency and Social Suffering', *Critical Social Policy*, 28(4), 438–60.

Garrett, P. (2013) *Social Work and Social Theory* (Bristol: Policy Press).

Giddens, A. (2003a) *Modernity and Self-identity: Self and Society in the Late Modern Age* (reprint) (Stanford, CA: Stanford University Press).

Giddens, A. (2003b) *The Consequences of Modernity* (Stanford, CA: Stanford University Press).

Kemshall, H. (2010) 'Risk Rationalities in Contemporary Social Work Policy and Practice', *British Journal of Social Work,* 40(4), 1247–62.

Klein, M. (1975) *Envy and Gratitude* (London: Routledge).

Kleinman, A. (1988) *The Illness Narratives: Suffering, Healing and the Human Condition* (New York: Basic Books).

Kleinman, A., Das, V. and Lock, M. (eds) (1997) *Social Suffering* (Berkeley, CA: University of California Press).

Lupton, D. (1999) *Risk* (London: Routledge).

Lupton, D. (2006) 'Sociology and Risk', in G. Mythen and S. Walklate (eds) *Beyond the Risk Society: Critical Reflections on Risk and Human Society* (Maidenhead, Berkshire: Open University Press), 11–24.

Miles, S. (2001) *Social Theory in the Real World* (London: Sage).

Mythen, G. and Walklate, S. (2006) 'Introduction: Thinking Beyond the Risk Society', in G. Mythen and S. Walklate (eds) *Beyond the Risk Society: Critical Reflections on Risk and Human Society* (Maidenhead, Berkshire: Open University Press), 1–7.

Orme, J. and Powell, J. (2008) 'Building Research Capacity in Social Work: Process and Issues', *British Journal of Social Work*, 38(5), 988–1008.

Rose, N. (1996) 'The Death of the Social? Re-figuring the Territory of Government', *Economy and Society*, 25, 327–56.

Rose, N. (1998) 'Governing Risky Individuals: The Role of Psychiatry in New Regimes of Control', *Psychiatry, Psychology and Law*, 5(2), 177–95.

Rose, N. (2000) 'Government and Control', *British Journal of Criminology*, 40(2), 321–39.

Stanford, S. (2010) '"Speaking Back" to Fear: Responding to the Moral Dilemmas of Risk in Social Work Practice', *British Journal of Social Work*, 40(4), 1065–80.

Stanford, S. and Taylor, S. (2013) 'Welfare Dependence or Enforced Deprivation? A Critical Examination of White Neoliberal Welfare and Risk', *Australian Social Work*, 66(4), 476–94.

Tew, J. (2014) 'Agents of Change? Social Work for Well-being and Mental Health', in J. Weinstein (ed.) *Mental Health: Critical and Radical Debates in Social Work* (Bristol: Policy Press), 39–48.

Webb, S. (2006) *Social Work in a Risk Society: Social and Political Perspectives* (Basingstoke: Palgrave).

Williams, C. and Briskman, L. (2015) 'Reviving Social Work Through Moral Outrage', *Critical and Radical Social Work*, 3(1), 3–17.

Wilkinson, I. (2005) *Suffering: A Sociological Introduction* (Cambridge: Polity Press).

INDEX